That Godless Court?
Second Edition

That Godless Court?

Second Edition

Supreme Court Decisions
on Church-State Relationships

Ronald B. Flowers

WESTMINSTER
JOHN KNOX PRESS
LOUISVILLE · KENTUCKY

Book design by Sharon Adams
Cover design by Eric Walljasper, Minneapolis, MN

Second edition
Published by Westminster John Knox Press
Louisville, Kentucky

This book is printed on acid-free paper that meets the American National Standards Institute Z39.48 standard. ♾

PRINTED IN THE UNITED STATES OF AMERICA

05 06 07 08 09 10 11 12 13 14 — 10 9 8 7 6 5 4 3 2 1

Library of Congress Cataloging-in-Publication Data is on file at the Library of Congress, Washington, D.C.

ISBN 0-664-22891-7

To the memory of our Granddaughter
Jodi Leigh Key
November 21, 1991–April 16, 2003
So lively–Suddenly gone

CONTENTS

Introduction

In 1962 and 1963, as a reaction to its decisions banning school-sponsored prayer in the public schools, the Supreme Court was frequently called "godless" by those who opposed those decisions. Is that a fair representation of the Court? Or is it more accurate to say that the Court was then and is now simply trying to maintain neutrality between church and state? My purpose in this book is to throw some light on such questions.

Why a book of this sort? First, the relationship between religion and civil authority in this country is a legal, ultimately a constitutional, concept. The Supreme Court is the final arbiter of constitutional issues. Second, there is frequently much confusion about what the Supreme Court has ruled, often because the primary information people get comes from the media. Unfortunately, media reports are usually brief and superficial and do not explain the scope or applicability of the Court's rulings. Furthermore, the nonlawyer is likely to be intimidated by the prospect of reading a Supreme Court decision, thinking that surely it will "read like an insurance policy," filled with legalese. Actually, the language of these opinions is often very clear and readable. My goal in this book is to try to help people get beyond those perceived barriers to better understand the Court and its church-state opinions. Church-state relations, and the decisions of the Court, have become considerably more complicated since the first edition of this book in 1994. I offer this revision and update because there is an even greater need today for a "user friendly" guide to this subject matter.

I have updated this book for several reasons. The first and most obvious is that since the previous edition went to press, the Court has decided twelve more church-state cases. Several of them are very important in that they illustrate a different course the Court has been taking on religious issues, especially on the Establishment Clause side. Not only have those cases illustrated the more accommodationist, that is, nonseparationist, attitude of the majority, but they have accelerated the pace at which the Court is moving in that direction. By the beginning of the 2005 term of the Court, the Establishment Clause, interpreted in a separationist way, was a mere shadow of its former self.

Second, the attitude of George W. Bush, whom some have called the most overtly religious president in our history, has strengthened a serious assault on a separationist interpretation of the Establishment Clause with his desire to fund religiously based charitable activities. Since the book attempts to explain some of the societal and political currents that provide the context in which the Court makes its church-state decisions, it has been necessary to make note of this trend.

A third reason to update the book has been to give a more complete explanation of what could be touched on only briefly in the first edition, the erosion of the Free Exercise Clause. As the first edition went to press, Congress had just passed the Religious Freedom Restoration Act. Subsequently, the Court found that law unconstitutional as it applied to the states. As a result, Congress made another attempt legislatively to guarantee a high standard of review in free-exercise cases, which itself is being challenged in the Court as this second edition goes to press.

I am both a professor of religion, now retired, and a committed church person. I am also a rather strict separationist in my view of church-state relationships. I am convinced that the Constitution demands substantial separation between religion and civil authority and, at the same time, mandates that religious freedom should be unfettered, limited only by the necessity of maintaining peace and order in society. Such a relationship is of benefit both to the state and to religion. Strict separation is not hostile to religion, as many have claimed, but will provide the best conditions for religion to flourish. Indeed, by keeping government out of religion, separation is best seen as a way to maximize the free exercise of religion.

It is important to realize that when church-state relationships are discussed, "church" and "state" are oversimplified, shorthand terms. On reflection, the reason for this is obvious. There is no single "church" in America; there is a multiplicity of religious bodies. Of course, there are groups that do not even use the word "church" when they speak of their places of worship, but may speak, rather, of "synagogue," "mosque," "Kingdom Hall," or "spiritual assembly." The pluralism of American religion makes the term "church" only an approximation. Likewise, there is not a single "state." The term encompasses the federal government, the various state governments, county and city governments, and governmental agencies such as boards of education, zoning commissions, regulatory agencies, and, frequently in time of war, draft boards. Any of these can interact with and impact religious people or groups. The better phrase for the subject at hand is "relationships between religion and civil authority." But here, for the sake of convenience and because of the familiarity of the phrase, I shall write of "church and state." Please remember that the phrase masks a much more complicated reality, on both sides.

Some readers may want to read one or more of the cases referred to in the book. Citations are given in endnotes and in the chronological table of cases. These references are not as intimidating or as opaque as those unfamiliar with them might think. Supreme Court opinions are printed by the federal government in *United States Reports*, which is designated by the "U.S." in the middle of the reference. If the reference says "S.Ct.," it means that the case has not yet been printed in *United States Reports* and can be found in *The Supreme Court Reporter*, published by West Publishing Company. The left-hand number refers to the volume number and the right-hand number designates the first page of the case. So, *Everson v. Board of Education* 330 U.S. 1 begins on page 1 of volume 330 of *United States Reports*. (Where a reference reads "1 at 5," the reference is to page 5 of a case that begins on page 1.) The books can be found in any law library and in many public and university libraries. The texts of cases can also be found on the Internet at http://www.findlaw.com.

Like living itself, the scholarly enterprise requires the help of others. I thank Yvonne Gillar, a second-career student at Brite Divinity School, Texas Christian University, for her assistance with some of the mechanics of this book. It is fun to see a person get "turned on" by a subject and volunteer to help her teacher with research/writing projects. My editor at Westminster John Knox Press, Stephanie Egnotovich, has both encouraged me in this project and sustained it with her considerable professional skills. As a wonderful added bonus, we have become good friends.

Finally, but far from least, a huge expression of gratitude goes to my wife, Leah, who endured more missed family time and blank stares during conversations than was proper or fair. And to Jennifer, Philip, and Paul, who, although now gone from home, still wonder how and why their father can get so excited about writing stuff. But, in spite of the puzzlement and missed togetherness, they all have been enormously supportive. I hope my appreciation has been evident.

1

The Court and Its Procedures

As Americans think of the three branches of their government, it is likely that the Supreme Court is more mysterious to most people than either the Presidency or Congress. This is because the Court is less public in its operations than either of the other two. Our first task, then, is to look at the inner workings of the Court.

SELECTING CASES: THE FIRST STEP

The Court makes its pronouncements on various issues, including church and state, by handing down opinions, which express decisions about cases. A case is a controversy between two parties (individuals or institutions, including the government), each of which has an interest in and will be affected by the outcome of the decision. The Court will not give opinions on abstract or merely philosophical questions. Only real controversies come before the Court: somebody *versus* somebody. A person may not challenge a law through a lawsuit unless his or her rights or welfare are somehow directly affected. This adversarial system of jurisprudence means that the Court does not set its own agenda, in the sense of going out and looking for controversies to resolve; it deals only with what is brought to it. However, as will be seen, the Court does set its own agenda by choosing from among the cases that come before it. The adversarial system also means that the questions before the Court will be formed more sharply and argued more vigorously than merely philosophical questions might be. Furthermore, a question of vital interest to two parties may be of importance to many others in the country. We know this is true from the public outcry Supreme Court decisions sometimes elicit.

Cases get to the Court through either the federal court system or the court system of a state. In the federal system, cases normally begin at the district court, or "trial court" level. There are currently ninety-four district courts. Here the controversy is fully aired by counsel for both sides, including the questioning of witnesses. A case involving religion will be heard by one federal judge. The judge virtually always hands down a written opinion. The losing party may appeal that opinion to a federal court of appeals, one of twelve that would hear religion cases. Here the judges do not rehear the witnesses, but rather examine the record of the trial in the lower court, including its opinion, read written statements by opposing counsel, and listen to arguments. On the basis of this evidence a decision is reached, again virtually always expressed in a written opinion. The decisions at this level may uphold the decision of the lower court or overturn it. The loser may want to appeal to the Supreme Court, but, as we shall see, the trip there is neither automatic nor easily traversed.

The courts of the fifty states hear the majority of cases in this country. Judicial systems vary from state to state, but it is possible to generalize about them. As in the federal system, there are trial courts and courts of appeal. In populous states, there are often four layers of courts, rather than three. Losers may appeal their cases upward. Of course, state courts hear cases involving state law. But state laws, either by their nature or by their enforcement, may have federal constitutional dimensions. So state courts may hear cases involving federal issues. If a case gets to a state supreme court and *involves a federal question* (as a church-state question would), it is a candidate for being heard at the U.S. Supreme Court.

In both the federal and state systems, appeal of a case from a trial court to a court of appeals is generally a matter of right to the loser in a case. That is, the appeals court must accept the appeal from the lower court. In the vast majority of cases, the decision of the appeals court is where the case stops, because appeal beyond one level is not a matter of right. The U.S. Supreme Court will be our example, since it is the focus of this book. There is a small category of cases, mostly having to do with conflicts between state laws and the federal Constitution, in which there is the right of appeal, that is, the Court must deal with those cases. But today, only about 1 percent of the Court's cases come on appeal.

The Court has "discretionary power" over some 99 percent of the cases that come to it; in short, it can refuse to hear them. This is the Court's way of managing its workload and focusing only on those cases that will clarify the law and/or have national significance. In the last quarter century the Court's workload has become almost unbearable. In the 1989–90 term, 5,746 cases came before it for consideration, but 9,176 cases in the 2001–2 term, 9,406 cases in the 2002–3 term, and 8,883 cases in the 2003–4 term.[1] Of course, it would be

impossible to give full consideration to all these cases. The procedure to win-
now out the less-important cases is called the "writ of certiorari." *Certiorari*
literally means "to be made more certain." The writ is a command "from a
higher court requiring the record of a case in the court below to be sent up to
itself for re-determination."[2]

When a case comes to the Court, it is accompanied by all the materials that
have been generated in the lower courts. The record of each case is examined,
and a preliminary judgment is made on the merit of the case. If a determination is made that a case is not worthy of discussion by the full Court, that case
goes on a "nondiscussion list." If all the nine justices have made that judgment,
the case is dismissed without any discussion. If any one of the nine believes
that a case is worthy of discussion, it is put on a list for conference. When the
justices come together in conference, a vote is taken on each case on the "discuss list." If four justices vote for a case ("the rule of four"), it is carried over
for oral arguments, "cert. granted." Even at the stage of conference, most cases
are denied certiorari and thus are never decided by the full Court. There are
many reasons why the Court refuses to hear a case. For example, the case may
not represent a real controversy, it may not present a federal question, or it
may not be of national importance. But the Court does not have to give reasons for refusing to hear a case and usually does not.

What does it mean when the Court refuses to hear a case, when the
response is "cert. denied"? It means only that. It should not be thought that
the refusal to hear a case is an endorsement of the decision of the lower court.
Certainly the decision of the lower court stands and becomes effective, because
the Supreme Court has chosen not to review it. But in denying certiorari, the
Court is not taking a position on the merits of the case or on the decision of
the court below. It means simply that, no matter how important the issue is to
the parties in the case, the Court, with a huge workload, cannot take all cases
and chose not to take this one. Perhaps this was best summarized by Chief Justice William Howard Taft:

> No litigant is entitled to more than two chances, namely, to the orig-
> inal trial and to a review, and the intermediate courts of review are pro-
> vided for that purpose. When a case goes beyond that, it is not
> primarily to preserve the rights of the litigants. The Supreme Court's
> function is for the purpose of expounding and stabilizing principles of
> law for the benefit of the people of the country, passing upon consti-
> tutional questions and other important questions of law for the pub-
> lic benefit. It is to preserve uniformity of decision among the
> intermediate courts of appeal.[3]

One of the main reasons the Court will accept a case for review is mentioned
in the last sentence of Chief Justice Taft's comment. Sometimes similar cases will

come up through two or more courts of appeal, and these courts will reach contradictory conclusions. Put simply, one court has decided yes and another court has decided no on the same issue. The Supreme Court will hear one of those cases (or combine two or more cases into one), in order to eliminate confusion and bring stability and consistency to the federal law on that subject. Examples of this procedure are the conscientious objector cases of 1965, discussed in chapter 5, and the public school prayer decisions of 1963, discussed in chapter 7.

This description of the procedure of winnowing out cases, particularly that the Court must decide between conflicting opinions from lower courts, brings up the fact that the Court gets hard cases. Usually the Court accepts for oral argument those cases that are most complicated and will have the most impact on American society. They are cases in which both parties seem to have persuasive arguments firmly based on law. They are very difficult cases to decide. One Supreme Court justice is reported to have said: "I can think of a thousand hypothetical cases that we could dispose of simply by reference to the words of the Constitution. But, doggone it, our Court never seems to get a case like that to decide."[4] Church-state cases are frequently of this most difficult type.

DECIDING CASES AND CLARIFYING THE LAW

As noted, the justices have already received the materials about each case from lower courts. When a case has been accepted for oral argument, the lawyers for each litigant submit additional briefs, arguing their viewpoint and marshaling all the legal rationale they can to persuade the justices to decide in their favor. Of course, because cases that come before the Court are often of great importance, parties or groups other than the litigants are frequently vitally interested in the outcome of a case. Such groups will often file amicus curiae, or "friend of the court," briefs. These may support either side in the suit and will sometimes ask the Court to look at other angles of the case than those articulated by the litigants.[5] Consequently, the justices may have a mountain of paper to read through to inform themselves about the case and ultimately reach a decision.

In oral arguments, the counsel for each side makes a presentation to the Court, summarizing the legal issues for the justices and telling them why they should decide for his or her client. They are expected not to read from a prepared text. Each side is allowed only thirty minutes to present its argument. Furthermore, the justices may—and do—break into the argument at any moment to ask questions. (The justices have already read much of the paperwork about the case and often come to the bench with a written summary of the case; they come prepared to ask questions.) It is a pressure-packed situation for the lawyers.

When oral arguments are over, the justices meet in conference to discuss the case. Only the nine justices attend these secret conferences. Given the caseload of the modern Court, the discussion of the case is not intense or meticulous. Its primary purpose is to see where the various justices stand in their view of how the case should be decided: is there consensus, or is the Court divided? It is here that the chief justice, whose vote is no more weighty than that of any other justice, may exercise the primary authority of the office, assigning opinions, although that authority is not absolute. If in the majority, the chief justice will assign one justice to write the opinion for the Court. If the chief is not in the majority, the assignment will be made by the most senior associate justice who is in the majority. In either case, the assigning justice may assign the case to him or herself.

The person assigned will write an opinion expressing the views of the majority, and this will become the decision in the case at hand. But, as suggested already, there may be justices who do not see the case that way. They are free to write dissenting opinions. No one assigns these opinions; any justice who is not with the majority may write a dissent. All these opinions are circulated to all the justices, who read them and react. Sometimes dissenters are won over to the majority and dissenting opinions are withdrawn. Sometimes some may break from the majority and join the dissenters. (Occasionally a dissenting opinion becomes the majority opinion.) The process is a debate on paper. Each justice who writes an opinion tries to be as persuasive to colleagues as possible, to win them to his or her position. Although they may talk about the case in conference on more than one occasion, it is through the opinion-writing process that the alignments of the justices are produced and the decision reached.

Sometimes justices agree with the result of the majority but not with the reasoning or legal principles by which they arrived at the result. These justices will frequently write concurring opinions. In extreme cases, a majority is not reached. For example, three justices may join "the opinion of the Court," and two others may "concur in the judgment," to produce a "plurality opinion" of 5–4. Such opinions tell who won and who lost but do not articulate a definite rationale. They therefore do not fulfill a major responsibility of the Court: clarifying the meaning of the law. When all the justices have decided where they want to be positioned in the result of a case, the decision is then made public. That is the "decision of the Court." That final decision may be of a unanimous Court (although that is rare[6]) or it may contain several concurring and dissenting opinions, the existence of which, particularly dissents, shows that it was impossible for the majority writer to persuade all colleagues to reach a consensus about the case. Dissent is important, however, because it compels the author of the majority opinion to be more precise and to try to answer the objections of the dissenters.

When the vote is 5–4, there is a tendency to think that one person decided the case. People are often concerned about this "law by one person" concept, particularly if they do not like the decision in the case. But although if one justice had voted differently the decision would have been different, in those close, split-vote decisions it was *five* or *six* justices who voted a particular way, not just one or two. It simply is not realistic to expect that all cases will be unanimous or voted preponderantly one way, especially given the complex world in which we live and the perplexing cases brought before the Court.

Law Clerks

The justices cannot handle the enormous amount of paperwork by themselves. Each may have up to four clerks, except for the chief justice, who may have five. The clerks are young lawyers, recent graduates from some of the best law schools in the country, who may have had experience clerking in a lower federal court. Clerks, chosen by each justice to work in his or her office for a year or two, are of immense help to the justices.

In the certiorari process described earlier, the clerks summarize each case and make a recommendation to the justice as to whether that case should be on the list for discussion. When a case is accepted for oral argument, the clerk will read the paperwork on it and prepare a summary for the justice to take to the bench on the day that case is argued. When a justice is assigned to write an opinion, or chooses to write a concurring or dissenting opinion, a clerk is responsible for doing the necessary research on the case. Some justices even ask their clerks to write first drafts of opinions for them to consider. Of course, the way clerks are used varies from justice to justice, but all the justices use their clerks to help bear the burden of a crushing workload.

The question is frequently raised as to whether this situation means that the business of administering justice for the nation has, in reality, passed from the justices to the law clerks. There is no doubt that the justices now give less attention to each case than they were able to in earlier times. (The first clerk was hired in 1882; prior to that time the workload was such that justices could do it all themselves. As recently as 1970, each justice had only two clerks.) But, even today, even with those justices who have clerks write first drafts of opinions, each justice looks carefully at the clerks' work, often edits it heavily or even rewrites it, and makes sure that the opinion says what the justice wants to say before he or she approves it. It is, in reality, the justice's decision.

So the situation seems to be not "justice by clerks" but "justice with the important help of clerks."[7]

Stare Decisis and Obiter Dicta

It is important to look at two legal concepts at this point. One is *stare decisis*, "let the decision stand." This is the principle of precedent, which is so important to the law. It is the principle of "not reinventing the wheel." This means that courts will routinely follow their previous decisions. So lower courts are bound to follow the precedents set by the Supreme Court, and the Supreme Court itself will ordinarily follow the precedents set by its previous decisions. This principle of precedent allows the Court more latitude in refusing to hear cases that raise questions well settled by previous decisions. It is this concept that enables lawyers to advise clients of their rights and their prospects of winning any proposed litigation. Precedent provides continuity to the law, giving the justices benchmarks and concepts that aid them in deciding on the litigation before them. A decided case and the rationale for the decision carry great weight in analogous cases before the Court.

The other principle of importance is obiter dictum (pl. dicta), "remark in passing." In writing opinions, the justices articulate legal principles that are central to the decision of the case. Often, however, they do not confine themselves to the technicalities of the case at hand, but comment more widely about history, philosophy, patriotism, and other topics that embellish the decision and enlighten its readers. Such comments, or dicta, do not have the same binding or precedential effect on future cases that the actual decision on the case has.

Sometimes people say about a statement in a decision, "Oh, that is just dictum," as if to minimize its importance. That is too bad, for often the dictum is quite wonderful, both in the sense of being good literature and in the sense of being instructive on matters of American history—even religious history, in the instance of church-state cases.

Dicta can influence later cases. For example, a dissenting opinion is clearly dictum, since it does nothing to decide the case and define the legal principles of the decision. But sometimes a dissent can be so persuasive that it can become the majority opinion in a later case on the same or a similar issue. A good example is the Jehovah's Witnesses flag salute cases, discussed in chapter 3. In *Minersville School District v. Gobitis*,[8] the Court ruled that school districts could compel Jehovah's Witness students to salute the American flag, even though it was contrary to their religious beliefs to do so. Justice Harlan Stone wrote a strong dissent. Three years later the Court reexamined the issue in *West Virginia Board of Education v. Barnette*.[9] The Court reversed itself, that is, it overruled the *Gobitis* case and said the Jehovah's Witness children had the constitutional right,

based on their religious belief and the Free Exercise Clause of the First Amendment, to refuse to salute the flag in the public school context. The majority opinion in *Barnette* was based largely on Justice Stone's dissent in *Gobitis.*

Occasionally, as in this example, the Court will reverse itself. The principle
of *stare decisis* is not absolute. And dicta often carry great force, even though
they may not focus precisely on the case at hand. We shall have occasion to
look at some stirring dicta in the chapters that follow. Indeed, I shall include
many direct quotes, because most who read this book have probably never
before read any Supreme Court opinions. I think it is important for you to get
a sense of how these opinions read. But, much more important, frequently
statements of the Court eloquently, even powerfully, articulate principles of
freedom and church-state separation. I hope you will be instructed by reading
the Court's own words. But first it is necessary to look at the background of
the religion clauses of the Constitution, which are critical to church-state relations in this country.

2

Background of
Constitutional Principles

Christianity became the official religion of the Roman Empire in the fourth century. In the language of church-state relations, it became the "established" religion. Throughout this book "establishment" means an official, formal, symbiotic relationship between religion and the civil authority. In those early days this relationship was assumed to be good for both the state and the church. It was beneficial for the state in that the moral precepts taught by the church provided an ideology and moral basis for government. It was good for the church in that it provided the church with political status and influence, protection from competition, and, in some eras, financial assistance from tax monies collected by the state for the benefit of the church.

The arrangement persisted for centuries in the Western world; the Catholic Church was the established church. One might think that when the Protestant Reformers broke with the Roman Catholic Church, they would also have abandoned its concept of establishment. But they did not. Because everyone was so immersed in the idea that it was necessary to have an establishment in order to have a stable political order, the new Protestant movements continued the practice. With the proliferation of religious movements, church-state alignments became much more complicated, but the principle and practice of establishment persisted in western Europe. The most prominent early examples were the Lutheran state churches in Germany and, later, Scandinavia, Henry VIII's Church of England (Anglican), and the established Reformed churches in Switzerland in Huldreich Zwingli's Zurich and John Calvin's Geneva.

The Anabaptists of Switzerland and the Low Countries are an exception to this generalization. They believed civil authority should have nothing to do with matters of religion. But this idea was regarded as heretical by the majority and was a major reason the Anabaptists were severely persecuted.

Because everything was complicated by the multiplicity of religious groups, in 1555 a treaty was signed, the Peace of Augsburg, which set forth, for Germany, the principle of *cujus regio, ejus religio*, "whose the rule, his or hers the religion." The actual phrase was not used until 1648, in the treaty called the Peace of Westphalia, which expanded the principle to apply to all of Europe. Under this principle, the ruler of a territory had the right to determine the religion of that territory. This proestablishment philosophy and this operating principle, "whose the rule, his or hers the religion," were transported to the New World with its earliest permanent settlers.

THE SEVENTEENTH CENTURY: A VARIETY OF CHURCH-STATE RELATIONSHIPS

It is frequently said that the founders of the first American colonies came to the New World for religious freedom. That is not entirely accurate. The earliest permanent settlers were those who created the colony of Virginia. They were members of the Anglican Church, which was the established church in England at the time. As such, in England they had not been persecuted or otherwise disadvantaged because of their religion. They came to the New World at least as much for its adventure and economic potential as out of missionary zeal. When they created a government for the Virginia colony, they established the Anglican Church; it was to be the only church in the colony. In the traditional style of an establishment, clergy were provided public support in the form of money or, more often, land and tobacco. "Dale's laws" (1610), named after one of the first governors of the colony, required attendance at Anglican worship by all citizens of the colony, and persistent violation of the law carried the death penalty. There were also laws against blasphemy and criticism of the Anglican Church or any of its particular doctrines. Depending on the seriousness of the offense, penalties could range from mutilation of one's tongue to death. There is no clear evidence that the laws were rigorously enforced or that the ultimate penalties were ever inflicted. But it is clear that there was no religious freedom in early Virginia.[1] Anglicanism was also at least nominally established in North and South Carolina, Georgia, and, in the eighteenth century, Maryland and New York.

There were in England, however, some people who did not conform to the Church of England. Although they disagreed among themselves about the extent to which they should separate from the national church, they agreed that it should be purified of what they considered to be the residue of Roman Catholicism within it—thus the name "Puritans." When it became clear the

Anglican Church would not follow their admonitions on the purification of the church and that they might lose their wealth or even their lives if they persisted in their criticism, they left for the New World.

Some Puritans landed at what is now Plymouth, Massachusetts, in 1620, and a larger group at Massachusetts Bay in 1628. Here they attempted to create the ideal church and state, a commonwealth based on the Bible, "a due form of Government both civil and ecclesiastical,"[2] an establishment. Because of the form of church government they followed, their church was called "Congregationalist." Puritan laws compelled the observance of Congregationalist faith and practice by all the citizens of the colony. They wanted to keep their religion pure. As one early leader, Nathaniel Ward, said, after naming a list of unacceptable religions, they "shall have free Liberty to keep away from us, and such as will come to be gone as fast as they can, the sooner the better."[3] Did the Puritans mean that? Yes; dissenters were often tried and physically punished, sometimes banished from the colony.[4] Between 1659 and 1661 four Quakers were executed by hanging, including Mary Dyer, the first woman martyr for religious liberty in the New World.[5] In short, these Puritans came to America for religious liberty, but when they got here they created an establishment just as repressive as that from which they had escaped.

> It is important to understand that they never intended to launch a colony that would be open to all persons of all religious persuasions— or none. The Puritans came to create a pure church and to conduct a holy experiment free of opposition, distraction, and error. They were not hypocrites who demanded freedom of religion then denied that same freedom to others. Freedom of religion across the board was never the plan, never the commission or errand. They came to prove that one could form a society so faithful, a church so cleansed, that even old England would be transformed by witnessing what determined believers had managed to achieve many thousands of miles away.[6]

The Congregationalist church was also established in Connecticut and New Hampshire.

Exceptions and Precursors

There were exceptions to the pattern of establishment, most notably Rhode Island and Pennsylvania. The former was founded by Roger Williams, the most vigorous advocate for religious freedom in the colonial period. He was concerned for the purity of the church and the spiritual welfare of those within it. To preserve its purity, he believed, the church should be separated from the corrupting influences of the state and the "natural man." Consequently, he founded Rhode Island in 1636 on the principle of religious liberty. The colony became a haven of freedom for those who were persecuted for their religion in other colonies.

Pennsylvania was founded in 1682 by William Penn, a Quaker. Quakers believed in the concept of the "inner light," something of God in each person, which both sanctified human life and potentially revealed God to the individual. Because one's experience with God could be direct and immediate and persons could understand the inner light differently, Quakers believed religion should be free from state-imposed uniformity in thought or practice. However, even in Pennsylvania, political office was available to Christians only. In spite of that restriction, Penn's "Holy Experiment" granted the broadest religious freedom in colonial America.

"Whose the rule, his or hers the religion." That principle was dominant in the early seventeenth century. Most governments chose to try to enforce religious uniformity and exclusivism, although the denominations differed from colony to colony. But others were willing to accommodate religious diversity. In any case, the shape of religion in a colony was dependent on the beliefs of those in power. However, as time progressed, several factors emerged to change this situation.

THE EIGHTEENTH CENTURY: THE PROCESS OF DISESTABLISHMENT

Pluralism

Pluralism is one of the principal features of American religion. "Pluralism" means that in this country we have a multiplicity of religions, each of which perceives itself as being different enough from others to merit separate existence. It has been that way from the country's beginning. Consequently, it may be artificial to introduce the concept of pluralism under the heading of the eighteenth century, for, as the seventeenth progressed, Dutch Reformed, Lutherans, Roman Catholics, Jews, Baptists, and many nonbelievers journeyed to America. In the eighteenth century, pluralism increased as groups like the Presbyterians, Mennonites, German Reformed, and Moravians began to arrive in numbers.[7]

With the increasing diversity of the population it became more difficult for any government to maintain religious homogeneity within its borders. Thus one of the traditional arguments for an establishment, a stable political order based on an official theology and set of moral ideas, became progressively irrelevant. Additionally, Rhode Island and Pennsylvania, which were flourishing, demonstrated that it was possible to have orderly government and a stable society even without religious uniformity. They were successful "laboratory schools" of religious pluralism.

Furthermore, from the perspective of the various religious groups, there was a very practical implication of this pluralism. None of them was large enough or powerful enough to become the dominant, much less the sole, religious group in an area. Groups perceived that if any one group was given political power, all others would be disadvantaged. Better that all religious groups be equal before the law. So pluralism was one of several factors in the eighteenth century that contributed to the eventual separation of church and state in America.

Religious Revivalism

Beginning in the 1720s with regional outbursts and reaching its peak from 1740 to 1742, the Great Awakening contributed significantly to the process of disestablishment. The Great Awakening was a revival movement that swept the eastern seaboard, spread primarily by the enormously talented preacher George Whitefield. The revival sought to enliven the churches, which many religious leaders saw as spiritually dead or at least in the doldrums, by preaching a message of spiritual renewal and discipline. It was not enough to be a lukewarm Christian; one should know that he or she was a sinful creature, estranged from God, before receiving God's forgiveness. But, by God's grace, salvation and spiritual revitalization were available. Much of this preaching was done not in churches, but in open-air meetings, thus reaching large crowds. Many people had conversion experiences. It is difficult to know how many conversions happened; eighteenth-century preachers were not much better at accurately reporting such numbers than modern ones. But historians are convinced that the churches of various denominations were revitalized and enlarged by the Great Awakening.

Religious leaders had historically argued that it was necessary to have an establishment to get people into the churches and that the police power of the state must be used to compel people to attend worship. (Remember "Dale's laws.") But those who responded to the revival preachers did so voluntarily, because they were attracted to the gospel. There was no coercion, yet people came to listen to preachers, worship, and join churches. Some began to wonder why, if it were possible to attract people to religion and churches through persuasion, it was necessary to continue the establishment pattern. Such thinking later contributed to the formulation of the concept of separation of church and state.

Pietism

In addition to the persuasive power of orthodox Christian preaching, many people at the time drew antiestablishment conclusions from the theology itself. This resulted in a style of religion historians know as pietism, which emphasized Christian identity based on the religious renewal of persons through a new birth, rather than having been born into an established religion characterized by lack of religious fervor.

Human beings are sinful; their stiff-necked pride causes them to rebel against God, thus distorting, if not destroying, the relationship between humans and God that God originally intended. This sin manifests itself in all sorts of ways, from minor peccadilloes to deeds of abject evil. Human beings cannot restore this relationship with God themselves. God, in an act of ulti-mate mercy, sent Jesus Christ to be the savior of humankind.

Those who heard this good news and in whom God ignited faith (Calvin-ist theology) or who responded to the message (Arminian theology) were brought into a restored relationship with God; they were Christian. But this was an individual experience. Without discounting the church as the place where the gospel was rightly preached and the sacraments rightly adminis-tered, as the community of the faithful gathered for mutual support and spir-itual nurture, nonetheless the experience of salvation was ultimately an individual experience.

In the American environment, some began to make a connection between the personal experience of salvation and political religious freedom. The expe-rience of becoming Christian was dependent on the work of the Holy Spirit within one, not the theological dictates of a state-controlled church. The lib-erating experience of salvation meant freedom from the "principalities and powers"—not only from sin, but the political powers as well. Furthermore, there was no guarantee that all should respond to the call of God in the same way. "Hence the pietist did not have the heart . . . longer to justify coerced uni-formity under Establishment."[8]

Rationalism

Another contributor to eventual separation was the opposite of pietism: rationalism. In this age of the Enlightenment, many became convinced of the virtual invincibility of human reason. Reason could perceive and understand all that was worth knowing; it could formulate ethical principles; it could devise systems of government. There was great emphasis on the worth and abilities of human beings. Rationalists were not unanimous in their views of religion. Some said reason took the place of God: by relying on reason, humans no longer had need for God; religion was only antiquated superstition. Others took the position that reason could demonstrate the existence of God; for example, the complexity and precision of the universe implied the existence of a Designer. This theistic form of rationalism was known as Deism and was the position of many of those great men who were responsible for writing the Constitution and shaping the early United States. Their Deism greatly influenced their views of church-state relationships. They believed any institution that hindered reason, interfered with free, creative thought, or shackled the minds of men and women was bad. They knew history well enough to know that established churches had had just such an impact. Theological orthodoxy imposed by law, the late medieval Inquisition, and the heresy trials and executions of the American colonies taught them that an established church was inimical to political and intellectual freedom. Consequently, they were not willing to make establishment a characteristic of the new nation they were creating.

The Virginia Experience

In sum, a variety of practical, theological, and philosophical factors contributed to constitutional disestablishment. A final factor was the almost laboratory experience of Virginia. By 1779 Virginia had become as religiously pluralistic as the other colonies, and many of its inhabitants were rethinking church-state relationships. The Anglican establishment was considerably weakened.

In 1784 a taxation bill was introduced in the Virginia legislature that was intended for the support of the Christian religion rather than any particular sect. The tax was to be collected by the civil authorities, but the taxpayer could designate which Christian group would receive the money. If one chose no Christian organization to receive the tax, it would go to education. The principal sponsor of the bill was Patrick Henry, who argued that governmental support of religion was necessary in order to have a moral society. The principal opponent of the bill was James Madison, who expressed his opposition in a document entitled "Memorial and Remonstrance against Religious Assessments" (see Appendix A). Madison marshaled rationalistic and philosophical arguments against any tax bill whatsoever, in the process making the case for religious freedom in a variety of forceful ways. No document has argued for religious freedom more eloquently; it is an American classic.

Madison's purpose in writing the piece was to sway public opinion against the taxation bill. In that he was extraordinarily successful. In 1785 the legislature defeated the taxation bill. Madison took advantage of this moment to reintroduce to the legislature Thomas Jefferson's "Bill for Establishing Religious Freedom" (Appendix B). Jefferson had first introduced this bill in 1779, and it had been tabled by the legislature every year since. But now, in the climate created by the Memorial and Remonstrance, the bill was enacted into law in January 1786. The importance of these events is not only that Virginia became a trailblazer in the American movement toward the separation of church and state, but also that it gave Madison the opportunity to crystallize and articulate his thoughts on the question of religious liberty before he went to Philadelphia to work on the Constitution.

THE CONSTITUTION

The statesmen who wrote the Constitution mentioned religion in only one place in the document, Article VI. They wrote a prohibition. Article VI, as a part of the requirement that state and federal officeholders take an oath or make an affirmation to support the Constitution, says: "but no religious Test shall ever be required as a Qualification to any Office or public Trust under the United States." There is no reference to God or to any religious tradition in the Constitution. Apparently this was not an oversight.

Does that mean that the founders were hostile to religion or even to Christianity? No, it means that they recognized, given the multiplicity of religions in the new nation and the distressing history of governmental oppression in the name of religion, that it would be better for them to leave the question alone. To avoid getting involved in a quagmire of competing religious loyalties, the government should remain neutral. Furthermore, it was a way of asserting the limited nature of government. The state had no powers that were not enumerated in the Constitution. By not mentioning religion, the founders were not expressing animosity toward religion, but rather keeping the sacred matter of religion from the reach of government. In the words of Madison, the Constitution was not to grant "a shadow of right in the general government to intermeddle with religion."[9]

> The political convictions of the men who struggled to ratify a godless Constitution were not products of personal godlessness. Far from it. Almost everyone who participated in the debates about the Constitution shared a concern about the health of religion. . . . Many of the men who championed the godless Constitution stayed aloof from dogmatic forms of Christian faith, but most of them believed in a God who rewarded good and punished evil in an afterlife. They respected the moral teachings of Christ and hoped that they would prosper among Americans and in the churches that Americans attended.[10]

They wrote a secular Constitution because they believed government should not be involved in matters of conscience. However, because the government obviously needed to set the requirements for public office, the authors addressed themselves to this question. Public office would be independent of religious belief or the lack thereof.

This provision of Article VI did not create the separation of church and state. But it went a long way to minimize in the new nation the possibility of the religious strife and oppression that had been known in the history of the Western world. Apparently the majority of Americans were satisfied with the Constitution's virtual silence on the question of religion, for it was ratified in 1789. But many were not satisfied by the silence of the Constitution on the larger question of the freedoms of citizens, including the freedom of religion. Consequently, the founders drew up a list guaranteeing particular freedoms: the Bill of Rights.

The Establishment Clause

The historical record on the process of writing the religion clauses of the First Amendment is not completely clear. The record of the debate in the House of Representatives is brief, perhaps more a paraphrase or summary than a verbatim report. The Senate debate was conducted in secret, although there is a record of the votes on various proposals. The information available indicates that the religion provisions of the Bill of Rights were modified several times before the final wording was decided on.

Several proposals, while clearly prohibiting the government from establishing one particular religious group, would have allowed it to aid all religions on a nondiscriminatory, nonpreferential basis. For example, these two proposals in the Senate: "Congress shall make no law establishing one religious sect or society in preference to others," and "Congress shall not make any law infringing the rights of conscience, or establishing any religious sect or society." Some of the proposals in the House were similar. But the First Congress rejected that language. When members of the House and Senate came together in conference committee, they produced the language that became the religion clauses of the First Amendment: "Congress shall make no law respecting an establishment of religion, or prohibiting the free exercise thereof." We shall return to this issue.

By the end of the eighteenth century, the colonial establishments described earlier had changed. No colony supported the establishment of a single religious group. No longer was the Anglican Church, the Congregational Church, or any other religious group exclusively established anywhere. As a result of many of the factors described earlier, especially pluralism, all the establishments had become "multiple establishments." By the time the Bill of Rights was ratified in 1791, only six states had any sort of establishment. Of those, three gave government support to Protestantism and three to Christianity—none to a specific denomination.

I mentioned earlier the bill proposed in the Virginia legislature in 1784 that would have levied a tax "for the Christian religion," in which each taxpayer could designate which group would receive the tax payment, so long as the group was Christian. The result would have been a "multiple establishment," and if Virginia had passed that bill, it would have brought to seven the number of states to have such an arrangement. The only variation among these states was that three excluded Catholicism by favoring only Protestant groups. Thus multiple establishment was the pattern at the time the First Congress was debating the language of the religion provisions of the Bill of Rights.

Some of the proposals presupposed this multiple establishment arrangement and wanted to preserve it by prohibiting the government from giving its favor and support to only one denomination. This is known as the "nonpreferential" view of establishment: establishment is permitted so long as it is nondiscriminatory, showing no preference between religions. This view is also known as the "accommodationist" approach: the proper relationship between church and state is for the state to accommodate the church.

But the final language of the First Amendment went beyond this view; it took the "separationist," or "no aid," approach. The founders were familiar with the no-preference approach, but they wrote that there was to be "no law respecting an establishment of religion." The government was not to establish one religion, neither was it to establish multiple religions. This was one more way the founders articulated their view that government was to be limited.

> Every bit of evidence goes to prove that the First Amendment, like the others, was intended to restrict Congress to its enumerated powers. Since the Constitutional Convention gave Congress no power to legislate on matters concerning religion, Congress had no such power even in the absence of the First Amendment. It is, therefore, unreasonable to believe that an express prohibition of power—"Congress shall make no law respecting an establishment of religion"—creates the power, previously nonexistent, of supporting religion by aid to one or all religious groups. The Bill of Rights, as Madison said, was not framed "to imply powers not meant to be included in the enumeration."[11]

The meaning of the Establishment Clause on this issue is currently a topic of intense debate. The debate is over what the founders originally intended by the First Amendment, especially the Establishment Clause. Although the evidence is strong, as just described, that the founders were "separationist" in their understanding of what they were doing, some argue that they were "non-preferentialists." This "original intent" controversy is covered in detail in chapter 9.

Application of Constitutional Principles by the States

When the Bill of Rights was ratified, it was understood by everyone that it applied only to the federal government, not to the states. The founders believed that each state should handle the issue of religion at the state level. The effect of this is easily illustrated. Most of the states wrote provisions into their constitutions that also provided for separation of church and state and guaranteed religious freedom. Sometimes the language was more detailed and stringent than the First Amendment. But three states—New Hampshire, Connecticut, and Massachusetts—continued their multiple establishments until long after the First Amendment became law in December 1791. Massachusetts, in 1833, was the last to abolish its establishment. So religious freedom was guaranteed against federal encroachment, but at the state level the concept still was basically "whose the rule, his or hers the religion."

After the Civil War, the Thirteenth, Fourteenth, and Fifteenth Amendments to the Constitution were ratified to eliminate slavery and to guarantee civil rights and the vote to freed male slaves. The following clause, known as the Due Process Clause, is in the Fourteenth Amendment, section 1: "[N]or shall any State deprive any person of life, liberty, or property, without due process of law." This demands that the *states* be diligent in preserving the liberties of their citizens.

In the twentieth century, the Supreme Court began to decide some cases by applying the liberties of the First Amendment to the states through the Due Process Clause of the Fourteenth Amendment. Lawyers call this "incorporation," meaning that the liberties of the First Amendment are incorporated into the Fourteenth. Specifically, because of the Fourteenth Amendment, the liberties guaranteed by the Establishment and Free Exercise Clauses are among the liberties the various states may not deny to their citizens. So, in the current understanding of the principle, no governmental unit, from Congress to the local school board, may make a law establishing religion or prohibiting its free exercise.

When Americans think of the late eighteenth century, they think of the Revolutionary War, by which independence was gained from Britain. But no less revolutionary was the separation of church and state. This was the first time in human history that a nation had written into its legal charter the idea of separation and religious freedom. Never before had a nation been bold enough to guarantee to its citizens the right to be religious or nonreligious, and, if religious, to practice that religion according to the dictates of their conscience. Revolutionary! That constitutional guarantee is preeminent among the features that make America the great country it is. But, of course, it has been necessary for the Supreme Court to interpret the meanings and boundaries of the guarantee. In chapter 3 we begin an examination of that exposition.

3

Defining the Scope of Religious Freedom Prior to 1963

A survey of the decisions of the Supreme Court on church-state relations should begin with the Free Exercise Clause, because cases about that clause came to the Court long before Establishment Clause cases. The First Amendment demands that "Congress shall make no law . . . prohibiting the free exercise [of religion]." The obvious meaning is that government may not prohibit religious activity. The religion clauses mean, at a minimum, that a person can believe what she or he wants in the area of religion. However, it would be a hollow freedom if one were told, "You can believe whatever you want, so long as you do not do anything about it." Religious freedom goes far beyond that. The Free Exercise Clause guarantees the right to implement one's religious beliefs, to put them into action. But does this mean that "anything goes," that whatever one does in the name of religion is constitutionally protected?

MORMON CASES

The Supreme Court began to confront the issue of the scope of free exercise in the late nineteenth century, in cases brought by the Church of Jesus Christ of Latter-day Saints, the Mormons. The controversy was over polygamy. The founder of the church, Joseph Smith Jr., had taught in the late 1830s and early 1840s that polygamy was divinely commanded and a religious obligation. That belief was part of the theology of the church for the rest of the century. When Mormons began to establish their communities in Utah and surrounding territories, Congress responded with laws forbidding plural marriages. The laws applied to federal territories, which enabled the Supreme Court to judge cases from Utah and Idaho even before the incorporation of the Free Exercise Clause

21

into the Fourteenth Amendment. The key case, decided in 1879, is *Reynolds v. United States*.[1] Reynolds, a Mormon who had two wives, was convicted for violating the antipolygamy law. But he asserted that the Free Exercise Clause protected his behavior because it was based on religious belief.

The Supreme Court rejected that argument. It held that one can believe whatever one wants, because the government may not interfere with religious belief, but one may not put those beliefs into action *if* those actions are somehow harmful to persons or even the moral structure of society: "Congress was deprived of all legislative power over mere opinion, but was left free to reach actions which were in violation of social duties or subversive of good order."[2] The Court held that the practice of polygamy tended to instill in people the attitude of despotism or authoritarianism (because a home with so many wives and children had to be "ruled with an iron hand"). Such an attitude was contrary to the needs of a democratic society. That is, the mentality of tyranny fostered by polygamy is incompatible with "government by the people." Furthermore, polygamy was historically unacceptable in the Western world because it was immoral. That was the reason Congress passed laws prohibiting plural marriages. Because the law and the Court assumed polygamy to be harmful to the moral fiber of society, the law was constitutional and Reynolds was not protected by the fact that his practice of polygamy was religiously based.[3]

In *Reynolds* the Court established a precedent that has persisted, in some form, to the present. Although religious freedom is a constitutionally guaranteed right, it is not absolute. It is subject to government interference if the government can show that a practice has harmful effects. In *Reynolds*, the Court held that government latitude is very wide in defining what is unacceptable to society. Although belief is protected, the government may prohibit any practice it determines has a negative impact on an individual, group, or society as a whole, even if it is religiously motivated. The Court did not give government officials any guidelines on how to define what was negative and what was not. So this case gave the government extremely broad authority to interfere with religious behavior, and the government retained that judicially defined power for more than sixty years.[4]

JEHOVAH'S WITNESSES CASES

In the 1930s and 1940s the Supreme Court heard a large number of cases brought by the Jehovah's Witnesses. This prompts a short but important discussion. Often cases are brought to the Court by groups, or individuals representing groups, that are looked down on by the general population. In the 1940s the Jehovah's Witnesses were widely despised, just as the Mormons had been in the late nineteenth century. They found many laws were written or enforced in a way that curtailed their religious liberty. Consequently, they initiated litigation to try to improve their situation. Of course, they had to invoke constitutional principles that applied to everybody (or were supposed to). The result was that in looking out for their own interests, the Witnesses elicited decisions from the Court that actually broadened the liberties of all Americans. So Americans all are in the debt of groups like the Mormons, Jehovah's Witnesses, Seventh-day Adventists, Native Americans, and individuals like Guy Ballard and Madalyn Murray O'Hair, who have braved the scorn of society to provide for clearer definitions and applications of the religion clauses of the First Amendment.[5]

Evangelizing on Public Property

Several of the Jehovah's Witness cases were about proselytizing or evangelizing on public property. The Witnesses believe that theirs is the only true religion and they are the only ones who understand God's activity in history. So it is their responsibility to tell as many people as possible about their faith. Furthermore, because they make no distinction between clergy and lay members, they believe that every baptized member of their organization is a minister with the obligation to evangelize. In the 1930s and 1940s they were especially vigorous in this activity, often going into the streets and parks of communities in large groups to proclaim the word of God as they understood it. Not only did many residents of these towns regard the Witnesses as a nuisance to be gotten rid of, but they sometimes resented their message so much that they retaliated. The issue was not so much that the Witnesses were proclaiming the impending return of Jesus Christ to judge the earth, but their assertion that that judgment would be inflicted on all who were not among God's true people, the Witnesses. In those days the Witnesses preached in no uncertain terms that all organized religion was evil and the Roman Catholic Church was the worst of the lot. This message frequently led to hostile responses rather than conversions. Consequently, communities tried to keep the Witnesses out, and the Witnesses responded by going to court, claiming free-exercise rights.

One of the cases that grew out of these confrontations, *Cantwell v. Connecticut*,[6] is such a significant case that it merits a detailed explanation.

Newton Cantwell and his two sons went to New Haven, Connecticut, to proclaim the Witnesses' message. A city statute required all outsiders to apply to a city official for a license to solicit funds or distribute material within the city limits. If the official determined that the cause was religious or a bona fide charity, the license would be given. If the cause was not, the license would be withheld. The Cantwells did not apply for a license because they believed obedience to God's command to evangelize was not contingent on any government official's approval. They simply proceeded to proclaim their religion on the streets and sidewalks. They spread their message by passing out literature to those who would take it and make a small contribution. They also played records on a small hand-held, spring-driven phonograph for those who would consent to listen. One of the records, entitled "Enemies," was a vigorous attack against the Roman Catholic Church. When some Catholics listened to the record, they threatened the Cantwells with violence if they did not leave. The Cantwells did leave, with no argument, but were later arrested for inciting a breach of the peace. They were also charged with not having obtained the required license. They were convicted of both offenses by a Connecticut trial court and the state Supreme Court. They asked the United States Supreme Court to hear their case.

Application to the States

The Supreme Court decided in 1940 in favor of the Cantwells. In the process, it set forth some very important principles. *Cantwell* is the first case in which the Court incorporated the Free Exercise Clause into the Fourteenth Amendment. Never before had the clause been applied to state law. No clearer explanation of the concept can be found than this statement from *Cantwell*, written by Justice Owen Roberts:

> We hold that the statute, as construed and applied to the appellants, deprives them of their liberty without due process of law in contravention of the Fourteenth Amendment. The fundamental concept of liberty embodied in that Amendment embraces the liberties guaranteed by the First Amendment. The First Amendment declares that Congress shall make no law respecting an establishment of religion or prohibiting the free exercise thereof. The Fourteenth Amendment has rendered the legislatures of the states as incompetent as Congress to enact such laws. The constitutional inhibition of legislation on the subject of religion has a double aspect. On the one hand, it forestalls compulsion by law of the acceptance of any creed or the practice of any form of worship. Freedom of conscience and freedom to adhere to such religious organization or form of worship as the individual may choose cannot be restricted by law. On the other hand, it safeguards the chosen form of religion. Thus the Amendment embraces two concepts,—freedom to believe and freedom to act. The first is absolute but, in the nature of things, the second cannot be. Conduct remains subject to regulation for the protection of society. . . . In every case the power to regulate must be so exercised as not, in attaining a permissible end, unduly to infringe the protected freedom.[7]

Impermissible Prior Restraint

The Court went on from this magnificent statement of what the freedom of religion is all about to say that New Haven, in attempting to attain a permissible end, had unduly infringed the Cantwells' religious freedom. The requirement to obtain a license to go into the streets to distribute literature and evangelize functioned as an impermissible prior restraint. A government official could not have the authority to decide what is a religion and what is not and accordingly issue or withhold an enabling license. Of course a city may maintain some control over what happens in its streets. "But to condition the solicitation of aid for the perpetuation of religious views or systems upon a license, the grant of which rests in the exercise of a determination by state authority as to what is a religious cause, is to lay a forbidden burden upon the exercise of liberty protected by the Constitution."[8] The effect of *Cantwell* was to broaden the liberty of all religious groups to be free from governmental prior restraint, that is, to be free from having to seek government approval to engage in religious activities, activities that may even determine their right to survive.

Clear and Present Danger

On the question of whether the Cantwells were guilty of incitement to breach of peace, the Court struck another blow for religious liberty. It ruled that before government may prohibit religious activity it must show the activity presents a "clear and present danger" or an "immediate threat" to public safety, peace, or order. In other words, the Court considerably narrowed the latitude given the government in *Reynolds v. United States* to interfere with religious activity. No longer could the government inhibit religious activity on the basis that it presented *some* danger to society. Now the government had to show the religious behavior presented a grave, significant, and current danger to society before it could be curtailed by government intervention. In short, since *Cantwell* religious freedom has been the rule, government interference the exception. It is a landmark case because it applied the Free Exercise Clause to the states and because it broadened the dimensions of religious liberty by both prohibiting prior restraints and articulating the clear and present danger test.

Taxing Evangelism Efforts

A variation on the effort to keep Jehovah's Witnesses, and anyone else who would attempt to evangelize in public places, from doing so was to levy a tax on the enterprise. Many cities in the late 1930s and early 1940s passed laws to require a permit and the payment of a tax for the permission to evangelize. The Court in the 1940s held such behavior also to be a form of prior restraint prohibited by the Free Exercise Clause (*Murdock v. Pennsylvania*).[9] But cities could maintain public order by placing time, place, and manner restrictions on the public evangelizing (*Cox v. New Hampshire*).[10] So government may not require the payment of a tax or the permission of a city official as a condition of evangelizing in public streets and parks,[11] but it may require the members of the evangelizing group to identify themselves and may have regulations on when, where, and how the evangelization is done. Thus cities are still in control of their streets and parks, in that they may insist that evangelization not be disruptive of a reasonably normal flow of traffic, not be harmful to citizens, and not overwhelm the police protection of the city.

Children as Evangelists

The Court also ruled that minor children may not be employed in preaching and literature distribution on public thoroughfares (*Prince v. Massachusetts*).[12] A Jehovah's Witness parent took her minor children into a downtown area to preach on the streets. This preaching included the distribution, in return for a voluntary contribution, of literature, principally *The Watchtower* magazine. The child labor laws in the jurisdiction in which Sarah Prince lived prohibited the sale of literature and other goods on the public thoroughfares by boys under twelve and girls under eighteen years of age. When Prince was arrested for the violation of child labor laws, she protested that the children were ministers of religion and their preaching was protected by the Free Exercise Clause. The Court ruled that whereas adults may practice their religion by preaching on the streets, children may not. Child labor laws, which are more restrictive of the kinds of work children may engage in than laws are about the labor of adults, show the state has a strong interest in the health and safety of children.[13] Consequently, the Free Exercise Clause cannot protect the activity of using children to evangelize on the public streets. In this case, the Court made a rather expansive statement: "Parents are free to become martyrs themselves. But it does not follow that they are free, in identical circumstances, to make martyrs of their children before they have reached the age of full and legal discretion when they can make that choice for themselves."[14]

Blood Transfusions

Prince has an application beyond evangelizing. Jehovah's Witnesses have believed for a long time that ingesting blood into the body in any way, including transfusions, is contrary to the will of God.[15] Consequently, while they accept modern medicine, they have not been willing to accept blood transfusions, even in the face of possible death absent the transfusion. But courts have ruled, based on *Prince*, that the children of Witnesses may be compelled to receive blood transfusions when adults may not.[16] Hospitals and physicians may obtain from judges legal authorization to administer blood to minors over the objection of their Jehovah's Witness parents. But beginning around 2000 the Witnesses began to change their policy on transfusions. This was principally to keep up with advances in medical technology. Witnesses still forbid transfusions of whole blood and any of its four primary components (red cells, white cells, plasma, platelets). But they now permit administration of blood fractions, derived from the primary components such as clotting factors from plasma and interferons from white cells, based on a personal decision by the believer. So the Jehovah's Witnesses entered the twenty-first century with confusion reigning in their blood transfusion policy. But the legal principle remains that the free-exercise rights of children are narrower than those of adults, if it can be shown that religious behavior is harmful to the physical or mental welfare of the child.[17]

Saluting the Flag

The Jehovah's Witnesses also have religious objections to saluting the flag of any country. They believe to salute a flag is to recognize the sovereignty of the country the flag represents. Jehovah's Witnesses believe there is only one sovereign worthy of the allegiance of humans—God. Their reason for not saluting the flag is not contrariness or lack of patriotism, but their adherence to the priorities they believe are taught by the Bible—loyalty to God should take precedence over loyalty to country. Furthermore, to salute a flag is to make a graven image and to engage in idolatry.[18] This practice became a legal matter when public school districts compelled Witness children to recite the Pledge of Allegiance and to salute the flag at the beginning of each school day.

On this issue, we see the Court's deliberative process at work. First, in 1940 the Supreme Court ruled that children could be forced to say the Pledge of Allegiance even though they claimed that the Free Exercise Clause protected their religious objections to the ceremony (*Minersville School District v. Gobitis*).[19] The Court's reasoning, written by Justice Felix Frankfurter, was that the nation needs the loyalty and unity of the people and the flag salute is a primary way of achieving it; a national interest of the highest importance was at stake. "National unity is the basis of national security. . . . The ultimate foundation of a free society is the binding tie of cohesive sentiment. . . . 'We live by symbols.' The flag is the symbol of our national unity, transcending all internal differences, however large, within the framework of the Constitution."[20]

However, three years later the Court examined the issue again, for at least two reasons. First, three new justices had come on the Court. Second, after *Gobitis* school districts across the country had made even more stringent rules requiring the recitation of the Pledge. When Witnesses remained faithful to their religious convictions and refused to salute the flag, shameful persecution was inflicted on them. This persecution included the burning of Witness meeting places, mob violence against Witnesses, at least one castration, and forcible removal from the communities where they lived. Sometimes they were made to drink castor oil and then paraded publicly through city streets.

In *West Virginia Board of Education v. Barnette*[21] the Court reversed *Gobitis*, Justice Robert Jackson writing for the majority. Arguing on both free speech and free exercise of religion grounds, the Court ruled that the state may not force one to say what one does not believe. Since the flag salute was a form of expression, Witness children could not be compelled to say the Pledge of Allegiance. Without denying the flag is the symbol of national solidarity, on which national security rests, the Court held freedom of religion and speech take precedent over even such important interests. Indeed, the very freedom the flag symbolizes includes the freedom not to salute it. Mindful of the terror of Nazism, which was sweeping Europe at the time, the Court said:

> Those who begin coercive elimination of dissent soon find themselves exterminating dissenters. Compulsory unification of opinion achieves only the unanimity of the graveyard. It seems trite but necessary to say that the First Amendment to our Constitution was designed to avoid these ends by avoiding these beginnings.[22]

Robert Jackson, one of the best writers to serve on the Court, went on to make what has become a famous statement about the scope of liberties Americans enjoy.

> But freedom to differ is not limited to things that do not matter much. That would be a mere shadow of freedom. The test of its substance is the right to differ as to things that touch the heart of the existing order.
> If there is any fixed star in our constitutional constellation, it is that no official, high or petty, can prescribe what shall be orthodox in politics, nationalism, religion, or other matters of opinion or force citizens to confess by word or act their faith therein.[23]

This is dictum at its finest, by which all Americans should be instructed!

THEOLOGY: A FORBIDDEN AREA

A final free-exercise case prior to 1963 did not involve the Jehovah's Witnesses but raised a very important issue of religious freedom. Guy Ballard was the leader of the "I Am Movement." He claimed to have had extraordinary spiritual experiences, including personal encounters with Saint Germain and Jesus. As a result, he claimed to know the spiritual secret of good health and to be able to heal people of even those diseases that doctors said were incurable. He and his family sent out mailings making these claims and encouraging people to send in money and partake of the healing the Ballards had available for them. The government claimed the Ballards knew the representations they made were not true and thus they were guilty of defrauding the public through the mail.

The question before the Court was whether the truth or falsity of the Ballards' theology could be presented to a jury. Stated differently, does a civil court or the government have the right to evaluate the religious beliefs of a person or a group? The Court answered that question with a resounding no in *United States v. Ballard*.[24] The fact that individuals or groups may believe what they want about religion means the government is not permitted to make a judgment about the validity of the beliefs. As Professor Harry W. Jones put it, "Could we tolerate for a moment a principle that the free exercise of religion means only the free exercise of 'true' religion, and that judges and juries are empowered to decide whose religious faiths are true and whose are untrue?"[25] Both the Establishment Clause and the Free Exercise Clause point in the direction of noninterference by government. Justice William O. Douglas, writing for the Court, clearly expressed the freedom that Americans enjoy:

> Freedom of thought, which includes freedom of religious belief, is basic to the society of free men. It embraces the right to maintain theories of life and of death and of the hereafter which are rank heresy to followers of the orthodox faiths. Heresy trials are foreign to our Constitution. Men may believe what they cannot prove. They may not be put to the proof of their religious doctrines or beliefs. Religious experiences which are as real as life to some may be incomprehensible to others. Yet the fact that they may be beyond the ken of mortals does not mean that they can be made suspect before the law. . . . Man's relationship to his God was made no concern of the state. He was granted the right to worship as he pleased and to answer to no man for the verity of his religious views. The religious views espoused by [the Ballards] might seem incredible, if not preposterous, to most people. But if those doctrines are subject to trial before a jury charged with finding their truth or falsity, then the same can be done with the religious beliefs of any sect. . . . The First Amendment does not select any one group or any one type of religion for preferred treatment. It puts them all in that position.[26]

Since from time to time Americans become concerned about "cults" and even want the government to take some action against them,[27] these words are important for us to remember. A similar idea was expressed in a dissenting opinion by Justice Robert Jackson:

> The chief wrong which false prophets do to their following is not financial. The collections aggregate to a tempting total, but individual

payments are not ruinous. . . . But the real harm is on the mental and spiritual plane. There are people who hunger and thirst after higher values which they feel wanting in their humdrum lives. They live in mental confusion or moral anarchy and seek vaguely for truth and beauty and moral support. When they are deluded and then disillusioned, cynicism and confusion follow. The wrong of these things, as I see it, is not in the money the victims part with half so much as in the mental and spiritual poison they get. But that is precisely the thing the Constitution put beyond the reach of the prosecutor, for the price of freedom of religion or of speech or of the press is that we must put up with, and even pay for, a good deal of rubbish.[28]

This concept, which prevents judicial or governmental evaluation of the merits of theology, is to the benefit of all those who are religious, not just to the "fringe" groups. *Ballard* does not mean that religions are immune from prosecution for fraud. For example, they may not promise to do one thing with money and then do another. Local churches or television evangelists may not solicit money, promising to send it to foreign missions, and then use it for local expenses, without running afoul of law against fraud. But, in every case, the government must proceed without making judgments about the veracity of the theology of the group.

By 1963 the free exercise of religion had been defined by the Court very broadly. Religious freedom was the rule, governmental interference in religious behavior was the exception. And in the area of religious belief, government intrusion was prohibited altogether.

4

The Uncertain Status of
Religious Freedom: 1963–2004

The year 1963 as the dividing point between the chapters on free-exercise cases was not chosen arbitrarily, for in that year the Court handed down a decision which "regularized" Free Exercise Clause jurisprudence for more than the next quarter of a century. Just as the "clear and present danger" test of *Cantwell v. Connecticut* prevailed from 1940 until 1963, the "*Sherbert* test" controlled free exercise cases until 1990. This balancing test preserved the broad scope of religious freedom for Americans while continuing to hold that government may interfere in religious behavior if conditions merit it.

THE "*SHERBERT* TEST"

Unemployment Compensation

The key case in this development is *Sherbert v. Verner.*[1] Adell Sherbert, an employee in the textile mills of South Carolina, was a Seventh-day Adventist. Adventists believe the seventh day of the week, Saturday,[2] is the proper day of worship. Their belief is based on two biblical ideas. First is the concept that God rested on the seventh day from the labors of creating the earth. That God rested at the end of the creative process means that this pattern of work and rest is built into the nature of reality and thus should be observed by humans. Second, the Fourth Commandment teaches that humans are to "remember the sabbath day, and keep it holy," thus adding the dimension of worship to the seventh day.[3] This observance of Saturday as a day of worship and rest is considered by Seventh-day Adventists to be a religious obligation.

Ms. Sherbert's troubles began when her employer changed her work week to include Saturday. She refused Saturday work because of her sincerely held religious beliefs, and she was fired. She looked elsewhere for work in her trade and discovered it was impossible to find employment that did not involve Saturday work. She then applied to state authorities for unemployment compensation. She was denied compensation on the ground the state supplied unemployment benefits for people for whom work was unavailable, not for people who were unavailable for work. Because Sherbert had essentially quit her job, albeit for religious reasons, she was not available for work, and thus not entitled to compensation. At that point Sherbert sued, claiming that this situation was an imposition on her free exercise of religion. She argued that she had been forced to choose between her employment and her religious practice. But when she had chosen the latter, she was denied state benefits and thus penalized for being faithful to her religion. The state supreme court ruled that her free exercise was not burdened. She could practice her religion as she chose; she just could not do that *and* receive unemployment payments. In an opinion by Justice William Brennan, the United States Supreme Court reversed that decision.

In the process of ruling on this case, the Court set forth a procedure for deciding free exercise cases. The procedure has become known as the "*Sherbert* test." This test balances government interests against the religious behavior at issue. The best way to understand this procedure is to think of it as a series of questions to be asked about the parties involved in the controversy:

1. Has the government placed a burden on the religious actions of the plaintiff (the one bringing the suit alleging government infringement on religion)? That is, has the government somehow impaired, interfered with, or prevented the person's or group's exercise of religion? If the answer is no, the case is over—the government has won and the plaintiff lost. But if the answer is yes, then the inquiry must go to a second question.

2. Does the government have a compelling interest that justifies burdening the religious activity in question? It is assumed the government is trying to accomplish some legitimate end or goal for the public good. The question is whether the government has a compelling interest in reaching that goal. "Compelling" means here "very important," "of the highest magnitude." The Court expressed it this way: "It is basic that no showing merely of a rational relationship to some colorable state interest would suffice; in this highly sensitive constitutional area, '[o]nly the gravest abuses, endangering paramount interests, give occasion for permissible limitation.'"[4] If the answer to the question is negative, the government loses the case, and the plaintiff wins. But if the answer is affirmative, the inquiry goes to a third question.

3. Even if the compelling interest exists, does the government have an alternative means to reach its legitimate goal without burdening religious action? Can the government do an "end run" around religious action and

still accomplish its objective? If the answer is affirmative, the government is obligated to employ the alternative procedure to reach its goal and cease its oppression of religious action. If the answer is negative, the government has won the case, and the plaintiff has lost.

In *Sherbert*, the inquiry stopped with the second question. The Court ruled the state had burdened Sherbert's exercise of religion. "To condition the availability of benefits upon this appellant's unwillingness to violate a cardinal principle of her religious faith effectively penalizes the free exercise of her constitutional liberties."[5] To be sure, the state had an interest in preserving unemployment compensation funds and thwarting fraudulent claims. But these interests were not compelling enough to override the constitutionally guaranteed right of free exercise of religion. Sherbert won, South Carolina lost.

This case replaced the "clear and present danger" test (*Cantwell v. Connecticut*; see chapter 3) without nullifying its benefits for religious liberty. The importance of *Sherbert* is that it set forth a more sophisticated procedure to decide free exercise controversies, designed to preserve the concept that freedom of religion is broad, the possibility of government interference narrow. This is not to say that "anything goes" in the name of religion; the government still has the authority to prevent harmful religious behavior. But in balancing religious freedom and government intervention, religious freedom is clearly the weightier. The existence of the Free Exercise Clause in the Constitution demands that it be so!

Compulsory Education Laws

A frequently cited example of the effect of the "*Sherbert* test" is *Wisconsin v. Yoder*, which in 1972 decided the question of whether government is obligated to accommodate the religious belief of the Amish about the education of their children.[6] The Amish, descendants of the sixteenth-century Anabaptists, believe that the world is evil and that it is imperative that the follower of Christ maintain distance from the world, in order to prevent being corrupted by the contact. Consequently, the Amish maintain a lifestyle specifically designed to emphasize their difference from the world. Two characteristics of this lifestyle are belief in separation of church and state and pacifism, the refusal to inflict violence on any human. The feature of their lifestyle most pertinent to this case is their refusal to allow their children formal education beyond the eighth grade. Any "book learning" beyond that time would expose their children to too much of the evil world. So the Amish withdraw their children after the completion of the eighth grade and continue their education at home, emphasizing domestic and farming skills, those things which are most needed for living in the Amish community.

Wisconsin, like most states, has a compulsory education law that demands that children continue in formal education beyond the eighth grade. The state demanded that Amish parents obey the law. The Amish refused, in spite of fines and short jail sentences, stating that their views on education are firmly based in their religious belief and claiming Free Exercise Clause protection.

The issue reached the Supreme Court in *Wisconsin v. Yoder.* The Court weighed the state's interest in public education against the Amish religious beliefs. It was clear that the state's interest in an educated citizenry was very weighty, but the constitutionally protected religious practices of the Amish were weightier still. In making this determination, but writing about the importance of the free exercise of religion in general, Chief Justice Warren Burger said for the Court: "The essence of all that has been said and written on the subject is that only those interests of the highest order and those not otherwise served can overbalance legitimate claims to the free exercise of religion."[7] Government may intervene in religious practice, but the burden is on the government to prove that it has an overwhelmingly important reason to do so. Religious freedom is the rule; government interference is the exception.

Additional Unemployment Issues

The Court rendered decisions on several other unemployment compensation cases after *Sherbert.* Although the facts were somewhat different, the issues were essentially the same.

Issues of Theology

A Jehovah's Witness who was employed in a steel mill was transferred to a department manufacturing turrets for military tanks. This activity was contrary to his religious belief.[8] Because his employer had moved to all military-related work, he quit his job. He was denied unemployment compensation and went to court, claiming Free Exercise Clause protection. The Supreme Court found in his favor in *Thomas v. Review Board of Indiana.*[9]

Two issues are worthy of note in this case. First, the state argued that Thomas should not be awarded unemployment compensation because other Jehovah's Witnesses working in the factory had no objection to making armaments. The Court held that a civil court could not determine who, within a group of believers, is more accurately holding the beliefs of the group. Furthermore, one should not be penalized because one does not express one's faith well. Chief Justice Burger wrote:

> Courts should not undertake to dissect religious beliefs because the
> believer admits that he is "struggling" with his position or because his

beliefs are not articulated with the clarity and precision that a more sophisticated person might employ. . . . Particularly in this sensitive area, it is not within the judicial function and judicial competence to inquire whether the petitioner or his fellow worker more correctly perceived the commands of their common faith. Courts are not arbiters of scriptural interpretation.[10]

This is a variation on and reaffirmation of the theme, articulated in *Ballard*, that the state, including its courts, may not get involved in theological/doctrinal issues. Freedom of religion demands the limitation of the state in this area.

Second, *Thomas* is important because the Court used it to reassert principles for interpreting the Free Exercise Clause, again taking the position that the state may not unduly burden the free exercise of religion, even indirectly:

Where the state conditions receipt of an important benefit upon conduct proscribed by a religious faith, or where it denies such a benefit because of conduct mandated by a religious belief, thereby putting substantial pressure on an adherent to modify his behavior and to violate his beliefs, a burden upon religion exists. While the compulsion may be indirect, the infringement upon free exercise is nonetheless substantial.[11]

This is an elaboration of the *"Sherbert* test," giving it more specificity, and reasserting the broad scope of religious liberty.

Religious Converts

In *Hobbie v. Unemployment Appeals Commission of Florida*,[12] involving a Seventh-day Adventist denied unemployment compensation when she refused to work on Saturday, the Court again decided in favor of the worker. What makes this case unique is that the worker converted to the Adventist faith after she was employed, in contrast to both *Sherbert* and *Thomas*, in which a previously acceptable job became religiously unacceptable because of changes brought about by the employer. Florida claimed that the worker rather than the employer was the "agent of change" and consequently the state should not have to pay the unemployment compensation. It was the decision of the worker, by converting to a religion that had stipulations about when a believer should work, that created the condition in the workplace that made continued employment impossible. Of course, if this contention became law, it would have a "chilling effect" on evangelism by churches. If employees thought they potentially were putting their jobs in jeopardy by converting to a religious belief, they would likely be much less receptive to evangelization. This would impose a subtle but real limitation on the religious freedom of individuals. The Court did not accept the "agent of change" argument; it would not give less favorable treatment to a convert. In another expression of the preeminence of religious freedom, Justice Brennan wrote: "The First Amendment protects the free exercise rights of employees who adopt religious beliefs or convert from one faith to another after they are hired."[13]

Personal Religious Belief

In *Frazee v. Illinois Department of Employment Security*,[14] a case in which a person refused to work on Sunday because of religious convictions, the state claimed that he was not entitled to unemployment compensation because he was not a member of a group that taught abstention from work on Sunday. In cases involving Seventh-day Adventists, for example, people who refused Saturday work did so because of the clear teaching of their church. But Frazee's refusal to work on Sunday was based only on his own personal theological convictions, not the doctrine of any organized group. The Supreme Court found in his favor anyway, because purely personal religious belief receives as much protection from the Free Exercise Clause as that tied to the theological propositions of an organized religious group.

One other unemployment compensation case is worthy of note, a Native American case, *Employment Division of Oregon v. Smith*. It is of crucial importance because it took away all the dimensions of free exercise just described. But, to put it in context and understand its argumentation, it is necessary to look at some other cases first, some of which began to interpret the Free Exercise Clause differently from the *Sherbert* test.

CLERGY AND PUBLIC OFFICE

Early in the history of this nation, it was widely held that clergy should not hold public office. There were laws to that effect in most of the states of the time. Seven of the original states and six more of the early additions to the Union had laws excluding clergy from holding public office. Two primary reasons usually were given for this. One was that the clergy had such a high calling and were engaged in such exalted activity, the proclamation of the Word of God and the care of souls, they should not be involved in the mundane and often messy activity of politics and governing. The other was that the nation had just begun the experiment of separation of church and state. One way to guarantee the success of disestablishment was to prevent clergy from holding office. The fear was that if they were in office, they might attempt to impose their religious views on the body politic.

However, even in these early days, some also argued against the exclusion of clergy. James Madison believed such a law punished a religious profession with the denial of a civil right, which struck at the heart of the concept of religious freedom. As time progressed, many were persuaded by that argument. Furthermore, many believed there were sufficient safeguards against establishment that the exclusion of clergy from public office was unnecessary. Consequently, clergy exclusion laws were gradually rescinded until, by 1977, Tennessee was the only state with such a law. The constitutionality of that was tested before the Supreme Court in *McDaniel v. Paty*.[15]

Tennessee's law that said nobody who was ineligible for service in the state legislature could be a delegate to a state constitutional convention. A Baptist minister named McDaniel ran to be a delegate and was elected. But in response to a suit by an opponent who claimed that his election was illegal, he was denied his place in the convention by the state supreme court. The U.S. Supreme Court reversed that decision. Although there was some disagreement among the justices about the rationale for the decision, the Court held that Tennessee's law denied McDaniel the free exercise of his religion. It had forced him to choose between his religious activity, which was also his profession, and a civil right. The Free Exercise Clause will not permit that. In Chief Justice Warren Burger's words:

> [T]he right to the free exercise of religion unquestionably encompasses the right to preach, proselyte, and perform other similar religious functions, or, in other words, to be a minister of the type McDaniel was found to be. . . . Tennessee has encroached on McDaniel's right to the free exercise of religion. "[T]o condition the availability of benefits [including access to the ballot] upon this appellant's willingness to violate a cardinal principle of [his] religious faith [by surrendering his religiously impelled ministry] effectively penalizes the free exercise of [his] constitutional liberties."[16]

The Court also observed that there was no record in American history in which a clergyperson had been less observant of the separation of church and state while holding public office than his or her unordained counterparts. Consequently, no unit of government may forbid a minister or other religious leader to hold public office. This case is very similar to *Torcaso v. Watkins*, an Establishment Clause case described in chapter 7.

THE MILITARY AND PRISONS

The following cases related to the military and prisons, heard before *Smith*, mark the beginning of the constriction of religious liberty by the Court made up mostly of justices appointed by Ronald Reagan or sympathetic to his conservative judicial philosophy. Given that the Court, in these cases, refused to explicitly apply the compelling state interest test and consistently decided

in favor of the government, *Smith* is not so surprising, though no less shock-
ing. The first of these cases, *Goldman v. Weinberger*,[17] involved an Orthodox
Jewish psychiatrist serving in the Air Force. Orthodox Jewish practice mandates that males cover their heads in the presence of God as a sign of respect
to God. Many Jews, reasoning that one is always in God's presence, choose to
wear a skullcap, or yarmulke, not only at worship, but at all times. The problem for Dr. Goldman was an Air Force regulation that prohibited someone in
uniform from wearing a head covering indoors. When he persisted in wearing
his yarmulke while in uniform and on duty in the base hospital, he was disci-
plined and threatened with a court-martial.[18] Goldman sued, claiming his Free
Exercise Clause right should supersede Air Force regulations.

The Supreme Court in 1986 decided in favor of the Air Force. Justice
William Rehnquist's opinion noted that the military wants to promote both
esprit de corps and a discipline that leads to instinctive obedience to orders.
Regulations about dress are part of those efforts. The Air Force argued the uniform subordinates personal preferences and identities (except rank) in people,
and this supports the group mission of the unit and the military as a whole. This
sense of group identity and subordination to authority is just as necessary in
peacetime as in time of war because the military must be always at the ready, in
case of national emergency. The military can allow no exceptions and still maintain the desired discipline. The Court ruled that in this special circumstance it
must defer to the expertise of military authority. Freedoms that are available to
the general citizen simply are not as available in the specialized environment of
the military. In this context, the free exercise of religion could not prevail.

> Our review of military regulations challenged on First Amendment
> grounds is far more deferential than constitutional review of similar
> laws or regulations designed for civilian society. . . . [W]hen evaluat-
> ing whether military needs justify a particular restriction on religiously
> motivated conduct, courts must give great deference to the profes-
> sional judgment of military authorities concerning the relative impor-
> tance of a particular military interest.[19]

A virtually identical decision was reached in *O'Lone v. Estate of Shabazz*.[20]
The issue in this case was whether minimum-security Muslim prisoners who
worked on a gang outside the prison walls during the day should be brought
back for Friday noon prayers, a religious obligation for Muslims. Prison
authorities argued that to do so would cause too many logistical and security
problems. Not all members of the work gang were Muslims. Non-Muslims
would have to be left behind while the Muslims were brought back to the
prison for prayers. That would result in different amounts of work being done
by different members of the gang, which would create morale problems. More

important for prison authorities, the procedure would require the assignment of extra guards, guards for the Muslim prisoners *and* for those who stayed behind. Bringing prisoners in and out the main gate at noon would require an extra security check. The Court decided against the prisoners, again arguing that in the special environment of a prison constitutional rights were not as broad as for regular citizens and that the Court needed to defer to the expert opinion of prison authorities.

In both these cases the Court weighed the interest of state institutions, which had specialized, out-of-the-ordinary populations, against the religious freedom of members of those populations. It determined that the state institutions had unique needs, and religious freedom was the loser.

NATIVE AMERICAN CASES

The Court continued its constriction of religious freedom, a process that would culminate in *Smith*, in some cases involving Native Americans.[21] In *Bowen v. Roy*,[22] the Court in 1986 was confronted with a member of the Abenaki tribe who objected to Pennsylvania's demand that his daughter be provided with a Social Security number to be eligible for aid under the Aid to Families with Dependent Children and food stamp programs. Roy's belief, based on his Native American religion, was that control over one's life was essential to spiritual purity and "becoming a holy person." Consequently, a number assigned specifically and uniquely to his daughter, whose name was Little Bird of the Snow, would "rob her of her spirit" and prevent her from gaining spiritual power as she grew older. That is, for Little Bird of the Snow to have a Social Security number would put her under the power and, to some degree, the control of the government. That would prevent her from growing into a unique spiritual being. Therefore Roy requested Pennsylvania to provide benefits to Little Bird of the Snow without requiring her to have a Social Security number. The state naturally declined and Roy brought suit, claiming a violation of his free exercise rights.

The Court decided against the Native American. Although it weighed government versus individual interests and found the government's heavier in the balance, Chief Justice Warren Burger articulated another rationale for the Court's decision. He argued that Roy was asking the government to alter its procedures in order to accommodate his religious practice. But the Free Exercise Clause did not demand that the government do that.

> Never to our knowledge has the Court interpreted the First Amendment to require the Government *itself* to behave in ways that the individual

believes will further his or her spiritual development or that of his or her family. The Free Exercise Clause simply cannot be understood to require the Government to conduct its own internal affairs in ways that comport with the religious beliefs of particular citizens.[23] (emphasis in original)

The Court illustrated this concept with the statement that Roy had no more right to determine the government's use of Social Security numbers because of his religious beliefs than he did to dictate the color of the filing cabinets the government used.[24]

A similar decision, based on the same rationale but this time written by Justice Sandra Day O'Connor, was handed down two years later in *Lyng v. Northwest Indian Cemetery Protective Association*.[25] A primary characteristic of Native American religion is belief in sacred lands. Land itself is regarded as sacred, living, and having spiritual qualities. Native Americans thus perform rituals on sites that are regarded as particularly holy for the purpose of honoring the land itself, for gaining "medicine" or spiritual power, for seeking curative powers for healing the sick, or for good luck in hunting or love. The ceremonies that are conducive of such things require silence and an aesthetic environment.

The issue in this case was that the Indians' sacred lands lay within a national forest and the United States government was building a road through those lands. The road was primarily to facilitate logging in the forest. In an attempt to prevent the defilement of their sacred lands, the Indians first had obtained a court injunction that halted construction before the road was finished. With this suit they were now trying to get the government to abandon the project, claiming that their religious practices would be destroyed if the road were completed.

The Supreme Court decided against the Indians. The Court acknowledged that the completion of the road would be devastating to their religious practice, and said that was regrettable. However, the Court argued that, as with the situation of Little Bird of the Snow in *Roy*, the Native Americans wanted the government to alter its procedures to fit their religious needs. The land, because it lay within a national forest, belonged to the government. Consequently, for the Indians to try to prevent the completion of the road was clearly an attempt to impose their religious needs on government procedures. The Free Exercise Clause does not allow that.

> However much we might wish that it were otherwise, government simply could not operate if it were required to satisfy every citizen's religious needs and desires. . . . Whatever rights the Indians may have to the use of the area, however, those rights do not divest the Government of its right to use what is, after all, *its* land.[26] (emphasis in original)

SOLICITATION IN PUBLIC PLACES

Another free exercise issue was solicitation for donations in public places by religious groups. These cases bore some resemblance to some of the Jehovah's Witness cases of an earlier generation. *Heffron v. International Society for Krishna Consciousness* (ISKCON)[27] involved the attempts of the Hare Krishnas, as they are more commonly called, to solicit funds at the Minnesota State Fair. Hare Krishna has a doctrine, *sankirtan*, which expects its members to evangelize the population by distributing or selling literature and soliciting donations for the support of the group. For them, *sankirtan* is a religious obligation and thus protected under the Free Exercise Clause. The Minnesota State Fair had a rule that all groups wanting to exhibit, distribute, or sell materials had to do so from a booth on the fairgrounds. The rationale for the rule was that it would be disruptive to crowd movement and crowd control for representatives of groups to be able to wander through the crowds distributing their literature and soliciting funds. So groups were confined to booths, although they could wander freely in areas adjoining the fairgrounds and solicit as they pleased. The Krishnas argued the rule was unnecessary and restrictive of their free exercise and free speech rights.

Justice Byron White, in his opinion for the majority of the Court, did not reach the constitutional issues of whether ISKCON's religious and speech freedoms were violated. The Court conceded, as did the Minnesota State Fair, that the group was entitled to exercise those freedoms. The real issue was whether or not the State Fair could impose reasonable time, place, and manner restrictions on First Amendment activity. The Court found such restrictions were appropriate. The fairgrounds were a special environment. Unlike a public thoroughfare, at the fair all the people had to go through gates and were concentrated within the grounds. The Court ruled that fair officials had a reasonable basis for requiring that solicitation take place from booths— crowd safety and traffic control made it necessary. The fair had not prevented distribution of literature or solicitation, nor had it placed restrictions on ISKCON different from those on other groups. Consequently, the State Fair's time, place, and manner rules did not violate the free exercise or free speech rights of anyone.

Some religious groups have seen airports as a potentially lucrative location to do solicitation. Airports have tried to inhibit such activity, on the basis that the solicitors were a nuisance to travelers. An important case in 1987 was *Airport Commissioners of Los Angeles v. Jews for Jesus*.[28] Airport officials had passed a resolution prohibiting *all* "First Amendment activities." On challenge from an evangelical Christian group, Jews for Jesus, the Supreme Court struck down the airport's prohibition as being entirely too broad. Noting that the rule had

the potential effect of banning talking, reading, and wearing symbolic clothing or campaign buttons, the Court said that it violated the free speech provision of the First Amendment.

In 1992 the Court considered a more sophisticated nonsolicitation rule
than the one from Los Angeles Airport. In *International Society for Krishna Consciousness v. Lee,*[29] the Court ruled that religious groups may distribute literature in the concourses of airports but may not solicit funds. Again, as in
Heffron, constitutional rights were not addressed, but rather the time, place,
and manner in which those rights could be exercised. The Court reasoned that
the traffic of an airport concourse was such that the distribution of literature
was not disruptive. Even people hurrying to their planes could take the literature on the fly and read it later. But if someone stopped them to solicit money,
it would disrupt the traffic of the concourse. Solicitees might stand for some
time listening to the "pitch" of the solicitor, they might want to explain why
they did not want to contribute, or, conversely, they might set down luggage
to get money out of their wallets or purses. In any case, solicitation would be
more intrusive into the normal flow of airport terminal activity than the mere
distribution of literature, so much so that airports could reasonably ban it.

LAWS OF GENERAL APPLICABILITY: DRUG USE

In 1990, an Oregon unemployment compensation case came to the Court, this
time involving not conscientious objection to workdays but the use of drugs.
Two counselors in a program for chemically dependent persons had agreed, as
a condition of employment, not to use any addictive substances. But they were
members of the Native American Church, an organization that has tradition-
ally used peyote as part of its worship service.[30] Peyote, a mild hallucinogenic
drug derived from the mescaline cactus, was on Oregon's list of illegal drugs.
When the drug counselors' employer discovered they used peyote, they were
dismissed from their jobs. Their application for unemployment compensation
was denied, because their firing was based on misconduct.

The issue came to the Supreme Court in *Employment Division of Oregon v.
Smith.*[31] Justice Antonin Scalia wrote the opinion. For the first time in an
unemployment compensation case, the Court found against the believer and
for the state. The reason is that Oregon's law proscribing certain drugs, peyote among them, was a "law of general applicability"; it applied to everybody,
not just religious groups. The Court ruled that the Free Exercise Clause cannot be used as a defense against laws of general applicability; that is, one cannot claim that one's free exercise of religion should take precedence over a law
that was not designed to burden religious behavior. A law specifically designed

to inhibit religious activity is unconstitutional, but a law of general applicability that has this effect is not. Justice Scalia cited the precedent of *Minersville School District v. Gobitis* (remember that *Gobitis* had been overturned by *West Virginia Board of Education v. Barnette*) and then said:

> Subsequent decisions have consistently held that the right of free exercise does not relieve an individual of the obligation to comply with a "valid and neutral law of general applicability on the ground that the law proscribes (or prescribes) conduct that his religion prescribes (or proscribes)."[32]

This decision also specifically discontinued the use of the *"Sherbert* test" except in a very narrow set of circumstances. No longer was the burden of proof on the government to show that it had a very important reason, a "compelling interest," to interfere with religious freedom. All it had to show was that it had a need to regulate citizen behavior by means of a law of general application. If that law had the effect of inhibiting or prohibiting religious activity, so be it.

> We conclude today that the sounder approach, and the approach in accord with the vast majority of our precedents, is to hold the test inapplicable to such challenges. The government's ability to enforce generally applicable prohibitions of social harmful conduct, like its ability to carry out other aspects of public policy, "cannot depend on measuring the effects of a governmental action on a religious objector's spiritual development." To make an individual's obligation to obey such a law contingent upon the law's coincidence with his religious beliefs, except where the State's interest is "compelling"—permitting him, by virtue of his beliefs, "to become a law unto himself," *Reynolds v. United States*—contradicts both constitutional tradition and common sense.[33]

The effect of *Smith* was essentially to declare the Free Exercise Clause null and void and to restrict religious liberty in the United States, except in a very narrow set of circumstances. The decision eliminated the advances in interpreting the Free Exercise Clause described in this chapter and took the status of the law back to 1879 and *Reynolds v. United States*, which had given civil authorities virtually unlimited right to interfere with religious freedom.

Justice Sandra Day O'Connor wrote an opinion concurring in the result of this case[34] but dissenting from the methodology of the Court. She declared the Court had done violence to its longstanding policy in support of religious freedom and deplored the abandoning of the compelling state interest test:

> In my view, today's holding dramatically departs from well-settled First Amendment jurisprudence, appears unnecessary to resolve the

question presented, and is incompatible with our Nation's fundamental commitment to individual religious liberty. . . . Given the range of conduct that a State might legitimately make criminal, we cannot assume, merely because a law carries criminal sanctions and is generally applicable, that the First Amendment never requires the State to grant a limited exemption for religiously motivated conduct. . . . As the language of the Clause itself makes clear, an individual's free exercise of religion is a preferred constitutional activity. A law that makes criminal such an activity therefore triggers constitutional concern—and heightened judicial scrutiny—even if it does not target the particular religious conduct at issue.[35]

We shall have occasion to look at this disastrous decision again in chapter 9.

ANIMAL SACRIFICE

Many thought and hoped the Court would use a case in 1993 as an opportunity to reverse the *Smith* decision, that is, to return to the use of the compelling state interest test and restore the Free Exercise Clause to its rightful place as a freestanding constitutional principle with some authority. The case was *Church of the Lukumi Babalu Aye v. City of Hialeah*.[36] The religion involved was Santeria, and the issue was its practice of animal sacrifice.

Santeria had its origin in Cuba in the nineteenth century. Many of the Yoruba tribe of western Africa were captured and brought to Cuba as slaves. The principal cultural task that faced these newly enslaved people was how to preserve their traditional African religion in Roman Catholic Cuba. The Yoruba accomplished this by adopting Catholic saints' names and some of the practices associated with them and applying them to the deities and spirits of their traditional religion. It is likely their captors thought the Yoruba had converted to Catholicism, but the Yoruba knew they were actually following their ancestral religion, only now under the guise of Catholicism. It was a defense mechanism by the Yoruba to prevent their traditional culture from being obliterated. Thus was born Santeria, "the way of the saints." It is a syncretism, a combining of two traditions into what is essentially a new religion.

A central belief of Santeria is the existence of *orishas*, or spirits. These spiritual beings influence the lives of human beings. It is necessary for one to maintain a personal relationship with the *orishas*, and one of the principal forms of devotion is animal sacrifice. Furthermore, although the *orishas* are powerful, they are not immortal. They derive vitality from the devotion of their worshippers. Consequently, it is a cardinal belief of Santeria that animal sacrifice is necessary for the survival of the *orishas*. So, among the adherents of Santeria, sacrifices are performed at the birth of a child, at marriage ceremonies and funerals, for the cure of the sick, and for the initiation of new members and consecrating of priests, among other reasons. Santeria devotees sacrifice chickens, pigeons, doves, ducks, guinea pigs, goats, sheep, and turtles. In every case, the animals are killed by cutting the carotid arteries in the neck.

Santeria was brought to the United States principally by exiles from the Cuban revolution. In Hialeah, Florida, it had usually been practiced in secret, in people's homes. But in the late 1980s the Church of the Lukumi Babalu Aye declared its intention to build a building for worship and to establish a cultural center and museum. In response to that announced intention, the city council of Hialeah in 1987 passed a series of ordinances that prohibited the killing of animals in religious rituals. There were several laws that came at the issue from a variety of directions, but the prohibition of sacrifice was the intent of them all. The church responded by filing suit, claiming that its free exercise of religion was violated by the city council's actions.

As noted above, many church-state watchers hoped the Court would use this case to revisit its recent gutting of the Free Exercise Clause by renouncing its *Smith* decision along the lines that Justice Sandra Day O'Connor had suggested in her opinion in that case. Their hopes were disappointed. The Court arrived at its decision by applying the *Smith* concept, that a neutral law of general applicability is not unconstitutional, even though it has the effect of hindering or even prohibiting religious activity.

But *Smith* had also said that if a law targeted religion specifically and hindered or prohibited that activity, then that law would be subjected to "strict scrutiny" (the compelling state interest test) by the Court. That was the case with Hialeah's laws. Justice Anthony Kennedy wrote the Court's opinion. He began with an admonition that applies not only to this case, but to religious freedom in general: "Although the practice of animal sacrifice may seem abhorrent to some, 'religious beliefs need not be acceptable, logical, consistent, or comprehensible to others in order to merit First Amendment protection.'"[37] When he turned to the issue at hand, it boiled down to this: Hialeah had passed laws that were aimed only at Santeria practice. This was obvious because they prohibited practices involved in animal sacrifice that were allowed if they were done for secular purposes. Two of many examples will illustrate the point.

A principal justification Hialeah put forth for its laws was the prevention of cruelty to animals. Thus, it prohibited the killing of animals in religious ritual. But it did not prohibit the killing of animals by slaughterhouses, in Jewish kosher slaughter, or even by individual hunters and people who fish, who may bring their prey home to kill it in their own houses. The city had also expressed concern about the disposal of the sacrificed animals, and so passed

laws prohibiting the disposal of the carcasses of sacrificed animals in open public places. But the laws did not prohibit hunters, fishers, or even the owners of
small farms within the city limits from disposing of animals in public places.
In short, the laws were discriminatory, as opposed to being of general applicability. That is unconstitutional even under the *Smith* interpretation of the
Free Exercise Clause.

> In sum, the neutrality inquiry leads to one conclusion: The ordinances
> had as their object the suppression of religion. The pattern we have
> recited discloses animosity to Santeria adherents and their religious
> practices; the ordinances by their own terms target this religious exer-
> cise; the texts of the ordinances were gerrymandered with care to pro-
> scribe religious killings of animals but to exclude almost all secular
> killings; and the ordinances suppress much more religious conduct
> than is necessary in order to achieve the legitimate ends asserted in
> their defense. These ordinances are not neutral, and the court below
> committed clear error in failing to reach this conclusion.[38]

As a result of this analysis, Justice Kennedy concluded his opinion with an
admonition to government officials (and to all Americans) to be sensitive to
that most precious of our liberties, freedom of religion. It is one of those
"quotable" passages because it expresses so well an important and durable
truth about the American system:

> The Free Exercise Clause commits government itself to religious tol-
> erance, and upon even slight suspicion that proposals for state inter-
> vention stem from animosity to religion or distrust of its practices, all
> officials must pause to remember their own high duty to the Consti-
> tution and to the rights it secures. Those in office must be resolute in
> resisting importunate demands and must ensure that the sole reasons
> for imposing the burdens of law and regulation are secular. Legisla-
> tors may not devise mechanisms, overt or disguised, designed to per-
> secute or oppress a religion or its practices. The laws here in question
> were enacted contrary to these constitutional principles, and they are
> void.[39]

LEGISLATIVE REMEDY TO *SMITH*

Even prior to *Babalu Aye*, efforts began to circumvent *Smith* and roll free exercise law back to pre-*Smith* standards. Opposition to and alarm about *Smith* was
wide and deep in both the religious and academic communities. Consequently,
a dramatically diverse coalition of religious and advocacy groups petitioned
Congress for relief from *Smith*. The groups represented the most liberal and
most conservative organizations and all points in between. The fifty-four

groups in the coalition represented all sorts of Christians, Jews, Hindus, Sikhs, and Muslims, and some secular groups.

Congress responded to the coalition's entreaty with the Religious Freedom Restoration Act (RFRA—pronounced "RIF-rah"). Both houses of Congress voted virtually unanimously for its passage, and it was signed into law by President Clinton on November 16, 1993.[40] Its purpose was to restore the "compelling state interest test" as the methodology courts used for adjudicating free exercise cases. It explicitly says it applied to all federal and state law, enacted before as well as after RFRA became law. The rationale and hope of RFRA is best understood from this statement by two lawyers who were leaders in the coalition that urged Congress to pass the law.

> RFRA is not a mere technical change from *Smith*. Rather, it restores a fundamentally different vision of human liberty. Religious believers acting on their faith are not suspicious characters seeking unprincipled special treatment. They are exercising a fundamental human right, and the American commitment is to let them exercise it unless there is an extraordinary reason to interfere—not a rational reason, or even a substantial reason, but a compelling reason. What is suspicious is not the believer practicing his faith, but the government seeking to stop him. RFRA can achieve its purpose only if the courts enforce this vision.[41]

Soon, however, some began to ask a serious question. Was RFRA unconstitutional? Indeed, some lower federal courts, deciding free exercise cases brought to them under the authority of RFRA, ruled it was, indeed, unconstitutional because it violated the constitutional principle of separation of powers. In short, Congress had no business telling courts, including the Supreme Court, how they were to decide cases.

The Supreme Court itself addressed the question in *City of Boerne v. Archbishop Flores*.[42] A Catholic parish in Boerne, Texas, experienced growing pains and decided to enlarge its sanctuary to accommodate the growing number of people attending worship. It was denied a building permit, however, because the church stood within a historical preservation district that had been created by the town. The parish could not modify the size or shape of its building and maintain its historical character. With the firm belief it was being denied a free exercise right (what could implicate freedom of religion more than a church's desire to change or improve its space for worship?), the church, in the person of P. F. Flores, archbishop of San Antonio, sued. Flores claimed the freedom of religion principle, enforced by RFRA, allowed it an exemption from the historical preservation ordinance. The city asserted that it had the right to preserve its historic nature and that RFRA was unconstitutional.

Justice Anthony Kennedy wrote a complicated opinion for the Court. The case involved an arcane, but very important, point of law. As we saw in chapter 2, the Fourteenth Amendment has to do with, among other things, the application of civil rights to the citizens of the various states. Section 5 of the Fourteenth Amendment says: "The Congress shall have power to enforce, by appropriate legislation, the provisions of this article." This means, the Court said in *Boerne*, Congress had authority under section 5 to "remedy" and "prevent" unconstitutional conduct by state and local governments. But RFRA went beyond that authority: by mandating courts to use the "compelling state interest test," it in essence made a substantive change in the Free Exercise Clause itself. Rather than enforcing the clause as interpreted by *Smith*, it had altered the meaning of the clause. Congress cannot do that. Stated two other ways:

> In the final analysis, the Court concluded that the RFRA represented an effort by Congress finally and authoritatively to determine what the Constitution means, thus usurping the power that our constitutional tradition has placed in the Supreme Court itself.[43]

> [T]he Court is the ultimate arbiter of what the Constitution requires, and legislation which can only be understood as a disagreement with the Court's understanding of what the Constitution requires is outside the bounds of Congress's Section 5 authority. That is what makes RFRA unconstitutional.[44]

So, the doctrine of separation of powers trumped Congress's attempt to undo *Smith* and restore broad religious freedom to the American people.

But the saga was not over with *Boerne*. Those still bothered by the effect and implications of *Smith* persuaded Congress to try again to provide relief legislatively from *Smith*, but within the limits announced in *Boerne*. The result was the Religious Land Use and Institutionalized Persons Act[45] (RLUIPA—pronounced "ar-LOOP-a"). As the long name implies, the law applies the "compelling state interest test" in interpreting land use, typically zoning disputes, and the rights of prisoners and others in government custody, when they implicate the Free Exercise Clause. Congressional hearings established that across the country, religious institutions were frequently discriminated against in the implementation of "generally applicable" zoning laws. RLUIPA requires that zoning boards cannot burden religious practice without a compelling reason to do so. That does not mean that communities must accede to any religious institution's request for zoning or other land use matters. But it does mean the government must at least treat religious institutions equally with secular ones and may not discriminate against any institution on the basis of religion or exclude religious organizations from a jurisdiction.

On the "institutionalized persons" side of the law, the effect is similar. The government may not place a burden on the religious practice of prisoners or persons living in other state institutions unless the burden is justified by a compelling purpose that cannot be reached by a less restrictive way. There was in the congressional hearings, and is today, a particular concern about how this plays out in prisons. Testimony was given that showed this standard did not compromise security and discipline standards in jails and prisons. Furthermore, it did not open the door to frivolous lawsuits by prisoners.[46]

Watchtower Bible and Tract Society v. Village of Stratton[47] is quite similar to many of the Jehovah's Witnesses proselytizing cases of the 1930s and 1940s. Indeed, some were surprised the Court agreed to hear it in 2002, thinking it was about issues already well settled. Stratton, Ohio, passed an ordinance that required, in broad description, salespersons, peddlers, canvassers, and other vendors of merchandise, services, or causes to register with the mayor prior to approaching residents. The inclusion of "services" and "causes" swept Jehovah's Witnesses and their evangelizing activity within the statute. The permissions to canvass in the village were routinely given at no cost, but the Witnesses did not register, because they believed they were under divine command to proclaim their message. They did not need government recognition or approval.

The village required solicitors to register with the mayor's office for three reasons: prevention of fraud, prevention of crime, and protection of residents' privacy. The Court recognized those as legitimate purposes. But Justice John Paul Stevens ruled the statute was too broad to accomplish those goals. That is, it covered spontaneous political comment between friends, prohibited communication by those who wished to remain anonymous, and burdened commercial, religious, and patriotic speech.

> The mere fact that the ordinance covers so much speech raises constitutional concerns. It is offensive—not only to the values protected by the First Amendment, but to the very notion of a free society—that in the context of everyday public discourse a citizen must first inform the government of her desire to speak to her neighbors and then obtain a permit to do so. . . . [A] law requiring a permit to engage in such speech constitutes a dramatic departure from our national heritage and constitutional tradition.[48]

The Court resolved the issue without reference to *Smith* or the "law of general applicability test." Neither was it covered by RLUIPA. It simply said the statute was broader than necessary to accomplish its announced purposes and was inconsistent with our "constitutional tradition."

Since 1963 the Court's view of the scope of the Free Exercise Clause, and consequently the amount of religious freedom available to the American people, has varied. Until 1990, when the "*Sherbert* test" was the principle for interpreting the clause, Americans enjoyed a large amount of freedom for religious practice. Those in specialized environments like the military did not enjoy the full range of this freedom, but decisions in these areas had little implication for the general population. Religious groups that tried to solicit in public places with large concentrations of people were restricted by considerations of how the solicitation would impact the movement of people. But with decisions such as *Bowen v. Roy* and *Lyng v. Northwest Indian Cemetery Protective Association*, that government procedures were not required to be sensitive to religious practices, in spite of the fact that those procedures might even virtually destroy a religion, the Court began to narrow religious freedom. With the *Smith* decision, which abandoned the "*Sherbert* test" and declared the Free Exercise Clause useless except in case of laws that specifically targeted religion, religious freedom received a virtually devastating blow. The implications of that will be explored in chapter 9.[49]

5

From Congregational Fights
to Pacifism

The Court has had to decide some cases over the years that were not specifically either Establishment Clause or Free Exercise Clause cases. If it can, the Supreme Court will decide a case on the language of a statute rather than the Constitution, simply because a constitutional interpretation has broader scope and greater weight. Some of the cases described in this chapter were decided on the basis of the interpretation of statutes, although some simply articulate principles for adjudication. This does not mean, however, that they are any less important in setting some of the boundaries of what is permitted in church-state relations.

CHURCH PROPERTY

Unfortunately, sometimes members of church congregations quarrel among themselves or congregations fight against their denomination. Frequently those disagreements involve the question of who owns the property of the local church, and at times they become so vituperative that the parties go to court. The Supreme Court has set some guidelines on how property ownership issues are to be settled.

Property, Not Theology

This issue first came to the Court in the nineteenth century, as an aftermath of the Civil War. A Presbyterian church in Louisville, Kentucky, had divided over the issue of slavery. The General Assembly of the Presbyterian Church in the U.S.A. had ruled that those members of the church who had supported slavery or aided in the rebellion against the Union were illegitimate church members until they repented of their proslavery beliefs and/or actions. In the congregation in Louisville, both the pro-Union and pro-Confederacy members claimed to be true Presbyterians and the rightful owners of the church property. The pro-Confederacy party, those at odds with the General Assembly, brought suit in civil court to gain control of the property. Their controversy finally made it to the Supreme Court in 1872 in *Watson v. Jones*.[1]

The Court decided not to decide on the controversy itself. This was not because of faintheartedness, but because the justices understood that the concept of separation of church and state did not permit civil courts to decide controversies when it would be necessary to make a decision based on doctrine. The litigants here were asking the Court to decide who were the true Presbyterians, in order to determine who should own the church property. That would require an investigation into theology and a judgment as to which party's theological beliefs were more correct. In our system of government, civil courts may not do that. (This is the concept we have already seen in *United States v. Ballard*, although *Watson* arrived at it much earlier from a different set of facts.) Justice Samuel Miller stated this for the Court in ringing language:

> In this country the full and free right to entertain any religious belief, to practice any religious principle, and to teach any religious doctrine which does not violate the laws of morality and property, and which does not infringe personal rights, is conceded to all. The law knows no heresy, and is committed to the support of no dogma, the establishment of no sect.[2]

But if civil courts may not solve church property disputes based on theological differences, how are the controversies to be decided? The Court gave some guidelines that depend on the way in which the church obtained the property, and on church governance.

1. In those circumstances where property has been given to the church through a bequest or some other instrument of donation, the civil court may make sure that the will of the donor is carried out. If there are theological stipulations to the donation, the civil court must enforce them in accord with the desires of the donor, even if the majority of the congregation now holds different theology. But in this situation, the civil court does not have to evaluate theology, only guarantee that the provisions of the donation instrument are implemented.

2. In those churches which are congregationally governed (in which there is no authority above the local congregation), the majority rules. The civil court may do no more than determine who the majority is and award the property to them. In such a situation it does not have to make a judgment about whose theology is correct.

3. In hierarchical churches, such as the one at issue in this case, the function of the civil court is not to decide, but to defer to the decision of the highest level of the church's government.

> In this class of cases we think the rule of action which should govern the civil courts . . . is, that, whenever the questions of discipline or of faith or ecclesiastical rule, custom or law have been decided by the highest of these church judicatories to which the matter has been carried, the legal tribunals must accept such decisions as final, and as binding on them, in their application to the case before them.[3]

The *Watson* rule was slightly modified in 1929 when the Court suggested that civil courts *might* become involved in church property disputes to determine if there had been fraudulent or arbitrary behavior on the part of ecclesiastical officials (*Gonzalez v. Archbishop*).[4] But the prohibition against decisions based on theology remained.

The prohibitions so far mentioned were raised to a constitutional level in 1952 in *Kedroff v. St. Nicholas Cathedral*.[5] This case was about the unusual situation in which a state legislature had taken sides in a church property controversy. There was a dispute between members of the Russian Orthodox Church in America as to who was the proper head of the church, the Patriarch of Moscow or a ruling committee formed by certain Orthodox persons in America. The committee called itself "The Russian Church in America." The New York legislature passed a law declaring that "The Russian Church in America" was the proper governing body of the Russian Orthodox churches in that state and the legitimate holder of St. Nicholas Cathedral in New York City. At the time of the legislation, the cathedral was held by those loyal to the Moscow patriarchate. The Russian Church in America brought suit to regain control of the cathedral from the Moscow group, which they believed the legislation authorized them to do.

The Supreme Court ruled that neither the Establishment Clause nor the Free Exercise Clause would allow the New York legislature to designate which of the groups competing for leadership was the true Russian Orthodox Church and rightful holder of the cathedral. The Moscow patriarchate was the highest judicial body of the Russian Orthodox Church, and the state legislature had to defer to its determination of the ownership of the cathedral. Because it was decided on the basis of the Establishment and Free Exercise Clauses, *Kedroff* converted the principle of *Watson* as modified by *Gonzalez* into a constitutional rule.[6]

Neutral Principles of Law

A case very similar to *Watson* is *Presbyterian Church in the United States v. Mary Elizabeth Blue Hull Memorial Presbyterian Church*.[7] Two local Presbyterian churches in Georgia had decided that the parent denomination had become too liberal and no longer conformed to traditional Presbyterian faith. They initiated proceedings to separate from the denomination and keep their local church property. The General Assembly (the highest denominational legislative body) had ruled that the congregations were no longer entitled to own the property. But a Georgia law addressed such issues, the main feature of which was a "departure from doctrine" concept: if, in a trial, a party in the controversy could convince the jury that the other party had departed from traditional church doctrine, the jury could award the property to the party that had remained true to tradition. In this case, a jury had decided that the General Assembly of the Presbyterian Church U.S. had departed from doctrine and thus could not deprive the local church of its property. However, with Justice William Brennan's opinion, the Supreme Court ruled that such a law is unconstitutional and that juries may not make determinations on the ownership of church property on the "departure from doctrine" concept. Civil courts simply may not delve into the theological issues:

> But First Amendment values are plainly jeopardized when church property litigation is made to turn on the resolution by civil courts of controversies over religious doctrine and practice. If civil courts undertake to resolve such controversies in order to adjudicate the property dispute, the hazards are ever present of inhibiting the free development of religious doctrine and of implicating secular interests in matters of purely ecclesiastical concern.[8]

Nevertheless, as if it were giving churches and/or denominations legal advice, the Court mentioned in passing that instruments of church property ownership could be written in such a way that courts could solve disputes without having to consider doctrinal issues. This could be done by basing ownership on "neutral principles of law." That means church charters or denominational rules could include language that specifies certain conditions under which the ownership of the church property might become disputed and what is to be done in each of those circumstances. So long as no theological interpretation was required, that procedure could be ruled on by a civil court. For example, in a hierarchical church, both the charter of the local church and the rules of the denomination could specify that if the congregation as a whole or a majority of the congregation chose to secede from the parent denomination, then local church property would automatically become the possession of the denomination. That would be a "neutral principle of law."

The Supreme Court addressed that question directly in 1979 in *Jones v. Wolf.*[9] The facts of the case were virtually identical to *Hull Presbyterian Church*. A Presbyterian church wanted to leave the parent denomination and keep its property. In the process of deciding this case, the Court explicitly endorsed what had previously only been hinted at: if the church property dispute can be decided on "neutral principles of law," the civil courts may render such a decision. Although the Court still held to the principle that civil courts may not adjudicate any dispute involving theological dimensions, it gave courts more latitude than had been granted before. Justice Harry Blackmun expressed this for the Court very well. Because this issue is potentially so important to local churches, an extensive passage from the opinion is quoted here.

> The primary advantages of the neutral principles approach are that it is completely secular in operation, and yet flexible enough to accommodate all forms of religious organization and polity. The method relies exclusively on objective, well-established concepts of trust and property law familiar to lawyers and judges. It thereby promises to free civil courts completely from entanglement in questions of religious doctrine, polity, and practice. . . . Through appropriate reversionary clauses and trust provisions, religious societies can specify what is to happen to church property in the event of a particular contingency, or what religious body will determine the ownership in the event of a schism or doctrinal controversy. In this manner, a religious organization can ensure that a dispute over the ownership of church property will be resolved in accord with the desires of the members.
>
> This is not to say that the application of the neutral principles approach is wholly free of difficulty. The neutral principles method . . . requires a civil court to examine certain religious documents, such as a church constitution, for language of trust in favor of the general church. In undertaking such an examination, a civil court must take special care to scrutinize the document in purely secular terms, and not to rely on religious precepts in determining whether the document indicates that the parties have intended to create a trust. In addition, there may be cases where the deed, the corporate charter, or the constitution of the general church incorporates religious concepts in the provisions relating to the ownership of property. If in such a case the interpretation of the instruments of ownership would require the civil court to resolve a religious controversy, then the court must defer to the resolution of the doctrinal issue by the authoritative ecclesiastical body.
>
> On balance, however, the promise of nonentanglement and neutrality inherent in the neutral principles approach more than compensates for what will be occasional problems in application. These problems, in addition, should be gradually eliminated as recognition is given to the obligation of "States, religious organizations, and individuals [to] structure relationships involving church property so as not to require the civil courts to resolve ecclesiastical questions." We therefore hold that a State is constitutionally entitled to adopt neutral principles of law as a means of adjudicating a church property dispute.[10]

Four justices dissented in this case, arguing that there should not be any reliance on neutral principles of law. That is, they believed the *Watson* rule should be interpreted broadly and strictly: civil courts should not adjudicate church property cases. Taking the view of the dissenters and the recognition by the majority that if there was any hint of theology in the church property dispute, civil courts could not proceed, plus *United States v. Ballard*, it is clear that it is still a basic rule that government, especially civil courts, should not become involved in the theological dimensions of religion. That part of the separation concept has remained inviolable.

WORKPLACE ISSUES

In chapter 4 several cases were discussed that were clearly workplace cases decided under the Free Exercise Clause. But other workplace cases do not as obviously fall under that clause. Some have free-exercise overtones, others have establishment dimensions, and some were decided on purely statutory grounds. Title VII of the Civil Rights Act of 1964 is the backdrop of some of these cases.

Undue Hardship

One of the provisions of the Civil Rights Act made it illegal for an employer to discriminate against an employee on the basis of religion. The 1972 amendment to the law specified that an employer was obligated to accommodate the religious practices of an employee *unless* such accommodation inflicted "undue hardship" on the employer.

The scope of the "undue hardship" provision was tested in *Trans World Airlines v. Hardison*.[11] Hardison became a member of the World Wide Church of God, a Sabbatarian group, while he was employed by TWA. He asked to be relieved of work assignments on his day of worship, sundown Friday until sundown Saturday. Making that accommodation became increasingly difficult for the company, especially because it had entered into labor agreements with a union. For the company to be able to accommodate Hardison's religiously based work requests meant it would have to violate some of the seniority rules of the labor agreement, which would impact other workers. Eventually Hardison was dismissed from employment. He sued, claiming TWA had not gone far enough to accommodate his religious practices.

The Supreme Court, in an opinion written by Justice Byron White, ruled against Hardison. An employer did not have to discriminate against some employees in order to accommodate the religious preferences of other employees. On the question of "undue hardship," the Court said that an employer should have to bear no more than minimal hardship or cost to be in compliance with the law. "To require TWA to bear more than a *de minimis* cost in order to give Hardison Saturdays off is an undue hardship."[12]

The Court seemed to confirm this ruling in *Ansonia Board of Education v. Philbrook*,[13] when it ruled that an employer did not need to accept the employee's preferred method in deciding how to accommodate the employee's religion. "[W]here the employer has already reasonably accommodated the employee's religious needs, the statutory inquiry is at an end. The employer need not further show that each of the employee's alternative accommodations would result in undue hardship."[14]

So, in spite of the law's prohibition against religion-based discrimination in the workplace, the Court interpreted the rule in such a way that employers seem to have the advantage over employees, and religious behavior carries little weight.[15]

Permissible Discrimination on the Basis of Religion

The original nondiscrimination provision of the Civil Rights Act prohibited religious groups from discriminating in hiring on the basis of religion, except that they could discriminate when hiring for jobs involving religious activity. For example, a Baptist church could consider only Baptists for the position of pastor. But Congress amended the law to say that religious institutions could also discriminate on the basis of religion when hiring for jobs not including religious activity. For example, under the earlier law a Methodist church seeking to employ a building superintendent would be required to hire a Lutheran or even an atheist if that person were best qualified for the job among all the applicants. But religious leaders complained that this law sometimes required them to hire someone whose different or nonexistent religious belief was disruptive or at least a bad influence on parishioners. Congress amended the law to allow churches to employ people of their own religion, even in nonreligious jobs; but some contended that this discrimination on the basis of religion was a violation of the Establishment Clause.

The issue came before the Supreme Court in *Church of Jesus Christ of Latter-day Saints v. Amos.*[16] A person employed in a secular job by the Mormon church was dismissed because he did not qualify for a "temple recommend," that is, a certificate that he was a member of the church in good standing and thus able to worship in Mormon temples. Justice Byron White, writing for the Court, argued that such discrimination was consistent with the law and that the law did not violate the no-establishment principle. A law is not an establishment when it requires the government to get out of the way of a religious group and allow it to practice its religion more freely. A religious institution ought to have leeway to define and carry out its religious mission without having to worry about whether the government will agree that a particular job is religious or secular. The amended law, by allowing religious groups to hire on the basis of religion for all their jobs, avoids that problem. In this regard, the Court gave some precision on how it understands establishment:

> A law is not unconstitutional simply because it *allows* churches to advance religion, which is their very purpose. For a law to have forbidden "effects" under *Lemon*, it must be fair to say that the *government itself* has advanced religion through its own activities and influence.[17] (emphases in original)

So religious institutions have the right to insist that their employees' religion be consistent with their own.[18]

Congressional Intent

Some teachers' unions expressed an interest in representing lay teachers in Catholic schools in the Chicago area. The National Labor Relations Board, in accordance with its procedures to oversee unionization elections, ordered elections to be held in the schools, even though Catholic school officials insisted that the NLRB had no jurisdiction in the matter. In the elections, the teachers voted to unionize, and that was duly certified by the NLRB. But the Catholic authorities refused to recognize the unions or to bargain. The NLRB ruled that the Catholic authorities, by refusing to bargain, had violated the National Labor Relations Act. At that point, Catholic school officials sued.

The Supreme Court decided the controversy in 1979 in *National Labor Relations Board v. Catholic Bishop of Chicago*.[19] The Catholic bishop contended that the action of the NLRB was a violation of the Establishment Clause, on the basis of excessive entanglement. But the Court, as it always attempts to do, was able to decide this case without having to reach the constitutional issue. It examined the debates in Congress when the National Labor Relations Act was passed and concluded that Congress had not intended for parochial schools to be covered by the legislation. Consequently, the NLRB could not compel the Catholic schools to bargain with the unions. In this particular labor dispute, the Court insulated religious institutions from interference from a government agency.

CONSCIENTIOUS OBJECTION

Historically, one of the most persistent conflicts between religion and the state has been over the question of the propriety of war. The Judeo-Christian tradition has a stream of thought that promotes pacifism. In the Ten Commandments one reads, "You shall not kill."[20] Jesus said, "Blessed are the peacemakers, for they will be called children of God," and "Do not resist an evildoer. But if anyone strikes you on the right cheek, turn the other also."[21] These and other passages have led some to adopt the position of pacifism. This has meant, at the very least, that neither individuals, nor groups, nor even nations should aggressively employ violence, although some hold that one might legitimately use violence in self-defense. Another position, more consistent but extreme, is nonresistance. That is, not only should one not be aggressively violent, but one should not even defend oneself against violence. This second view is the commonly accepted understanding of pacifism. Conversely, frequently war has been justified with religious arguments. Indeed, as in the Crusades, warfare even has been waged in the name of God. So there is a tension about what is the proper thing for a religious person to do, wage war or be a pacifist. Pacifists are virtually always in the minority. In principle, the state maintains a military on the ground that it must at least defend itself and its citizens. Sometimes the state uses its military aggressively to try to expand its power and territory through conquest. The majority of the population virtually always supports the military and its functions and thinks of the conscientious objector as at least unpatriotic, if not traitorous.

The position of the pacifist in the United States has been somewhat more problematic than the previous paragraph might suggest. The Preamble of the Constitution says that one of the purposes for that charter of government is to "provide for the common defense." Furthermore, Article I, Section 8, empowers Congress "To declare War," "To raise and support Armies," "To provide and maintain a Navy," and "To provide for calling forth the Militia to execute the Laws of the Union." So the nation's basic law provides for national self-defense, at the very least. Of course, the assumption is the nation will need to call on its citizens to serve in these various military bodies. For the pacifist, a dilemma results: how to be loyal to the nation and still be obedient to the belief that God's law prohibits violence. The Supreme Court has rendered decisions that have set some boundaries about how far one can carry one's pacifism before running afoul of the state's need for military service.

The Issue of Citizenship

Strangely enough, the issue first came before the Court in the cases of pacifist aliens who applied for citizenship in the United States. The first of these, in 1929, was *United States v. Schwimmer*.[22] The oath of naturalization contained the phrase "I will support and defend the Constitution and laws of the United States of America against all enemies, foreign and domestic." Rosika Schwimmer was an atheist, but she was conscientiously opposed to war in any form. She declared that she would not be willing to take up arms for the nation. Even though she was both female and fifty-one years old at the time of her Supreme Court case, both of which would have disqualified her from military service, the Court denied her citizenship. Although Schwimmer said that there were other ways that one could defend the country without bearing arms—through words, for example—the Court said taking up arms was the only way the country could be defended. Those whose conscience would not allow them to do that could not be naturalized.

In 1931 two other similar naturalization cases were handed down, *United States v. Bland*[23] and *United States v. Macintosh*.[24] Marie Averil Bland was a Christian (Episcopalian) and opposed to all war. Douglas Clyde Macintosh, a Northern Baptist and a theology professor at Yale Divinity School, wanted to decide whether or not particular wars were morally justified before he would agree to participate; he wanted to pick and choose his wars. Despite these differences in the facts of the cases, the Court used *Schwimmer* as precedent. Noncitizens opposed to participation in war could not become United States citizens because, in the words of the naturalization law, they were not "attached to the principles of the Constitution of the United States, and well disposed to the good order and happiness of the same."[25]

A statement in *Macintosh* illuminates the latter part of this chapter. One of the arguments made by these naturalization candidates was that they ought to be awarded citizenship because the government had previously passed laws exempting native-born conscientious objectors from military service.[26] All they were asking was they be given the same privileges as those who were already American citizens. Macintosh's lawyer wrote in his prepared brief to the Supreme Court that it was a "fixed principle of our Constitution" that a citizen should be allowed to be a conscientious objector. The Court, Justice George Sutherland for the majority, responded to that assertion:

> This, if it means what it seems to say, is an astonishing statement. Of course, there is no such principle of the Constitution, fixed or otherwise. The conscientious objector is relieved from the obligation to bear arms in obedience to no constitutional provision, express or implied; but because, and only because, it has accorded with the policy of Congress to relieve him. . . . The privilege of the native-born conscientious objector to avoid bearing arms comes not from the Constitution, but from the acts of Congress. That body may grant or withhold the exemption as in its wisdom it sees fit; and if it be withheld, the native-born conscientious objector cannot assert the privilege.[27]

The Will of the State, the Will of God

A second statement in *Macintosh*, somewhat parenthetical to this chapter, reflects an attitude that has been and still is widespread in this country: somehow America is God's favored nation. It was noted above that Macintosh was not an absolute conscientious objector; he wanted to judge the moral value of the war he was asked to serve in before he would agree to serve. In his own words:

> I do not undertake to support "my country, right or wrong" in any dispute which may arise, and I am not willing to promise beforehand, and without knowing the cause for which my country may go to war, either that I will or that I will not "take up arms in defense of this country," however "necessary" the war may seem to the government of the day.[28]

Justice Sutherland responded to Macintosh's attitude with a remarkable statement:

> When he speaks of putting his allegiance to the will of God above his allegiance to the government, it is evident . . . that he means to make *his own interpretation* of the will of God the decisive test which shall conclude the government and stay its hand. We are a Christian people according to one another the equal right of religious freedom, and acknowledging with reverence the duty of obedience to the will of God. But, also, we are a nation with the duty to survive; a nation whose Constitution contemplates war as well as peace; whose government must go forward upon the assumption and safely can proceed upon no other, that unqualified allegiance to the nation and submission and obedience to the laws of the land, as well those made for war as those made for peace, are not inconsistent with the will of God.[29] (emphasis in original)

The will of the State is essentially equivalent with the will of God! There could hardly be a clearer statement of the negative side of what some now call "civil religion." I use the phrase "negative side" because it is precisely this attitude, that "*unqualified* allegiance to the nation . . . [is] not inconsistent with the will of God," which commonly leads patriots to baptize their nations' wars, that is, to wage wars in the name of God as well as country. Because the opponents automatically become enemies of God, such an attitude historically has led to unnecessary destruction, atrocities, and a demand for total victory that often disregards the humanity or civil rights of the vanquished.

Court Reversal Rooted in Previous Dissents

Finally, in 1946, the Supreme Court reversed itself on the question of the naturalization of conscientious objectors in *Girouard v. United States*.[30] Girouard was a Seventh-day Adventist whose position was the same as his denomination's: he would be willing to serve in the military, but only as a noncombatant. He recognized the need of the nation to wage war sometimes, but he also felt strongly that God's will is that one should not kill. He was willing to serve in the military, but to try to preserve life rather than take it.

The Court found in Girouard's favor. In *Schwimmer* Justice Oliver Wendell

Holmes had written a strong dissent, and in *Bland* and *Macintosh* Chief Justice Charles Evans Hughes had vigorously dissented. The majority opinion in *Girouard*, written by Justice William O. Douglas, picked up many of the themes of those dissents. The principal one was that the oath of naturalization actually does not require aliens to promise to bear arms. In fact, that oath is virtually identical to that required of all native-born government officehold- ers, who are allowed to be conscientious objectors. There was simply no evi- dence that Congress had set a higher standard for those applying for citizenship than it did for those citizens who take the oath in order to hold some government office. Another theme was that it is certainly possible to serve the welfare of the country in ways other than by bearing arms.

> Refusal to bear arms is not necessarily a sign of disloyalty or a lack of attachment to our institutions. One may serve his country faithfully and devotedly, though his religious scruples make it impossible for him to shoulder a rifle. . . . The effort of war is indivisible; and those whose religious scruples prevent them from killing are no less patriots than those whose special traits or handicaps result in their assignment to duties far behind the fighting front.[31]

As the result of *Girouard* and the Immigration and Naturalization Act of 1952,[32] the law now is that noncitizens who have objections to war based on religious training and belief may take alternative forms of the oath. One form will admit them to citizenship and allow them to serve in the military as non- combatants. The other form will permit them to avoid military service alto- gether, provided that they do nonmilitary work of national significance when required by law.

On the question of the relation of the state to the will of God, the Court made the following observation:

> The struggle for religious liberty has through the centuries been an effort to accommodate the demands of the State to the conscience of the individual. The victory for freedom of thought recorded in our Bill of Rights recognizes that *in the domain of conscience there is a moral power higher than the State.*[33] (emphasis added)

Here the Court recognizes the proper relationship between the will of God and the state. In fact, *Macintosh* was the last time the Court ever articulated the Christian nation heresy.[34]

Citizen Conscientious Objectors

The other line of conscientious objection cases taken up by the Court involves the citizen (as opposed to the applicant for naturalization) who refuses to participate in the military. As noted above, in *Macintosh* the Court clearly expressed that any exemption from military service must come from Congress; it certainly is not a constitutionally given right.[35] But, in fact, Congress has made provision for conscientious objectors. Such laws first were passed during the Civil War. In 1864 both the Union and the Confederacy exempted from conscription those people who were members of well-recognized denominations that taught pacifism, groups such as the Society of Friends (Quakers) and the Mennonites. People not members of the "peace churches" were not eligible for the exemption. The same exemption was reenacted in the Draft Act of 1917,[36] so long as the objection was to "war in any form." The law required that all eligible persons be inducted into the armed forces, but members of "peace churches" were allowed to perform noncombatant service.

In 1940 the law was revised again.[37] Now it was not necessary to belong to a peace church, so long as one's objection to war in any form was based on "religious training and belief." Those who qualified were not inducted but allowed to perform alternative service useful to the nation. Some believed, however, that such criteria were broad enough to include intellectual or humanist objections to war. So, in 1948, Congress refined the category to say that

> religious training and belief . . . means an individual's belief in a relation to a Supreme Being involving duties superior to those arising from any human relation, but does not include essentially political, sociological, or philosophical views or a merely personal moral code.[38]

With the advent of the Vietnam War, perhaps America's most unpopular war, draft boards were deluged with applications for conscientious objector status. Some of those applications involved people who claimed to have sincere conscientious objections to participation in war, but who were not religious in a conventional sense. Not only were they not participants in some organized religious group; some did not even believe in a personal God. Did these people qualify for conscientious objector status, given the wording of the law? The Supreme Court first faced this question in 1965 in *United States v. Seeger*,[39] a case that actually combined the appeals of three different young men.

Redefining Religious Belief

How unconventional were these people? Rather than answer yes or no, Seeger preferred to leave open the question of whether he believed in a personal God. But that did not mean that he believed in nothing whatsoever. He had a "belief in and devotion to goodness and virtue for their own sakes and a religious faith in a purely ethical creed," and cited Plato, Aristotle, and Spinoza as support for such a belief. An appellant named Jakobson said he believed in "Godness" which was "the Ultimate Cause for the fact of the Being of the Universe." He believed in a relationship to Godness in two directions, "vertically, toward Godness directly," and "horizontally, toward Godness through Mankind and the World." He preferred the latter. The third applicant, Peter, said that for him religion was "the supreme expression of human nature; man thinking his highest, feeling his deepest, living his best." He said he supposed one could say such a belief was grounded in a Supreme Being or God, but "[t]hese just do not happen to be the words I use."[40] In all three cases, the young men said the beliefs thus articulated were the basis of their sincere objection to participation in war.

The question the Supreme Court faced in this case was whether the conscientious objection of these men resulted from "religious training and belief . . . in relation to a Supreme Being," as demanded by the statute. Justice Tom Clark, writing for the Court, began his discussion by noting that Congress had used the phrase "Supreme Being" rather than the word "God" in the statute. By making this choice of words, it intended to accommodate something broader than a traditional belief in a personal God. Taking a kind of "ultimate concern" view of religion, the Court argued that the statute did not insist on a traditional concept of God, but would be satisfied with a belief in a being or impersonal power upon which all else is dependent or to which all else is subordinate. In the light of Congress's expansive language, the three men in this case fit the category of being in "relation to a Supreme Being involving duties superior to those arising from any human relation."

The Double Sincerity Test

But was this really "religious training and belief" as required by the statute? The Court set forth a test for determining religious belief: "The test might be stated in these words: A sincere and meaningful belief which occupies in the life of its possessor a place parallel to that filled by the God of those admittedly qualifying for the exemption comes within the statutory definition."[41] I call this a "double sincerity test." In evaluating the application of a conscientious objector with unconventional "religious" beliefs, the officials at the draft board (or a judge) have to think of some conscientious objector with conventional religious beliefs they have known (or, if they have not known any, hypothesize about one), say, a Quaker. They are to think about the sincerity of religious belief of that person, that is, the role that a personal God plays in his or her life. Then they are to think about the unconventional applicant and try to determine if that person's unconventional beliefs are held as sincerely, or play as large a part in that person's life, as those of the Quaker. If they are parallel, then the unconventional person can be granted conscientious objector status. This is not an easy assignment.

I mentioned earlier that the government (courts) is not permitted to eval-

uate or determine the truth or falsity of theology under our system of separation. In general that is true. But the *Seeger* case's double sincerity test pushes
at the constraints, because it asks government officials to evaluate one applicant's beliefs in comparison with another's more conventional beliefs. Some
may argue that the procedure defies the principle. But others may argue, and
the Supreme Court would agree, that it is not the content of the belief that is
being evaluated, but the sincerity with which it is held. The distinction is very
fuzzy. The Supreme Court has never defined religion, because of our system
of separation, but *Seeger* comes as close as the Court ever has come. And the
definition is very broad.

The Result: An Elastic Law

Welsh v. United States[42] illustrated how broad the definition was. In terms of
the statements made on his application for conscientious objector status,
Welsh was even less religious, in any conventional sense, than Seeger and the
others in that case. On the application form for conscientious objector status,
the question was asked as to whether the applicant's views on war were based
on "religious training and belief." Seeger had put quotation marks around
"religious," but Welsh marked out the word. Although he later did say that he
was religious "in the ethical sense of the word," he never thought of himself
as being a religious person. He certainly had no clearly defined theological
views or a belief in a personal God. He characterized his beliefs as having been
formed "by reading in the fields of history and sociology."

Still, the Supreme Court upheld Welsh's qualification to be classified as a
conscientious objector, on the ground he was more religious than he knew.
That is, Justice Hugo Black wrote, few people knew of the broad interpretation given to the word "religious" in *Seeger*. Without knowing that definition,
they might think they fall outside the category when, in reality, they could be
included:

> [V]ery few registrants are fully aware of the broad scope of the word
> "religious" as used in § 6(j) [as interpreted in *Seeger*], and accordingly
> a registrant's statement that his beliefs are nonreligious is a highly
> unreliable guide for those charged with administering the exemption.
> Welsh himself presents a case in point.[43]

Recall that the statute specified that one's objections to war could not be
based on "essentially political, sociological, or philosophical views or a merely
personal moral code." The government, which opposed Welsh's application,
claimed that he fell within this forbidden territory. But the Court, having said
Welsh was actually religious under the *Seeger* definition, disagreed. It said the
exclusion mentioned in the law should not include persons who have strongly

held beliefs about America's domestic or foreign policy or whose objection to war is based on considerations of public policy.

> The two groups of registrants that obviously do fall within these exclusions from the exemption are those whose beliefs are not deeply held and those whose objection to war does not rest at all upon moral, ethical, or religious principle but instead rests solely upon considerations of policy, pragmatism, or expediency.[44]

Welsh qualified as a conscientious objector.

With these two cases, the conscientious objector provision of the draft law became the most elastic of laws, able to be stretched to include almost anyone. Furthermore, Congress did not react by rewriting the law to make it more precise, but essentially accepted the interpretation of *Seeger* and *Welsh* without a whimper.[45] Some did wonder, however, if even these broad interpretations did not function to eliminate inarticulate applicants, those with too little education to be able to cite the likes of Plato and Aristotle, and those who had not read in history and sociology.

Selective Conscientious Objection

Finally, *Gillette v. United States*[46] is another important case. Some native-born citizens who applied for conscientious objector status were not opposed to all wars. Guy P. Gillette said that although he was opposed to the war in Vietnam, he could conceive of wars in which he would be willing to participate, such as wars of national defense or those fought under the auspices of the United Nations. He considered America's efforts in Vietnam to be unjust, however, and had conscientious objections to participation therein.

The Court made short work of this application for conscientious objector status. Remember the statute specified that, in order to qualify, the applicant must be "conscientiously opposed to participation in war in any form." The Court took those words literally; no elastic definition here. Indeed, the Court's opinion, written by Justice Thurgood Marshall, held that there can be only one reading of the words. Gillette did not fit the statutory requirement; thus his application must be denied. Even though the Court had been most generous in its interpretation of who could fall within the boundaries of conscientious objector status, even those who might otherwise qualify under the loose standards cannot pick and choose their wars. To the argument that this interpretation might discriminate against certain denominations, those which have just war/unjust war theories, for example, the Court disagreed. The statute is religion-neutral and is not designed to single out any religious organization or creed for special treatment or discrimination.

Now that the nation no longer has conscription, but rather relies on voluntary armed service, these cases are moot. One can assume that if conscription were resumed under the same statutory framework as formerly, the definitions of these cases would become operative again.

6

Aid to Church-Related Schools

The propriety of the presence of religion in public schools has been and continues to be one of the most volatile issues in the church-state decisions of the Supreme Court. Americans take education very seriously. Historically, schools have been seen to be crucial to the national welfare. Americans have seen the education of children as essential for a strong and vital nation. The knowledge and skills the schools give youth enable them to earn a living for themselves. But such training also is fundamental to a strong economy, which makes America the world power that it has been. Furthermore, the schools have served the important purpose of passing on American values to successive generations—values such as democracy, capitalism, and, with notable exceptions, a diluted form of Protestant Christianity. The notable exceptions, of course, exist because some of those schools are operated by non-Protestant or non-Christian religious groups. There are parochial schools in this country as well as public schools. Both kinds of schools are involved in the church-state decisions of the Supreme Court.

The first educational institutions in this country were all church-related and had as their primary objective the education of clergy. In the early seventeenth century, once the Puritans established a colony at Massachusetts Bay, "[O]ne of the next things we longed for, and looked after was to advance Learning, and perpetuate it to Posterity, dreading to leave an illiterate Ministry to the Churches, when our present Ministers shall lie in the Dust."[1] With this motivation they founded Harvard College in 1636. They also founded "a fair Grammar School, for the training up of young Scholars, and fitting of them for Academical Learning."[2] Likewise, the Massachusetts School Act of November 11, 1647, declared:

It being one chief project of that old deluder, Satan, to keep men from
the knowledge of the Scriptures, . . . that learning may not be buried
in the grave of our fathers in the church and commonwealth, the Lord
assisting our endeavors,—

It is therefore ordered, that every township in this jurisdiction, after
the Lord hath increased them to the number of fifty householders,
shall then forthwith appoint one within their town to teach all such
children as shall resort to him to write and to read.[3]

The assumption that if ignorance is the work of Satan, then education must
somehow be the work of the Lord undergirds all church-sponsored education.
This law established the educational pattern for the rest of the colonial period.
The pattern was denominationally sponsored schools along the eastern
seaboard and, later, on the frontier. Although educational goals were broadened beyond training for the ministry, the curricula of all the schools included
a large component of Christianity, taught from the perspective of the sponsoring denomination.

After the country won independence, virtually all recognized that education was essential to the development of the new nation. Democracy could survive only if there were informed debate about national issues. Informed debate
could take place only if the citizenry were educated. But many believed it was
inappropriate for the nation to reap the benefit from something for which it
did not pay. Furthermore, the various denominational schools, each perpetu-
ating its own creed, would lead to fragmentation in the body politic. That was
not good for a democratic society. In response to these two concerns, in the
early 1830s the idea of the public school developed. Schools would be paid for
by the various local and state governments. They would not teach the theology of any religious group, and thus presumably would be free from sectarian
differences and divisiveness.

A nation desires, of course, law-abiding, moral citizens. Clearly, then, the
new public schools should teach civic morality along with "reading, writing,
and arithmetic." But what would be the source of this civic morality, since the
public schools were to be free from sectarian religious teaching? School leaders decided it would be religious virtue, derived from those virtues common
to all Judeo-Christian religions, namely, a belief in God and a life of morality
based on the ethical teachings of the Bible. Surely all people could agree on
those as being essential to the content of public school curricula.

But all did not agree. Some of the Protestant groups that operated schools
believed the public schools, even with their "common religion" approach to
morality, were not religious enough. These Protestants wanted more emphasis
on religion, denominationally proclaimed, than the public schools were able to
give. So they continued their parochial schools. Lutherans are a major example.

Beginning about 1830 and continuing throughout the rest of the century (the Civil War years excepted), massive waves of immigrants poured into America. Many of these people were Roman Catholic. Catholics were convinced that the public schools were purveyors of "lowest common denominator Protestantism" (which surely they were). Even though it was a watered-down Protestantism, the public schools were too Protestant for the Catholics. Consequently, the Catholic Church began a parochial school movement, into which it has poured enormous amounts of money, energy, and talent.

Given this history, the Supreme Court has had to deal with two kinds of school cases. One involves government aid to parochial schools, the subject of this chapter. The other is about religion in the public schools, in the form of religious instruction or devotional exercises. These cases are the subject of chapter 7. In both instances, the Establishment Clause is involved, because that clause especially is the guardian of separation of church and state; that is, it demands that government be neutral toward religion, neither aiding nor hindering it.

GOVERNMENT AID TO PAROCHIAL SCHOOLS

Once Roman Catholics decided to have an extensive school system, they also tried to get public funding for it. This was, after all, an immigrant church in the nineteenth century, and resources were scarce for the development and maintenance of its schools. The church's principal rationale for seeking public assistance was that the parochial schools served the public good; they contributed to the educated citizenry necessary to the democracy and also relieved population pressures on the public schools. Consequently the church felt that it was only right that some government money should help support its schools. This effort to gain government aid began as early as the 1840s, with the efforts of Archbishop John Hughes of New York.[4]

Before examining these aid cases, it is important to look at a challenge to the very existence of parochial schools. In 1922, in a fit of anti-immigrant passion, Oregon passed a law requiring all able-bodied and educable children to attend the public schools of the state, because private and parochial schools tended to perpetuate differences between people. That law, a way of trying to assimilate immigrants, was challenged by a parochial school and a military academy. In *Pierce v. Society of Sisters*[5] the Court ruled on the basis of the Fourteenth Amendment (the First was not applied to the states until the 1940s). Remember the Fourteenth Amendment contains the phrase "nor shall any State deprive any person of life, liberty, or property, without due process of law." The Society of Sisters and Hill Military Academy claimed the law impermissibly denied private and parochial schools the liberty to do business (which is essentially property), in violation of that clause. The Court agreed with that contention, and further held that Oregon's law interfered with the freedom of parents to educate their children as they wanted. States could not prohibit private and parochial schools from existing. The Court did say, however, that the educational standards in parochial schools had to conform to the standards of quality demanded by the state. This case is often called the Magna Carta of parochial schools.

The Child Benefit Theory

Given that lease on life, parochial schools continued to seek public funding. The first case challenging that funding, *Cochran v. Louisiana State Board of Education*,[6] came before the Court in 1930. Louisiana had a program that provided state-financed textbooks used in public schools to students in parochial schools. The program was challenged on the ground that it took private (tax) money (property) and used it for a private (parochial school) purpose, as opposed to a public purpose. This use of tax money was alleged to be illegal under the Fourteenth Amendment. The Court disagreed with that contention and in the process articulated an important concept in church-state relations: the "child benefit theory." The Court ruled that the state benefit went only to the children enrolled in parochial schools, not to the schools themselves, and certainly not to the churches that operated the schools. Chief Justice Charles Evans Hughes wrote, "The schools, however, are not the beneficiaries of these appropriations. They obtain nothing from them, nor are they relieved of a single obligation, because of them. The school children and the state alone are the beneficiaries."[7] The "child benefit theory" has appeared from time to time in subsequent cases.

A prime example of its application is the 1947 landmark case *Everson v. Board of Education*.[8] Ewing Township, New Jersey, consistent with state law, passed a regulation that permitted the parents of children attending public and Catholic schools to receive a reimbursement from public money for the expense of having their children transported to and from school on public buses. A taxpayer of the community sued, claiming that the program was a violation of the Establishment Clause of the First Amendment. He argued that this transportation program at state expense aided church schools and thus violated the separation between church and state demanded by that clause.

Everson is important for two reasons. First, it was the case in which the Court applied the Establishment Clause to the states through the Fourteenth Amendment.[9] Second, Justice Hugo Black, the author of the majority opinion, wrote an expansive, strict separationist description of the scope and power of the Establishment Clause. This important paragraph, or portions of it, have been quoted in Supreme Court decisions ever since:

> The "establishment of religion" clause of the First Amendment means at least this: Neither a state nor the Federal Government can set up a church. Neither can pass laws which aid one religion, aid all religions, or prefer one religion over another. Neither can force nor influence a person to go to or to remain away from church against his will or force him to profess a belief or disbelief in any religion. No person can be punished for entertaining or professing religious beliefs or disbeliefs, for church attendance or non-attendance. No tax in any amount, large or small, can be levied to support any religious activities or institutions, whatever they may be called, or whatever form they may adopt to teach or practice religion. Neither a state nor the Federal Government can, openly or secretly, participate in the affairs of any religious organizations or groups and *vice versa*. In the words of Jefferson, the clause against establishment of religion by law was intended to erect "a wall of separation between church and state."[10]

This 1947 statement has set the tone for Establishment Clause decisions of the Court since then. The justices have wrestled with the principles and implications of this statement ever since, and although some of them recently have wanted to modify or abandon it, it is still quoted in decisions.

Justice Black concluded his opinion with another strict-separationist statement, which seems to echo and summarize the paragraph just quoted. "The First Amendment has erected a wall between church and state. That wall must be kept high and impregnable. We could not approve the slightest breach. New Jersey has not breached it here."[11]

Yet, amazingly, the majority approved of the public-financed bus transportation for children going to parochial schools and agreed that the program did not violate the Establishment Clause. How could this happen, given the sentiments that form the core of the opinion?

The Court reached its conclusion by using a variation of the "child benefit" approach, although it did not use the phrase. Bus transportation of children to schools, public and parochial, is a kind of public welfare program similar to police and fire protection or sewage lines and sidewalks. These other government services are made available to churches just as they are to all other segments of the community. They provide for the public's safety. Just so with the public transportation of children to school. The program was to protect children from the dangers of walking to school or even riding with their parents in private cars. For the city to pay for transportation to church-related schools on public buses was not aid to religion but a way to protect children from the dangers of public thoroughfares. The child was the beneficiary, not the school or the church that operated the school.

This child benefit approach had grounding in the religion clauses of the Constitution. (This gave the theory more weight in reference to religion than the *Cochran* decision did, since that case was decided only on Fourteenth Amendment grounds.) In a passage less frequently quoted, but no less important, than the one cited above, Justice Black wrote of the First Amendment:

> That Amendment requires the state to be a neutral in its relations with groups of religious believers and non-believers; it does not require the state to be their adversary. State power is no more to be used so as to handicap religions than it is to favor them.[12]

Because the result of the decision was so anomalous with its reasoning, two strong dissents were written, joined by four justices. But all of the dissenters agreed with either the application of the Establishment Clause to the states or the strict-separationist description of the scope of the clause. So it was left to later justices to dispute the Establishment Clause philosophy expressed in this case.

EXCURSUS 1: THE *"LEMON* TEST"

A Three-Part Test for Interpreting the Establishment Clause

In order to discuss the procedures the Court used to decide post-*Everson* aid to parochial school cases and other Establishment Clause cases, it is necessary to understand a test that was developed to interpret the clause. In 1963, the Court decided *Abington Township School District v. Schempp*,[13] a case about prayer and Bible reading in the public schools, which is examined in chapter 7.

In *Schempp* the Court generated the "secular purpose test" and the "primary effect test." In order for a law to be judged constitutional under the Establishment Clause, it must have a secular purpose, and its primary effect must neither advance nor hinder religion. The secular purpose test refers to the intention of the legislative body. Was the legislature's intent to pass a law that would give aid or sanction to a religion or to religion in general? If so, the law is unconstitutional. The primary effect test has to do not with the purpose of the law but with its implementation or enforcement. The tests are independent of each other, because it is possible to enforce a secular law in a way that advances or hinders religion.

In 1970 the Court handed down a decision in *Walz v. Tax Commission of the City of New York*,[14] a case about property tax exemptions for churches explained in chapter 8. In that case the Court crafted a third test for interpreting the Establishment Clause, one prohibiting "excessive entanglement": if a program or law creates more than minimal interaction between a religious institution and civil authority, then it is unconstitutional. The Establishment Clause demands the intercourse between church and state be as limited as possible. In this time of rapidly expanding government, there can be no such thing as absolute separation of church and state. But the involvement must be kept slight; anything more is a violation. The "excessive entanglement test" permits the courts to determine whether a violation has occurred.

The entanglement test was added to the other two, thereby formulating a three-part test for interpreting the Establishment Clause. The first time these tests were used together, as a unit, was in 1971 in an aid to parochial school case called *Lemon v. Kurtzman*:[15]

> In the absence of precisely stated constitutional prohibitions, we must draw lines with reference to the three main evils against which the Establishment Clause was intended to afford protection: "sponsorship, financial support, and active involvement of the sovereign in religious activity."
>
> Every analysis in this area must begin with consideration of the cumulative criteria developed by the Court over many years. Three such tests may be gleaned from our cases. First, the statute must have a secular legislative purpose; second, its principal or primary effect must be one that neither advances nor inhibits religion; finally, the statute must not foster "an excessive government entanglement with religion."[16]

This three-part test has come to be known as the "*Lemon* test." Considerably more is said of this elsewhere in this book.

Note that the elements of the test are subjective. They are not hard-and-fast rules, but what the Court once called "no more than helpful signpost[s]."[17] They require judgment calls. What is a secular purpose as opposed to a religious one? What is a primary effect to either advance or hinder religion as opposed to, say, an indirect effect? What does it take to make entanglement excessive? All these are questions of interpretation, the sort of things on which courts are supposed to rule. But they are also issues on which people, even Supreme Court justices, disagree, which will become abundantly clear.

EXCURSUS 2: STANDING

In order to be able to understand many of the parochial school issues that follow, it is necessary to become familiar with the legal concept of "standing." Standing has to do with whether the one who files a suit has the right to do so.

We have an adversarial system of jurisprudence in this country. Article III,

Section 2 of the Constitution says the judicial power of the government shall extend to "cases" and "controversies" between parties who have real interests in conflict with each other. One question involved in the issue of standing is whether one's interest is substantial and actually protected under the law. Furthermore, will the decision of the court make a difference to the parties in the suit—will they be affected by the outcome? If the answer to these questions is negative, then the one bringing the suit does not have standing. If one lacks standing, one cannot come to court; that is, the suit presented to the court will not be considered.

A principal example, and one pertinent to this book, is that of taxpayer suits. The best way to understand this is to look at a famous case, *Frothingham v. Mellon*.[18] Ms. Frothingham filed suit in federal court challenging the constitutionality of the Maternity Act of 1921. That law sent federal money to the states to improve prenatal and infant care. She claimed this act inflicted on her the burden of paying taxes in support of an unconstitutional program. To put it another way, she had to pay taxes for a government program she believed was wrong and illegal. The Supreme Court responded to this complaint by saying that Frothingham could not raise the constitutional question about the program because she did not have standing as a taxpayer. The amount of federal taxes she paid was a minuscule part of the total federal budget. Given that only a small percentage of the federal budget actually went to fund the maternity program, her personal involvement as a taxpayer in that particular program was even smaller—infinitesimal. That small level of involvement meant she really did not have a personal stake in the funding of the program or in the outcome of her suit. She did not have standing. Consequently, the Court never considered her constitutional challenge to the maternity law, because she was not qualified to be a litigant.

The rule derived from *Frothingham* is that taxpayer suits are not permitted in federal courts. State courts, however, frequently did and do allow taxpayer suits. Occasionally the Supreme Court accepts a taxpayer suit that came through a state court system and presents an important federal question, in spite of the *Frothingham* rule. Both *Cochran v. Louisiana State Board of Education* and *Everson v. Board of Education* were such cases.

An Exception to *Frothingham*: *Flast v. Cohen*

The question of standing was raised in the church-state area in *Flast v. Cohen*.[19] In 1965 Congress passed the Elementary and Secondary Education Act, which, among other things, allowed federal money to go to church-related schools for instruction and materials. In New York seven individuals brought suit in federal court, challenging the constitutionality of the part of the law that aided religious schools. Their only qualification to be plaintiffs was that they were payers of federal taxes. The government contended they did not have standing and that the suit should be dismissed. The plaintiffs claimed they did have standing. The case was diverted from being a challenge to the constitutionality of the Education Act and was turned into a standing suit; that is, the Court was now to decide if a taxpayer has standing when the challenge is made to a law alleged to violate the Establishment Clause.

Chief Justice Earl Warren, writing for the majority, slightly modified the *Frothingham* rule on standing, saying that a federal taxpayer has standing if two requirements are met. First, the taxpayer has to prove that the law challenged was passed under the Taxing and Spending Clause of the Constitution (Article I, Section 8).[20] That is, one may not challenge expenditures under a regulatory program of government, but may challenge legislation involving expenditures from taxation. Second, the taxpayer must show that the law challenged involves a constitutional limitation on congressional taxing and spending, such as the Establishment Clause. Because the Establishment Clause prohibits government sponsorship or sanction of religion, it is a constitutional restriction on congressional taxing and spending for religious programs. The taxpayer/plaintiff must show that such a provision is involved in the lawsuit. If both these conditions are met, the plaintiffs have standing to sue. Obviously, if either requirement is not met, the suit is dismissed from court.

The importance of this case lies in the determination that taxpayers who challenge government expenditures to aid church-related schools as a violation of the Establishment Clause have met both the conditions. The *Frothingham* rule was not eliminated; generally taxpayer suits are not yet allowed in federal courts. But an important exception to the rule was created. Virtually all of the parochial school cases after 1968 were taxpayer suits and could not have been brought if it were not for *Flast v. Cohen*. It was clearly a landmark case in church-state relationships.

Preserving but Not Expanding on a Precedent

Although the result of *Flast* is the point of this excursus from the narrative of this chapter, given its implication for challenges to government aid to church-related schools, one other standing case is worth mentioning. In 1949 Congress enabled the government to dispose of its surplus property for the benefit of American society. Property that is no longer useful to the government can be given to public or private entities for their use. Under that law, in 1976 the government gave a seventy-seven-acre tract of property with several buildings on it to Valley Forge Christian College, which was owned and operated by the Assemblies of God. Because the government believed that it had gotten its money's worth from the property, it was given to the college free of charge.

Sometime after the transfer, some employees of Americans United for Separation of Church and State learned of the transaction through a news release. The organization and four individual employees filed suit in federal district court, asking that the transaction be voided and that the college give the property back to the government. Their claim was that they were federal taxpayers, and furthermore, as citizens they wanted assurance that the Establishment Clause was not being violated. The Supreme Court in 1982 addressed the complaint in *Valley Forge Christian College v. Americans United for Separation of Church and State.*[21]

Justice William Rehnquist, writing for the Court, rejected the objection to the government giveaway by holding that the objectors did not have standing to bring suit. Even though *Flast v. Cohen* said federal taxpayers could challenge acts of Congress when the Establishment Clause was involved, it specified that the congressional acts had to be pursuant to the Taxing and Spending Clause of the Constitution, Article I, Section 8. But the congressional act challenged in *Valley Forge* was under the authority of the Property Clause of the Constitution, Article IV, Section 3, Clause 2. Because their challenge did not meet the narrow requirement of *Flast*, those challenging the transfer of property did not have standing. The Court preserved the precedent of *Flast*, but did not go an inch beyond it.

Thus the window of opportunity for taxpayers to sue in federal court is a small one. The challenge must be specifically targeted at how Congress spends money and be based on a constitutional limitation on the exercise of the congressional taxing and spending power. But by preserving that holding in *Flast*, the Court still left open the possibility of taxpayer challenges to government money being spent to aid church-related schools. As noted earlier, this made possible a number of cases involving that issue.

Many of the aid cases focus on specific kinds of aid provided to church-related schools. It is prudent and will be less tedious not to look at each case in detail, telling how it came to the Court or from where it came, but rather simply to describe the services the Court has permitted and those it has forbidden, with the case name in each instance.

First, however, the Court—certainly in its post-*Everson* cases if not before— assumes a church-related school is pervasively religious. A church-related elementary or secondary school exists not just to teach secular subjects, for that service can be and is supplied by public schools. Its principal reason for existence is to teach religion, and to teach it from the perspective of the sponsoring church. It can do this by having worship in the school, by teaching courses that are exclusively religious in content, and by including religious content or themes in secular instruction. So the Supreme Court, as it has had to make decisions on a variety of efforts to supply government aid to church-related schools, has approached the enterprise with the assumption that the schools are principally religious in nature. One statement, from *Meek v. Pittenger*, illustrates this view. Speaking of the aid program to "religion-pervasive institutions" involved in that case, the Court said:

> The very purpose of many of those schools is to provide an integrated secular and religious education; the teaching process is, to a large extent, devoted to the inculcation of religious values and belief. Substantial aid to the educational function of such schools, accordingly, necessarily results in aid to the sectarian school enterprise as a whole.[22]

It will become apparent, however, that recently the Court has moved away from this assumption and become increasingly lenient in approving programs of government aid to parochial schools.

PERMITTED GOVERNMENT AID

Lending Textbooks

It was noted earlier that the Court has approved of providing, by the expenditure of state funds, secular textbooks to the pupils in church-related schools (*Cochran v. Louisiana State Board of Education*). The "child benefit theory" was developed in that case and indeed made possible the Court's approval of the program. The provision of books was reaffirmed later in *Board of Education v. Allen*.[23] *Allen* is different from *Cochran* in that it was decided under the Establishment Clause rather than just the Fourteenth Amendment. Although it used "child benefit" language, it also held that the loan of textbooks law had a secular purpose under the Establishment Clause. *Allen* is important because it raised the loan of textbooks to parochial school students to a higher level, finding such a program constitutional under the First Amendment. Subsequently, textbooks for parochial school students were approved in two other cases, *Meek v. Pittenger*[24] and *Wolman v. Walter*.[25] We have also seen that the Court used child-benefit or public-welfare language in approving city-financed bus rides for children going to parochial schools (*Everson v. Board of Education*).

Standardized Testing, Diagnostic Services, and Therapy

Some states authorized the administration of state-prepared standardized tests to students in parochial schools, as well as the grading of those tests, at public expense. The Court in 1980 held such a program constitutional (*Wolman v. Walter* and *Committee for Public Education and Religious Liberty v. Regan*[26]). The reasoning was that state-prepared tests are for subjects routinely taught in public schools and thus contain no religious content. Consequently, the administration and grading of such tests at state expense would not put the state in the posture of aiding religion.

Similar reasoning approved of diagnostic services for parochial school students. The program funded examinations of students to detect speech and hearing problems. Health professionals under contract to the board of public education diagnosed students in parochial school buildings. The Court ruled that in the process of diagnosis by doctors and nurses no commentary or indoctrination about religion could take place at government expense, even though the services were in the parochial school. Diagnosis is religion-neutral (*Wolman v. Walter*).

Diagnosis may be religion-neutral, but therapy has the potential not to be. Conversation, perhaps even in-depth interaction, takes place during therapeutic services. There is the possibility that conversation, even exhortation, about religion could take place during sessions providing speech or hearing therapy, guidance counseling, or remedial services. That would be unconstitutional if the therapy were being done by government-paid therapists at religious schools. However, the Court permitted such services to be administered to parochial school students by such therapists as long as the therapy occurred away from the parochial school. That is, a neutral site minimized the possibility of religious indoctrination to the satisfaction of the Court (*Wolman v. Walter*). "It can hardly be said that the supervision of public employees performing public functions on public property creates an excessive entanglement between church and state."[27]

Standardized testing, diagnostic services and therapy, along with lending textbooks and bus transportation and aid to handicapped students, discussed below, are the sum total of what the Court to 1994 had declared to be constitutional and permissible to provide to parochial schools at government expense. But these services did not represent the total of programs and services that various states attempted to make available to parochial schools. Several states made vigorous efforts to provide a wide variety of other forms of aid to church-related schools, efforts that were rejected by the Court.

PROHIBITED SERVICES

The list of services prohibited begins with the "purchase of secular educational services." In one case, the state recognized that it could not pay for the teaching of religion, but believed it could "purchase" secular instruction. This involved the direct reimbursement of parochial schools for teachers' salaries, textbooks, and instructional materials. The Court declared such a program unconstitutional under the "excessive entanglement" test: the surveillance required by public officials to guarantee the state money was used only for secular education in the parochial schools would create an impermissible level of interaction between religion and civil authority (*Lemon v. Kurtzman*[28]).

A program to pay salary supplements from public funds to teachers in parochial schools met the same fate for the same reason. Here, although the bulk of the teachers' salaries was paid by the church-related school, the law authorized supplementary payments from public funds to bring their salary levels up to minimum standards. The law specified that the teachers could teach only those subjects offered in public schools, that is, secular subjects. Furthermore, as a condition for getting the salary supplements, teachers had to promise in writing not to inject any religious content into their classroom presentations. But in spite of these safeguards against the state's paying for religious instruction, the Court ruled against the program. Although it assumed the honesty and integrity of the teachers, the Court noted that they were, after all, paid by and teaching in a church-related school. Furthermore, many of them were members of religious orders. Given that, it would require regular and frequent surveillance by public officials to make sure that religion did not creep into their teaching. Such surveillance was impermissible entanglement (*Lemon v. Kurtzman*).

New York State initiated a program to give parochial schools money to maintain and repair buildings. Under the theory that the state has an interest in the health, safety, and welfare of students in parochial as well as in public schools, the program provided money for janitorial services, utilities, necessary upkeep and renovation of buildings, and a variety of other such services. Although this kind of program has a child-benefit sound to it, the Supreme Court declared it unconstitutional (*Committee for Public Education and Religious Liberty v. Nyquist*[29]). The problem was that the money was not confined to the upkeep of buildings or rooms used only for secular purposes; it could be used for the school chapel as well as the gymnasium, for example. Given that lack of restriction, the Court ruled the law had the primary effect of advancing religion with state money. "If the State may not erect buildings in which religious activities are to take place, it may not maintain such buildings or renovate them when they fall into disrepair."[30]

Funding of teacher-prepared examinations in parochial schools was also declared unconstitutional. Unlike state-prepared standardized tests, which were devoid of religious content, the content of teacher-prepared tests could not be controlled by the state. Because such tests might have religious content, to provide state money to underwrite their preparation had the primary effect of advancing religion (*Levitt v. Committee for Public Education and Religious Liberty*[31]).

Some states tried to aid parochial schools by supplying them, at state expense, with instructional materials and equipment such as maps, globes, and film projectors. The Court held such a program to be unconstitutional because it had the primary effect of advancing religion. Because religious instruction is so intertwined with secular instruction in the church-related schools, the Court argued, it is impossible to believe that the equipment can be used for secular purposes only. "Even though earmarked for secular purposes, 'when it flows to an institution in which religion is so pervasive that a substantial portion of its functions are subsumed in the religious mission,' state aid has the impermissible primary effect of advancing religion."[32] This form of aid was denied parochial schools in both *Meek v. Pittenger* and *Wolman v. Walter*.

When services such as remedial and accelerated instruction, speech and hearing assistance, and guidance counseling were offered to parochial school students *on the premises*, the program was unconstitutional. Although the service providers were public employees, the fact they rendered their services in the parochial schools at least raised the possibility that some religious instruction would take place. It would require continuing surveillance to make sure that their services remained entirely secular. That surveillance would foster excessive entanglement between government and religion, a violation of the Establishment Clause (*Meek v. Pittenger*).

For reasons similar to those marshaled against the loan of instructional equipment to parochial schools, the Court refused to approve instructional field trips. Although the statute at issue in the case specified that public money could be used to finance only those field trips comparable to those taken by public school students, the Court noted that such trips are still led by parochial school teachers. The teachers determine how the trips fit with the curriculum being presented in the parochial schools and interpret the site to the students. Such trips are an integral part of the educational experience. When the educational experience is pervaded with religious themes, it is likely the field trips will be affected by that. Consequently, the Court ruled, publicly funded field trips by church-related schools have the primary effect of advancing religion (*Wolman v. Walter*).

The Court also considered programs in which public school teachers actually came to parochial schools to teach supplementary and enrichment courses or even traditional academic courses to educationally deprived children. In one case, *Grand Rapids School District v. Ball*,[33] some of the state-paid teachers came to the church schools to teach art, music, physical education, reading, and mathematics during the regular school day. Other teachers came after the school day to teach such things as arts and crafts, yearbook production, chess, and nature appreciation; most of these latter teachers were parochial school teachers hired by the city. The Court held that this program had the primary

effect of advancing religion. State-paid teachers—many of whom were identified by their students as their parochial school teachers—teaching in the context of the church school might indoctrinate students in religion or, at the least,
symbolize state support for religion.

In another case, *Aguilar v. Felton*,[34] the teachers were public school teachers hired with money supplied by the federal government to come to the
parochial schools to teach traditional subjects to educationally deprived, low-
income students. The teachers were instructed not to teach religion. The
Court ruled that it would take supervision to guarantee that they, in fact, did
not teach religion and that supervision would create impermissibly excessive
entanglement between church and state. Public school or state-paid teachers
could not teach in the context of the parochial school.

States and occasionally the federal government have been creative in trying
to find ways to provide specific programs to aid church-related schools. The
Supreme Court, using particularly the primary effect and excessive entanglement tests to interpret the Establishment Clause, until recently took a fairly
hard line against such efforts. Although not all forms of aid through services
to parochial elementary and secondary schools were considered unconstitutional, most were.

TUITION TAX CREDIT PLANS

In addition to trying to provide specific services to church-related schools,
some states have tried to create a general funding program for them. The
Court in 1973 ruled on one such attempt in *Committee for Public Education and
Religious Liberty v. Nyquist*,[35] a case about tuition supplements and tax credits.
The first part of the plan tried to help low-income parents send their children
to parochial schools. If a parent had an annual taxable income of $5,000 or
below, for New York State income-tax purposes, the state would reimburse the
family $50 for each grade school child and $100 for each high school child who
attended a parochial school.[36] The program was designed to be a supplement:
the grants could not exceed 50 percent of the actual amount the family paid in
parochial school tuition. The second part of the plan was for those whose taxable income was over $5,000. Parents whose income was between $5,000 and
$9,000 could subtract from their adjusted gross income on the state income-
tax form $1,000 for each dependent up to three who was enrolled in parochial
school. For those whose taxable income was above $9,000, the amount of the
deduction per child decreased on a sliding scale until there was no deduction
at all for families with a taxable income of $25,000 or more. The design of the
plan was a variation on the child-benefit theme, a kind of a "parent benefit"

concept in which the parents of children in parochial schools received either a payment from the state or a tax credit, depending on their income. Neither the church school nor the church sponsoring the school received money directly from the state. (In fact, the parents did not even have to use the money to pay parochial school tuition. They could do anything they wanted to with the money. But the fact that they had a child or children in church-related school triggered their receipt of the supplement or tax credit.)

In spite of the apparent insulation from any state money going directly to the church schools, Justice Lewis Powell, writing for the Court, found the program unconstitutional. The program had the primary effect of aiding religion in that it provided a state incentive for parents to send their children to parochial schools.

> The qualifying parent under either program receives the same form of encouragement and reward for sending his children to nonpublic schools. The only difference is that one parent receives an actual cash payment while the other is allowed to reduce by an arbitrary amount the sum he would otherwise be obliged to pay over to the State. We see no answer to Judge Hays' dissenting statement below that "[i]n both instances the money involved represents a charge made upon the state for the purpose of religious education." . . . Special tax benefits . . . cannot be squared with the principle of neutrality established by the decisions of this Court. To the contrary, insofar as such benefits render assistance to parents who send their children to sectarian schools, their purpose and inevitable effect are to aid and advance those religious institutions.[37]

It should be noted here, at the end of this long series of rejections of attempts to supply state aid to parochial schools, that the Court did not intend to show hostility to the schools. It now and again remarked with appreciation that church-related schools make a significant contribution to America. But the Court is responsible for interpreting the Establishment Clause, which was regarded at the time as prohibiting state sponsorship and sanction of religion. More often than not, state efforts to aid the schools fell on the forbidden side of the line of permissibility. That the Court enforced that prohibition should not be interpreted as animus toward church-sponsored education. The two sides of this are illustrated by this passage from *Lemon v. Kurtzman*:

> Finally, nothing we have said can be construed to disparage the role of church-related elementary and secondary schools in our national life. Their contribution has been and is enormous. Nor do we ignore their economic plight in a period of rising costs and expanding need. Taxpayers generally have been spared vast sums by the maintenance of these educational institutions by religious organizations, largely by gifts of faithful adherents.

The merit and benefits of these schools, however, are not the issue before us in these cases. The sole question is whether state aid to these schools can be squared with the dictates of the Religion Clauses. Under our system the choice has been made that government is to be entirely excluded from the area of religious instruction and churches excluded from the affairs of government.[38]

A decade later, in 1983, the Court considered a similar tax credit plan in *Mueller v. Allen.*[39] The program in that case had one principal difference from the plan struck down in *Nyquist.* In *Mueller* the tax deduction from Minnesota income tax was available to all parents who had children in school, be it parochial, private, *or public.* The deduction was to cover the expenses incurred in paying for tuition, textbooks, and transportation. The deduction could not exceed $500 per child in grades kindergarten through six and $700 in grades seven through twelve. The factual difference from *Nyquist* made the result different. Justice William Rehnquist, writing for the majority, said the fact that the tax deductions were available to the parents of all schoolchildren negated or avoided all church-state problems. The law creating the tax deduction has a secular purpose, namely, undergirding the creation of a well-educated citizenry. It does not have the primary effect of advancing or inhibiting religion, since the money is not aimed only at the parents of parochial school pupils. (This decision thus left *Nyquist* intact; it is still unconstitutional to have a tax law that benefits only parochial school parents.) It does not create excessive entanglement between church and state, because the decision to access the tax credit is a decision made only by the parent without any interaction with a state official. This became a very important concept in Establishment Clause cases.

Many believed, after *Mueller,* that many states and perhaps even the federal government might pass legislation that would provide aid to parochial school parents by provisions in the income-tax codes that would allow all parents with children in school, of whatever kind, to make a deduction. It did not happen, perhaps because in difficult economic times most governments are not willing to deprive themselves of the revenue they would lose by the tax deductions. It may also be that many legislators were convinced by the vigorous dissent written by Justice Thurgood Marshall and joined by three others. The idea which had bamboozled the majority, Marshall argued, that all parents were helped by this "evenhanded" tax deduction, is a fiction. The deduction is not evenhanded, because only under the most unusual circumstances do public schools charge any tuition or fees for their books. Only those parents who send their children to private or parochial schools are anything beyond minimal beneficiaries of the plan. Whatever its neutral qualities on the surface, the program was designed to provide incentives for, or to aid, parents who send their children to sectarian schools.

Aid to the Physically Disabled

If *Mueller* did not result in expansive plans for tax deductions for parochial schools in other states or in federal law, it was a turning point in Establishment Clause decisions. Its acceptance of private decisions triggering government money going to religious entities started a trend away from *Everson*-type strict separationism. (Justice Marshall's dissent in *Mueller* did not dissuade the Court in subsequent cases from "running with" the private choice concept.) Good examples are two cases in which state aid flowed to disabled persons in parochial schools.

A Washington State statute provided aid to the visually impaired in the form of financial assistance for vocational training. The purpose of the law was to assist persons with sight disabilities to be productively employed and to contribute to society. Larry Witters enrolled in a private Christian college with the goal of becoming a pastor, missionary, or youth minister. When he applied for state funds authorized under the law, he was denied on the ground that the use of state money in a clearly theological educational program was improper. When he sued to obtain the funds, the Washington Supreme Court ruled that the state had properly denied him the money; using state money to support religious education violated the Establishment Clause. The United States Supreme Court reversed the decision in 1986, however, in *Witters v. Washington Department of Services for the Blind*.[40]

In a decision written by Justice Thurgood Marshall, the Court ruled it was permissible for Witters to receive government money. Vocational assistance to the blind clearly had a secular purpose, to help those persons become productive members of society. On the question of whether Witters's use of the money for ministerial training had the primary effect of advancing religion, the Court said it did not. The fact that state money went to a theological school was because of the choice of the recipient, not because of any decision of the state. The state money went to students because of their circumstance in life, that is, their blindness. If a recipient used it for ministerial training, it was not the state's doing. Furthermore, Witters's use of the money seemed to be an isolated incident; there was no evidence that others would use state funds under this program for ministerial education. "[The program] is in no way skewed toward religion. . . . It creates no financial incentive for students to undertake sectarian education."[41] Consequently,

> On the facts we have set out, it does not seem appropriate to view any aid ultimately flowing to the Inland Empire School of the Bible as resulting from a *state* action sponsoring or subsidizing religion. Nor does the mere circumstance that [Witters] has chosen to use neutrally available state aid to help pay for his religious education confer any message of state endorsement of religion.[42]

(In his opinion, Justice Marshall did not refer to *Mueller v. Allen*, because he had written a blistering dissent against it. But three other justices, in concurring opinions in *Witters*, specifically called attention to the fact that *Witters* followed the reasoning of *Mueller*.)

The other case about a disabled person, in 1993, was *Zobrest v. Catalina Foothills School District*.[43] Here the issue was whether a state could pay for a sign-language interpreter for a deaf student enrolled in a parochial high school. The federal Individuals with Disabilities Education Act (IDEA) provided money to be administered by states for the education of disabled persons. James Zobrest, deaf from birth, attended a public middle school in Arizona, and the state, using federal IDEA funds, had paid for a sign-language interpreter for him. When he reached high school age, James's parents enrolled him in a Roman Catholic school and requested that the state continue to provide the interpreter. The state refused, on the ground that in the parochial school environment a government subsidy for the interpreter would violate the Establishment Clause. The Zobrest family sued. The Supreme Court ruled in their favor, Chief Justice William Rehnquist writing for the majority.

The Court relied on *Mueller v. Allen* and *Witters v. Washington Department of Services for the Blind* as precedents. In each of those cases, state benefits (tax deduction or vocational training) were made available to all eligible recipients, whether they utilized parochial or state educational institutions. Furthermore, the decision to use church-related schools was made by the recipients, not by the state. The same was true here. IDEA was designed to facilitate education of disabled persons, regardless of where they chose to receive that education. In *Zobrest*, given that the parents chose a religious school for their son, that a state-paid sign interpreter communicated religious content could not be attributed to a decision by the state; it was the result of the private decision of individual parents with no prior incentive from the state. The Court concluded:

> When the government offers a neutral service on the premises of a sectarian school as part of a general program that "is in no way skewed toward religion," it follows under our prior decisions that provision of that service does not offend the Establishment Clause.[44]

Witters and *Zobrest* exhibit a definite "child benefit theory" flavor reminiscent of much earlier cases: *Cochran v. Louisiana State Board of Education* and *Everson v. Board of Education*. A fairly consistent theme of the Court in aid-to-parochial-school cases is if the aid flows directly to the student rather than directly or indirectly to the school, the Establishment Clause is not violated. Those results were greatly facilitated by the "private individual choice rather than government decision" concept first introduced in 1983, in

Mueller v. Allen, and followed consistently in later cases. It served as a perfect tool for accommodationist, nonpreferentialist justices to reshape the older, separationist interpretation of the Establishment Clause.

GOVERNMENT AID TO CHURCH-RELATED UNIVERSITIES

The efforts to provide government aid to parochial schools discussed so far involve elementary and secondary schools. When the Court pondered the question of government assistance to church-related universities, its position was very different from its attitude about aid to lower-level schools. The best way to explain this is to look at *Tilton v. Richardson*,[45] a 1971 case involving various forms of federal aid to church-related universities. Title I of the Higher Education Facilities Act of 1963 authorized the federal government to provide money to colleges to construct buildings, as long as neither religious instruction nor worship was to take place there. However, the law said, after twenty years, when the government had gotten its money's worth,[46] the government-financed building could be used for a religious purpose. When some church-related colleges in Connecticut received some money to build and improve buildings on their campuses, a taxpayer suit was filed.

The Supreme Court, Chief Justice Warren Burger writing for the majority, found this law to be constitutional for the most part. The act had a secular purpose, in that it aimed to help improve the quality of higher education in America. It did not have the primary effect of advancing or inhibiting religion, because the buildings were to be secular buildings (no college chapels), used for secular purposes only. The Court declared, however, the twenty-year reversion clause of the law to be unconstitutional; at no time in its existence could a government-financed building be used for religious activities or purposes. But to strike down that section of the law did not nullify it entirely.

When it came to the excessive entanglement test, Chief Justice Burger articulated the heart of the case. Challengers to the law argued that even if the buildings were supposed to be used for secular purposes, it would take continual surveillance to assure they were used for such purposes—and this would create impermissible excessive entanglement. The Court disagreed. Continual surveillance would not be required because of the nature of a college. Unlike an elementary or secondary school, a church-related college is not pervasively religious. Courses—even courses in religion—are usually taught, not for the purpose of initiating or nurturing faith, but for stimulating inquiry, seeking to encourage critical thinking by students. Both students and faculty enjoy the academic freedom that is characteristic of probing inquiry. Furthermore, college students are older and less impressionable than younger students. For all these reasons, the Court decided, it is not necessary to investigate colleges to determine if they are improperly using their government-funded buildings. Thus, impermissible entanglement between church and state would not be a problem.

The Court took the same approach in two other cases. In 1973 it upheld a South Carolina law that enabled church-related colleges to borrow money at a lower rate of interest through purchase of state-issued bonds (*Hunt v. McNair*[47]). The Court held that by simply issuing bonds at an interest rate lower than commercial and allowing church-related colleges to buy them, the state had no significant involvement with church-related colleges and did not advance or entangle itself with religion. This was particularly true since the colleges were not pervasively religious, as it had described in *Tilton*.

Similarly the Court in 1976 upheld a Maryland program that was broader and more beneficial to church-related universities than *Tilton*. Whereas government money in *Tilton* was available only for building construction, the Maryland program imposed hardly any restrictions on the use of government funds. The statute prohibited a school from offering only theological degrees (so seminaries were excluded) and required a school to promise not to utilize the funds for sectarian purposes. Outside those two limitations, the church-related colleges could use the state funds for any purpose they wanted. The Court still found the law constitutional, in *Roemer v. Board of Public Works of Maryland*.[48] The law had a secular purpose, in that it sought to contribute to an educated population; it did not advance or hinder religion, because of the character of colleges described in *Tilton*; and it did not suffer from entanglement, because the inspections required to see if the schools had kept their promises would be infrequent and brief, rather like those for reaccreditation.

In 1995 the Court heard a different kind of university aid case. It was not about whether or not government could give aid to a church-related university, but rather whether a state university could give aid to religious publications on campus. So the case was more like *Widmar v. Vincent* (chapter 7) than like *Tilton v. Richardson* and *Roemer v. Board of Public Works of Maryland*.

The case is *Rosenberger v. Rector and Visitors of the University of Virginia*.[49] The University of Virginia used funds from a student activity fee to pay for, among other things, the printing of student-run publications. However, the school did not fund student activities that were political or philanthropic, would in some way endanger its tax-exempt status, or—to avoid violating the Establishment Clause—religious. A religious activity was defined "as any activity that 'primarily promotes or manifests a particular belie[f] in or about a deity or ultimate reality.'"[50]

An evangelical Christian magazine, *Wide Awake: A Christian Perspective at the University of Virginia*, applied for student activity funds to pay its printing costs, but the request was denied under this policy. Ronald Rosenberger, the founder and editor of *Wide Awake*, sued on the grounds that the university had denied the paper's rights to freedom of speech and press, free exercise of religion, and equal protection under the law (since other kinds of student publications received funding). The university relied primarily on its no establishment policy.

The Supreme Court, in an opinion by Justice Anthony Kennedy, found in favor of Rosenberger and *Wide Awake*. The decision has two parts. The first relies on the freedom of speech; the second examines the university's Establishment Clause defense.

The University of Virginia, by being a university dedicated to the study and expansion of knowledge and, as a corollary, steadfast in its commitment to lively debate on virtually any topic, had created a limited public forum. (It was "limited" because it was not available to the general public but, rather, confined to the faculty, staff, and students of the university and their invited guests. But within that population, virtually any subject could be discussed.) The Court ruled that, under freedom of speech principles, government could prevent discussion of topics that were not appropriate to the forum it had created; that was permissible "content discrimination." But it could not prevent discussion of certain topics within the categories it had already approved. That was impermissible "viewpoint discrimination."[51] The university was guilty of viewpoint discrimination. Because the university paid the expenses of publications on a wide range of topics, it consequently could not refuse to pay those of *Wide Awake:*

> When the government disburses public funds to private entities [in this case, *Wide Awake*'s printer] to convey a government message, it may take legitimate and appropriate steps to ensure that its message is neither garbled nor distorted by the grantee.
>
> It does not follow, however, . . . that viewpoint-based restrictions are proper when the University does not itself speak or subsidize transmittal of a message it favors but instead expends funds to encourage a diversity of views from private speakers. . . . The University's regulation now before us, however, has a speech-based restriction as its sole rationale and operative principle. . . . Having offered to pay the third-party contractors on behalf of private speakers who convey their own messages, the University may not silence the expression of selected viewpoints.[52]

The Court disagreed with the university's claim that the Establishment Clause required its restriction. Justice Kennedy asserted that the Establishment Clause requires government neutrality toward religion. This is another way of expressing the accommodationist belief that government may aid religion so long as it is evenhanded and nonpreferential. The university was neutral in its attitude toward religion. It did not seek to advance religion, but to create and finance a forum to encourage the expression of all sorts of ideas characteristic of a diverse student body. *Wide Awake* sought funding not because it was a religious publication, but because it was an eligible student journal. Consequently, the university illegitimately used fear of Establishment Clause violation as a rationale for denying the Christian newspaper funding.

Justice Kennedy's concluding paragraph integrated the two sides of the decision:

> To obey the Establishment Clause, it was not necessary for the University to deny eligibility to student publications because of their viewpoint. The neutrality demanded by the State by the separate Clauses of the First Amendment was compromised by the University's course of action. The viewpoint discrimination inherent in the University's regulation required public officials to scan and interpret student publications to discern their underlying philosophic assumptions respecting religious theory and belief. That course of action was a denial of the right of free speech and would risk fostering a pervasive bias or hostility to religion, which could undermine the very neutrality the Establishment Clause requires. There is no Establishment Clause violation in the University's honoring its duties under the Free Speech Clause.[53]

Rosenberger, an example of how the free speech principle overrode the traditional Establishment Clause values expressed in *Everson v. Board of Education*, manifested exactly what Justice White feared in his dissenting comment in *Widmar v. Vincent*.

Locke v. Davey[54] in 2004 raised the question of whether a state may deny scholarship money to otherwise qualified students if they are studying for the ministry. Washington State provides "Promise Scholarships" to college students who meet certain income and academic criteria who attend accredited colleges, even church-related colleges. But it excludes from benefits students pursuing a degree in theology. Joshua Davey enrolled in an Assemblies of God college with the intent of studying for the ministry. When he was told he could not receive scholarship funds, he sued, claiming his exclusion violated the Establishment, Free Exercise, and Free Speech Clauses and denied him equal protection of the law. The Supreme Court framed the question as whether Washington could deny ministerial students scholarship money without violating the Free Exercise Clause.

One might think *Witters v. Washington Department of Services for the*

Blind would serve as precedent for this case. The Court had decided that Witters, studying for a ministerial career, could use state vocational rehabilitation funds to support his study because his private choice caused the money to be used for that purpose. But *Witters* played no role in this case. Davey made his case on the precedent of *Church of Lukumi Babalu Aye v. Hialeah*, the case in which Hialeah, Florida, had targeted the Santeria church with laws aimed at its practice of animal sacrifice. The Court said laws that single out religion for discriminatory treatment deny those religions their free exercise rights. Davey claimed the same was true here; Washington had targeted students working for a degree in theology for adverse treatment, which he charged was unconstitutional treatment under the *Lukumi* precedent.

Chief Justice William Rehnquist, writing for the Court, did not see it that way. He said this case illustrated the "play in the joints" between the Establishment and Free Exercise Clauses. Unlike the city's action in *Lukumi*, Washington's restriction did not impose any criminal sanctions on religious behavior and did not compel students to choose between their religious beliefs and getting government money. It had simply chosen not to fund a distinct category of academic study. Because pursuing a degree in theology is a religious calling and leads to the religious vocation of ministry, the state, under its antiestablishment interest, is justified in not funding that kind of study:

> [T]he subject of religion is one in which both the United States and state constitutions embody distinct views—in favor of free exercise, but opposed to establishment—that find no counterpart with respect to other callings or professions. That a State would deal differently with religious education for the ministry than with education for other callings is a product of these views, not evidence of hostility toward religion. . . . In short, we find neither in the history or text of Article I, § 11 of the Washington Constitution, nor in the operation of the Promise Scholarship Program, anything that suggests animus toward religion. Given the historic and substantial state interest at issue, we therefore cannot conclude that the denial of funding for vocational religious instruction alone is inherently constitutionally suspect.
>
> Without a presumption of unconstitutionality, Davey's claim must fail. The State's interest in not funding the pursuit of devotional degrees is substantial and the exclusion of such funding places a relatively minor burden on Promise Scholars. If any room exists between the two Religion Clauses, it must be here.[55]

It is clear that the Court has adopted a different standard for church-related colleges than for parochial elementary and secondary schools. That different standard derives primarily from the character of the students. College students are older and less impressionable than elementary and secondary school students in reference to authority figures. In addition, the nature of the teaching at the college level is more objective and fostering of critical thinking, while at the lower levels there is more faith nurturing and pervasively religious teaching. Certainly the consideration of the university as a place of robust discussion of diverse viewpoints contributed to the provision of government money to the religious newspaper in *Rosenberger*. Consequently, whereas the Court has been relatively unbending in not allowing government aid to lower-level church-related schools, under the Establishment Clause, it has been rather free in approving such programs at the university level. *Locke v. Davey* is an exception to that generalization.

PROHIBITED SERVICES REVISITED

When the Court decided *Aguilar v. Felton*, described earlier in this chapter, Justice O'Connor expressed outrage in a strong dissent. She was upset because the program declared unconstitutional in that case was to aid educationally disadvantaged children from low-income families. To deprive them of public school teachers to teach remedial subjects in their private school environments would, she observed, be harmful to their development as educated persons.

Twelve years later, in 1997, she got an opportunity to rectify the situation when the Court accepted *Agostini v. Felton*,[56] a frontal attack against the earlier decision. Federal Rule of Civil Procedure 60(b)(5) was the mechanism that allowed the Court to review and modify an earlier case if the law had changed in the meantime. The Board of Education of New York City and some parents challenged *Aguilar* on the ground the Court's Establishment Clause jurisprudence had changed since it was decided and thus it was no longer good law. The Court agreed; Justice O'Connor wrote the opinion.

She began by noting the plaintiffs had good reason to challenge *Aguilar*, for her prediction had come true. The Board of Education had spent millions of dollars buying "mobile instructional units," vans, to use in providing instruction in off-campus settings. That expenditure reduced the number of children who received remedial instruction by 35 percent.

Justice O'Connor reviewed *Aguilar v. Felton* and its companion case, *Grand Rapids v. Ball*. The holdings in those cases could be reduced to four propositions: (1) any public employee working in a religious school will inculcate religion; (2) public employees in a religious school symbolize a union between church and state; (3) public money used in religious schools impermissibly finances religious indoctrination; and (4) public teachers in religious schools must be closely watched to make sure they do not teach religion, thereby creating excessive entanglement between church and state. The Court no longer considered those presumptions true, however, because of its decisions in *Witters v. Department of Services for the Blind* and *Zobrest v. Catalina School District*. In *Witters* money flowed to a religious organization because of the private choice of an individual, thus showing that not all aid to religious schools is invalid. *Zobrest*, by holding that a state-financed sign language interpreter in a Catholic school was permissible, rejected the premises that a public employee in a religious school will inevitably inculcate religion or symbolizes a link between church and state. One could logically infer from these holdings that, under these circumstances, excessive entanglement disappeared, also. It was clear that cases subsequent to *Aguilar* had, indeed, changed the jurisprudence on the Establishment Clause. Two results came from that recognition. First, the mechanism of Rule 60(b)(5) was a proper way to challenge the earlier decision. Second, in light of the recent cases, *Aguilar v. Felton* and the remedial and enrichment classes portion of *Grand Rapids v. Ball* were no longer good law and explicitly overturned.

> To summarize, New York City's Title I program does not run afoul of any of three primary criteria we currently use to evaluate whether government aid has the effect of advancing religion: it does not result in governmental indoctrination; define its recipients by reference to religion; or create an excessive entanglement. We therefore hold that a federally funded program providing supplemental, remedial instruction to disadvantaged children on a neutral basis is not invalid under the Establishment Clause when such instruction is given on the premises of sectarian schools by government employees pursuant to a program containing safeguards such as those present here. The same considerations that justify this holding require us to conclude that this carefully constrained program also cannot reasonably be viewed as an endorsement of religion.[57]

Note carefully the three criteria mentioned in the first sentence, for they were important in the next case discussed.

The interpretive criteria articulated in *Agostini* were utilized in an enormously complicated and densely written case, *Mitchell v. Helms*.[58] This case was about the constitutionality of the use of federal money by state and local boards of education to lend instructional materials and equipment to public and private, including religious, schools. The case arose in Louisiana, where the money was used to provide library and media materials and computer hardware and software to public and private schools to implement, in the language of the statute, "secular, neutral, and nonideological" programs. The challenge, of course, was whether the Establishment Clause would permit this government aid to go to religious schools.

Justice Clarence Thomas wrote a "plurality opinion."[59] To answer the question of constitutionality, he focused on the second part of the *Lemon* test, whether or not a law has the effect of advancing or hindering religion. The first *Agostini* criterion to determine effect was whether any religious indoctrination is the result of government action. The answer was no in this case. Justice Thomas asserted an interpretive principle for Establishment Clause cases—neutrality. If a program is neutral in its application, its effect does not advance religion. If the government aid is available to the religious, irreligious, and areligious, no one would think government intends to indoctrinate religion. Indoctrination may happen, but if the aid is given evenhandedly to religious and secular recipients, then one cannot attribute the indoctrination to the government. Furthermore—and here Thomas used precedent that began with *Mueller v. Allen*—if government aid flows to religious recipients because of the private, individual, independent choice of parents or students, government does not grant special favors that would be an establishment. Private choice helps guarantee neutrality by preventing a program from preferring religion over irreligion or favoring one religion.[60]

The second *Agostini* method of determining the effect of a law is whether a program defines its recipients by reference to religion. The principle of neutrality inevitably leads to a negative answer.[61] Having answered those two questions, Thomas began to elaborate on the principle of neutrality.

He made a distinction between direct and indirect aid; not just an obvious distinction, but a constitutional distinction. Justice Thomas began by asserting that if aid to schools is neutrally available and passes through the hands of numerous private citizens who could use the money elsewhere, the government has not supported religion. This is clearly indirect aid and permissible. But where government gives money directly to religious schools or entities, this creates what Thomas called "special Establishment Clause dangers." Such direct payments are unconstitutional. But that impermissible form of government aid was not an issue in this case.[62]

Those challenging this law feared that this "neutral" aid might be diverted to religious purposes. The Court did not agree, but actually said it would not make any difference. Justice Thomas stated a means, not results, test. So long as the aid was also appropriate for use in public schools (guaranteeing its neutrality), and eligibility for aid passed the *Agostini* criteria, "any use of that aid to indoctrinate cannot be attributed to the government *and is thus not of any constitutional concern*"[63] (emphasis added). The issue is not divertability, but the content of the aid. If it is suitable for public school use, the aid is insulated from "Establishment Clause concerns that exist if aid is actually diverted to religious uses."[64] Basically, the results of aid are of no concern to the Court, if the procedures for providing aid and its content are correct.

In previous cases, religious schools were sometimes labeled as "pervasively sectarian," with the result that government aid could not go to such schools.[65]

Justice Thomas abandoned such language. The religious nature of the recipient of aid does not matter, so long as the aid advances government's secular purpose. If aid is given to all schools, regardless of their relationship to religion, "it is a mystery which view of religion the government has established, and thus a mystery what the constitutional violation would be." Furthermore, for courts to examine the recipients' religious beliefs is "unnecessary and offensive." Finally, Thomas said, labeling schools as "pervasively sectarian" began with the anti-Catholic movement of the nineteenth century. The designation was "born of bigotry" and "should be buried now."[66]

The statute in this case required that the aid should be "secular, neutral, and nonideological." Given that the aid was mostly computers and software and library books, government had complied and the program was constitutional. Justice Thomas concluded by saying that to the extent *Meek v. Pittenger* and *Wolman v. Walter* (see above) conflicted with the holding in *Mitchell v. Helms* (which they surely did), these earlier judgments were overruled and no longer good law.[67]

Justice Sandra Day O'Connor, joined by Justice Breyer, wrote an opinion "concurring in the judgement." O'Connor believed, however, that the plurality's neutrality principle was entirely too broad and could open all sorts of ways for government to give aid to religious entities and that government aid that uses a third person to essentially launder (my word) the money is not sufficient to pass the no-establishment principle. She agreed with the private choice argument, but stated that programs of aid must provide "true private choice," that is, a true variety of options. She also was not ready to abandon "pervasively sectarian" language.

Three justices dissented from the case. They agreed with Justice O'Connor's reservations, although they could not agree the result of the decision was correct. So they, plus Justices O'Connor and Breyer, formed the majority in terms of the definitional and procedural matters of the case. They agreed neutrality (with all its permutations Justice Thomas described) is not the only factor in analyzing whether government aid may be given to religious institutions. They additionally believed the pervasively sectarian standard is still applicable to monetary benefits given directly to religious institutions.

So, *Mitchell v. Helms* illustrates how the Court entered the twenty-first century with no clear standard on how to interpret the Establishment Clause, although a majority of the Court had accommodationist leanings. The dispute between them was principally over how far to go in accommodating religion. The strict separationist view, articulated in that famous paragraph in *Everson v. Board of Education*, was just a distant, and unfortunate, memory to most of the Justices. *Zelman v. Simmons-Harris* illustrates this generalization.

THE GRAND GOAL OF ACCOMMODATIONISTS: VOUCHERS

As we have seen, state legislatures have tried in a variety of ways to provide government aid to church-related schools. For years, however, the goal of such efforts was to provide money payments for students attending parochial schools, and normally such bills were beaten back by opponents of government aid to parochial schools. Finally, because the public schools in Cleveland had deteriorated to abysmal depths, the Ohio legislature passed a bill to provide vouchers to allow students to attend nonpublic schools, including religious schools. This comprehensive law allowed students to remain in public schools, to remain in public schools with a tutor, to attend public schools outside their district, to attend magnet or community schools, or to attend private schools, either secular or religious. (A magnet school is a public school that focuses on a particular subject matter, such as science, foreign languages, or drama; community schools receive state funds, but are governed by their own boards.) In every case, public money was available, although the amounts varied according to the income level of a student's family and the kind of school a student attended. Participating private schools were required not to discriminate on the basis of race, religion, or ethnic background and not to advocate hatred or unlawful behavior.

Given that most of the participating private schools were religious and that students received public money to enable them to attend, the law was challenged as a violation of the Establishment Clause. The case was *Zelman v. Simmons-Harris*.[68] The decision, written in 2002 by Chief Justice William Rehnquist, found the law constitutional. It had a secular purpose, namely, to provide a quality education to students whose school system had become dysfunctional. The primary effect of the law was neither to advance nor to hinder religion. This was obvious from the features of the plan. Because students could attend all sorts of schools, public and private, where they attended was the choice of the students and their parents. If public money went to the religious schools, it was because of individual, private choice, not the decision of government or any government official. Citing the precedents of *Mueller v. Allen*, *Witters v. Washington Services for the Blind*, and *Zobrest v. Catalina School District*, Chief Justice Rehnquist wrote:

> [W]e have repeatedly recognized that no reasonable observer would think a neutral program of private choice, where state aid reaches religious schools solely as a result of the numerous independent decisions of private individuals, carries with it the *imprimatur* of government endorsement. . . . The Establishment Clause question is whether Ohio is coercing parents into sending their children to religious schools, and

that question must be answered by evaluating *all* options Ohio provides Cleveland schoolchildren, only one of which is to obtain a program scholarship and then choose a religious school.[69] (emphasis in
original)

(Because attendance was based on parental choice, and the check was made out
to the parents, who then endorsed it over to the school, no government payments were made directly to religious schools. Direct payment would be
unconstitutional.)[70] The same features meant that the recipients were not
defined by religion, an Establishment Clause criterion introduced in *Agostini
v. Felton*. The Court concluded:

> In sum, the Ohio program is entirely neutral with respect to religion.
> It provides benefits directly to a wide spectrum of individuals, defined
> only by financial need and residence in a particular school district. It
> permits such individuals to exercise genuine choice among options
> public and private, secular and religious. The program is therefore a
> program of true private choice. In keeping with an unbroken line of
> decisions rejecting challenges to similar programs, we hold that the
> program does not offend the Establishment Clause.[71]

In *Zelman v. Simmons-Harris* the Supreme Court, for the first time, approved
the use of vouchers to deliver substantial amounts of government money to
religious schools.

7

Religion in Public Schools

In chapter 6 I noted that as public schools developed in this country, the role religion should play in them became a subject of debate. Historian Sidney E. Mead argued that the public schools have functioned as the established church of America,[1] noting that the traditional role of an established church is to supply the civic ideology of a culture, or at least a major portion of it. In Western culture, the Catholic Church and, later, the various Protestant churches in the countries where they were established articulated the moral basis for national life and citizenship. That is the principal role of the official religious body in any culture where an establishment exists.

But when America separated church and state by means of the First Amendment, the question arose as to who or what would supply this civic ideology. For most Americans, the public schools were the answer. The schools would instill in children, native-born and immigrant alike, the ideas of Americanism: democracy, capitalism, fair play, and respect for freedom. Sectarian religion in the public schools, as noted earlier, became a kind of "lowest common denominator Protestantism." With the increasing pluralism of society because of immigration, the development of new religions, and, coincidentally and somewhat paradoxically, the growing secularization of the American psyche, in the twentieth century the public schools became less and less obviously religious. Even the "lowest common denominator Protestantism" diminished. But there has been a sense of nostalgia among some for a greater presence of sectarian (or at least nondenominational Judeo-Christian) religion in the public schools. Probably, without using Mead's terminology, some have picked up on his idea of the public schools as the nation's established church, but have wished that it could be more specifically religious than it has been. There have been attempts to introduce a

more overtly religious presence in the public schools, either through the teaching of religious ideas or by means of prayer and Bible reading as a required part
of each school day. Many believe that only by having religion present in public schools can they fulfill their necessary role of instilling civic virtue in young
American citizens. Consequently, the Supreme Court has decided a variety of
cases in which it had to balance this desire for religion in the public schools
against the limitations imposed by the Establishment Clause.

RELEASED TIME

Instruction inside the School Building

McCollum v. Board of Education[2] in 1948 presented the question of the constitutionality of "released time" as a method of teaching religion in public
schools. The school board of Champaign, Illinois, invited a group of clergy to
teach classes on religion in its public school buildings to students in grades
four through nine. Classes were held weekly, thirty minutes for the lower
grades, forty-five minutes for the higher. Parental permission was required for
students to attend the religious instruction. The classes were taught by ministers from various Protestant denominations, Roman Catholic priests, and
Jewish rabbis. Participating students could choose which denominational
instruction to attend. Students who did not participate were not excused from
school attendance, and were required to go to some other place in the school
building. During this time they received no academic instruction, because that
would put them ahead, in their regular schoolwork, of those who attended the
religion classes. One assumes they spent their time in study hall. Attendance
was recorded in religious classes and reported to the students' regular teachers, as was that of the nonparticipants.

Mrs. Vashti McCollum, an atheist and the mother of a student, contended
the program violated the Establishment Clause. The Supreme Court agreed,
in an opinion written by Justice Hugo Black. The program had two closely
related problems. First, the enterprise was unconstitutional because the religion classes were taught in rooms in a tax-supported building. Second, because
students were required by truancy laws to be in school and attendance was
monitored to make sure children were either in the religious classes or in study
hall, the program delivered a captive audience to the clergy. Here is the essence
of the opinion:

> Pupils compelled by law to go to school for secular education are
> released in part from their legal duty upon the condition that they
> attend the religious classes. This is beyond all question a utilization of

the tax-established and tax-supported public school system to aid religious groups to spread their faith. . . . Here not only are the State's tax-supported public school buildings used for the dissemination of religious doctrines. The State also affords sectarian groups an invaluable aid in that it helps to provide pupils for their religious classes through use of the State's compulsory public school machinery. This is not separation of Church and State.[3]

Instruction outside the School Building

McCollum did not lay to rest the issue of released time, however. In 1952 the Court decided *Zorach v. Clauson.*[4] The facts of the case were virtually the same as in *McCollum:* classes were taught by clergy, parental permission was required, roll was taken, nonparticipants had to remain at school, biding their time, during the time of religious instruction. The *only* difference was that in *Zorach* the classes were conducted at locations away from the public school, not in school buildings. For the majority, that made all the difference.

The opinion was written by Justice William O. Douglas, usually a strict separationist, who in this case deviated from his normal views. Obviously no tax-supported buildings were involved in this program of religious instruction. That eliminated one fatal flaw in *McCollum.* Justice Douglas disagreed with the contention that released time programs gave a captive audience to religious teachers. All the schools had done here was adjust their schedules to accommodate the desires of those who wanted to attend religious instruction. He agreed the First Amendment commands that church and state be separate, but said that does not mean the state should be the adversary of religion. The amendment does not say the separation should be absolute. Religion has played an integral part in American history, and this may be acknowledged in the interaction between religion and the public schools. So long as the public schools do not promote or sponsor religion but merely cooperate with it, as they did in this program, there is no problem. Justice Douglas brought these themes together in a dictum that is a rather eloquent statement of accommodationism, one that has been referred to frequently by accommodationists in subsequent years.

> We are a religious people whose institutions presuppose a Supreme Being. We guarantee the freedom to worship as one chooses. We make room for as wide a variety of beliefs and creeds as the spiritual needs of man deem necessary. We sponsor an attitude on the part of government that shows no partiality to any one group and that lets each flourish according to the zeal of its adherents and the appeal of its dogma. When the state encourages religious instruction or cooperates with religious authorities by adjusting the schedule of public events to

sectarian needs, it follows the best of our traditions. For it then respects the religious nature of our people and accommodates the public service to their spiritual needs. To hold that it may not would be to find in the Constitution a requirement that the government show a callous indifference to religious groups. That would be preferring those who believe in no religion over those who do believe. . . . But we find no constitutional requirement which makes it necessary for government to be hostile to religion and to throw its weight against efforts to widen the effective scope of religious influence. The government must be neutral when it comes to competition between sects. It may not thrust any sect on any person. It may not make religious observance compulsory. It may not coerce anyone to attend church, to observe a religious holiday, or to take religious instruction. But it can close its doors or suspend its operations as to those who want to repair to their religious sanctuary for worship or instruction. No more than that is undertaken here.[5]

The three dissents in this case are noteworthy. They argued that this program still delivered a captive audience to religion teachers through the mechanism of the public school. The schools were still in session during the religious instruction, and the students had to choose between going to religion classes and staying in school in study hall, cleaning erasers, or doing whatever nonacademic activity the teachers could find to keep them busy. The dissenters said the schools should simply close one afternoon a week and let the students go free. It would be interesting to see how many went to religion classes in that circumstance. The fact they either had to go to religion classes or stay in school was a stimulus for them to take religious instruction. That was unconstitutionally using the power of the state to aid religion, in the view of the dissenters. Two dissenters, Jackson and Frankfurter, wrote dicta worth thinking about. At the conclusion of his opinion, Justice Felix Frankfurter asserted:

> The unwillingness of the promoters of this movement to dispense with such use of the public schools betrays a surprising want of confidence in the inherent power of the various faiths to draw children to outside sectarian classes—an attitude that hardly reflects the faith of the greatest religious spirits.[6]

Justice Robert Jackson wrote:

> It is possible to hold a faith with enough confidence to believe that what should be rendered to God does not need to be decided and collected by Caesar.
>
> The day that this country ceases to be free for irreligion it will cease to be free for religion—except for the sect that can win political power. . . . We start down a rough road when we begin to mix compulsory public education with compulsory godliness.[7]

Justice Jackson had such contempt for the majority opinion he concluded his dissent with the comment that the majority opinion would be more interesting to students of psychology than to students of constitutional law.

As a result of *McCollum* and *Zorach* a community may provide religious instruction for public school students, during the school day on a released-time basis, so long as it is not done in the public school building. If such instruction is done off-campus, even in a church, synagogue, or other ecclesiastical structure, it is acceptable under the law. Nothing in these cases would prevent clergy from teaching the classes.

PRAYER AND TEACHING RELIGION

In the 1960s the Court was presented with a matter that became, and continues to be, one of the most volatile, emotion-laden issues of the last forty years—prayer in the public schools. No church-state issue has produced more heated debate and misunderstanding than this one.

Required Classroom Prayer

The issue of prayer first came to the Supreme Court in 1962 in *Engel v. Vitale*,[8] a case about a state-written prayer. Acting under authorization from the state legislature, the Board of Education of New Hyde Park, New York, adopted a prayer written by the State Board of Regents, which had supervisory power over the state's public schools. Apparently concerned about a perceived decline in morality among schoolchildren, the Regents had initiated a program of moral and spiritual training in the schools, which included a prayer. Mindful of the religious pluralism in the state, the Regents had tried to make the prayer nonsectarian and general enough so as not to offend any denomination or religious person. The prayer was: "Almighty God, we acknowledge our dependence upon Thee, and we beg Thy blessings upon us, our parents, our teachers and our Country."[9] (One commentator called it a "To whom it may concern" prayer.) Not only was the prayer written by state education officials, but its recitation was required at the beginning of each school day in the New Hyde Park school district. Students could be excused from praying with a written request from their parents.

The parents of ten students enrolled in the schools filed suit in a state court, claiming this required prayer was contrary to their religious beliefs and practices and their children's. More importantly, they argued that a prayer written by state officials and said at the beginning of each school day as required by law was a violation of the Establishment Clause. Hardly anything could be a clearer example of state sponsorship.

The Supreme Court agreed with the plaintiffs' contention. Justice Hugo Black wrote the opinion, which is short and to the point. It was clear the state and the school district had violated the Establishment Clause by writing the prayer and imposing it on the schoolchildren and their teachers by law. That it was nondenominational and could be avoided by children with parental excuses made no difference. A law authorizing such a prayer, even if there is no compulsion to say the prayer, violates the Establishment Clause. As is frequently so, there are quotable and memorable dicta in this opinion:

> [W]e think that the constitutional prohibition against laws respecting an establishment of religion must at least mean that in this country it is no part of the business of government to compose official prayers for any group of the American people to recite as a part of a religious program carried on by government.[10]

What is the Establishment Clause for? Why should the Court, and Americans, be so diligent in strictly maintaining the separation of church and state for which it calls? The Court wrote:

> Its first and most immediate purpose rested on the belief that a union of government and religion tends to destroy government and to degrade religion. . . . The Establishment Clause thus stands as an expression of principle on the part of the Founders of our Constitution that religion is too personal, too sacred, too holy, to permit its "unhallowed perversion" by a civil magistrate. Another purpose of the Establishment Clause rested upon an awareness of the historical fact that governmentally established religions and religious persecutions go hand in hand.[11]

Apparently counsel for the Board of Education had argued in briefs, at oral argument, or both, that to declare the Regents' prayer unconstitutional would mean the Court was hostile to religion and prayer. Justice Black vociferously rejected that contention as neither true in fact nor the attitude of the Court. Its decision striking down the state-written required prayer should not be construed as antireligious. The Establishment Clause demands the state should stay out of the religious lives of Americans. That is not hostility to religion; it actually shows great respect for it.

> It is neither sacrilegious nor anti-religious to say that each separate government in this country should stay out of the business of writing or sanctioning official prayers and leave that purely religious function to the people themselves and to those the people choose to look to for religious guidance.[12]

In spite of this disclaimer, *Engel v. Vitale* provoked strong reactions across America—most of them negative. There was considerable demagoguery in Congress. Many religious groups and religious leaders speaking for themselves released statements. Some statements were positive, but most opposed the decision. Representative of many reactions to this case, and to many other separationist decisions since then, was this by the Rev. Billy Graham: "This is another step toward the secularization of the United States. . . . The framers of our Constitution meant we were to have freedom of religion, not freedom from religion."[13]

In spite of the criticism heaped on the Court (or perhaps because of it), in the very next year, 1963, it agreed to hear another school prayer case. *Engel* was a narrow decision, involving only state-written prayers. The new case, *Abington Township School District v. Schempp*,[14] had a much broader scope: required prayer, including the Lord's Prayer, and Bible reading in public school classrooms.

Schempp combined two cases, one from Maryland and one from Pennsylvania. The Maryland case was brought by Madalyn Murray (later O'Hair) on behalf of her son, who was enrolled in a public school. Maryland law mandated that in the public schools in the state each day had to begin with the "reading, without comment, of a chapter in the Holy Bible and/or the use of the Lord's Prayer."[15] Mrs. Murray, an outspoken atheist, sued the school board in Baltimore, claiming the requirement interfered with her and her son's First Amendment rights because it preferred religious belief over nonbelief.

The law in Pennsylvania was similar to that in Maryland. It required that the day in every public school begin with the reading of ten verses from the Bible, without commentary. The Bible reading was routinely followed by a recitation of the Lord's Prayer. Mr. and Mrs. Edward Schempp, whose three children were enrolled in public schools, filed suit, claiming the religious exercises were a violation of the Establishment Clause. The Schempps were a religious family and regularly attended worship at their local Unitarian church.[16] So their suit was motivated not by hostility to religion but rather by a concern for constitutional values and a belief that mandated religious practice tended to trivialize religion. The Supreme Court combined these two cases under one title.

The Court, in an opinion written by Justice Tom Clark, declared the religious exercises to be unconstitutional. The two states argued that the required Bible readings and prayers were not intended to be religious, but rather were a way to promote moral values, combat the materialistic tendencies of our times, perpetuate American institutions, and teach literature. The states claimed that these were secular reasons for having the requirement. The Court responded that they had chosen religious means to accomplish their allegedly secular purposes, which the Establishment Clause forbids. That the

laws specified that the Bible be read "without comment" showed the legislators knew the Bible is quintessentially religious literature and wanted to avoid
sectarian interpretation. Furthermore, as Justice William Brennan wrote in a
concurring opinion, the secular objectives of the state could just as easily have
been accomplished with secular literature, for example, readings from major
documents in American history. But the school board chose only religious literature and prayer, obviously a religious expression. The state's choice of these
obviously religious documents/practices to the exclusion of all others belied
its profession of secular goals.

That students could be excused with parental permission did not minimize
the Establishment Clause violation. The no-establishment principle was violated by the law mandating religious exercise in the public schools; it was not
necessary that coercion be shown for a violation to happen. That is, the violation occurred with the enactment of the legislation requiring the religious
exercises; that students could absent themselves was irrelevant to this exercise
of state power.

As noted in chapter 6, in reaching its decision the Court articulated two
tests for interpreting the Establishment Clause. In order for a law to be constitutional under the clause, it must have (1) a secular purpose and (2) a primary effect that neither advances nor hinders religion. The first test has to do
with the intention of the legislative body, the second test with the implementation or enforcement of the law. A law or program must conform to both tests
to be constitutional; if it fails either one, it is unconstitutional.

The prayer laws at issue in *Schempp* failed both tests. Because only religious
readings and prayers were required, it was clear that the legislatures' purpose
in passing the laws was religious, not secular: they wanted to instill religion in
the public school students of their states. Furthermore, the laws had the primary effect of advancing religion. The required actions were clearly religious
or devotional exercises. To require them by law advanced religion by state
authority. Thus the prayer and Bible reading laws were unconstitutional.

It is important that this decision be carefully analyzed and understood,
because so much demagoguery, misunderstanding, and silliness has been evident about it since it was announced. The Supreme Court never said, in either
Engel or *Schempp*, that young people or their teachers may not pray in the public school context. It struck down only devotional exercise mandated by state
law. The Constitution forbids a "law respecting an establishment of religion";
therefore, any law that *requires* public school students or teachers to engage in
religious exercise is unconstitutional. But if students or teachers want to pray
silently and individually, they have perfect freedom to do so. If a student wants
to pray before or during a math exam, he or she may do so. Nothing in the
Constitution or the Supreme Court's opinions prohibits it. The prayer should

not be disruptive of the educational process. The student cannot pray loudly during the math test, for example, but that is a matter of school discipline and decorum, not of constitutional law. Teachers may not lead pupils in prayer, or even pray audibly before them, because teachers are authority figures, symbolize the public schools, and are public employees. But if teachers want to pray in the faculty lounge or silently even in the classroom while students are studying, that is acceptable. It is absolutely incorrect to say the Supreme Court "took God out of the classroom" or banned prayer from the public schools, as some journalists and more politicians have proclaimed.

Especially after the negative uproar across the country following *Engel*, the Court recognized that *Schempp* would elicit similar critical reaction. Counsel for the respective school boards in the case had apparently argued that if the Court found against the required prayers, it would be "establishing a religion of secularism." The Court responded to that argument by denying it and spelling out a positive role for religion in public schools:

> It is insisted that unless these religious exercises are permitted a "religion of secularism" is established in the schools. We agree of course that the State may not establish a "religion of secularism" in the sense of affirmatively opposing or showing hostility to religion, thus "preferring those who believe in no religion over those who do believe." We do not agree, however, that this decision in any sense has that effect. In addition, it might well be said that one's education is not complete without a study of comparative religion or the history of religion and its relationship to the advancement of civilization. It certainly may be said that the Bible is worthy of study for its literary and historic qualities. Nothing we have said here indicates that such study of the Bible or of religion, when presented objectively as part of a secular program of education, may not be effected consistently with the First Amendment.[17]

The Court explicitly endorsed the teaching of religion as an academic study within the public schools![18] Even though the media and the public have never given due attention to this dimension of the opinion, the Court clearly showed that it was not hostile to religion. It offered the opportunity for the schools to help their students understand more about religion. Although it did not mention it, the Court in *Schempp* implicitly endorsed the dicta by Justice Robert Jackson in his concurring opinion in *McCollum v. Board of Education*:

> I think it remains to be demonstrated whether it is possible, even if desirable, to comply with such demands as [McCollum's] completely to isolate and cast out of secular education all that some people may reasonably regard as religious instruction. Perhaps subjects such as mathematics, physics or chemistry are, or can be, completely secularized. But it would not seem practical to teach either practice or

appreciation of the arts if we are to forbid exposure of youth to any religious influences. Music without sacred music, architecture minus the cathedral, or painting without the scriptural themes would be eccentric and incomplete, even from a secular point of view. Yet the inspirational appeal of religion in these guises is often stronger than in forthright sermon. Even such a "science" as biology raises the issue between evolution and creation as an explanation of our presence on this planet. Certainly a course in English literature that omitted the Bible and other powerful uses of our mother tongue for religious ends would be pretty barren. And I should suppose it is a proper, if not an indispensable, part of preparation for a worldly life to know the roles that religion and religions have played in the tragic story of mankind. The fact is that, for good or for ill, nearly everything in our culture worth transmitting, everything which gives meaning to life, is saturated with religious influences, derived from paganism, Judaism, Christianity—both Catholic and Protestant—and other faiths accepted by a large part of the world's peoples. *One can hardly respect a system of education that would leave the student wholly ignorant of the currents of religious thought that move the world society for a part in which he is being prepared.*[19] (emphasis added)

Fifteen years after this was written in *McCollum*, the Court, in *Schempp*, said "Amen" to its sentiment. Instruction in religion is an integral part of the educational process, and in calling attention to that, the Court showed that it was not hostile to religion in its school prayer decision.

As the Court anticipated, there was great negative reaction to the *Schempp* opinion. By May of 1964, for example, more than 145 proposed constitutional amendments had been submitted in the United States House of Representatives to reverse *Schempp*.[20] That kind of legislative initiative has occurred in spurts to the present day, usually around election time. Some centrist-to-liberal denominations, however, began to understand that the decision was very narrow (prohibiting only state-required religious exercises) and was not hostile to religion, and began to express approval of it. (Representatives of the following churches testified in the late 1960s against a constitutional amendment mandating school prayer: American Baptist, American Lutheran, Christian Church (Disciples of Christ), Episcopal, Greek Orthodox, Lutheran Church–Missouri Synod, United Church of Christ, United Methodist, and United Presbyterian.) Nonetheless, on the issue of school prayer and Bible reading there has been an emotional and political tug-of-war ever since.

A Moment of Silence in Schools

In 1985 the controversy was intensified by the Court's decision in *Wallace v. Jaffree*.[21] The issue was a moment of silence in the public schools of Alabama.

In 1978 the state had passed a law authorizing a minute of silence in public schools "for meditation." In 1981 the law was modified to authorize the minute of silence "for meditation or voluntary prayer." Soon thereafter a suit was filed that argued the addition of the words "or voluntary prayer" made the minute of silence law unconstitutional because the activity of prayer now received state endorsement.

The Court, in an opinion written by Justice John Paul Stevens, agreed. Applying the "secular purpose" test, the Court found the legislation that added the words "or voluntary prayer" had the sole purpose of characterizing prayer as a favored practice, which is not consistent with the Establishment Clause.

Jaffree is interesting because the authors of the majority opinion, two concurring opinions, and three dissents all agreed that a minute of silence at the beginning of each school day was an acceptable concept that states were perfectly free to legislate. Furthermore, all acknowledged that students and/or teachers could say silent prayers during that minute of silence if they so chose. In fact, the schoolchildren of Alabama had had that opportunity to pray after the first, 1978, legislation, if not before. So, argued the majority, the legislation adding the phrase "or voluntary prayer" was redundant. But redundancy is not a constitutional offense; giving state endorsement to prayer is. Because it was unnecessary to add those words to give young people the opportunity to pray during the moment of silence, it was clear that the only purpose of explicitly adding the words was to characterize the activity of prayer as a favored practice.[22]

The *Jaffree* ruling is very narrow. It applies only to the addition of the words "or voluntary prayer" to legislation. But it gave the justices the opportunity to show again that they were not hostile to religion and that they had never outlawed all forms of prayer from the public schools. They were able to do this by pointing out that students or teachers may pray during the minute of silence with no constitutional problem.

Commencement Prayers

In 1992 the Court addressed the question of prayers at public school commencement exercises, in *Lee v. Weisman*.[23] In Providence, Rhode Island, public middle and high school principals were permitted to invite clergy to say invocations and benedictions at graduation exercises. In *Weisman*, a principal invited a rabbi to offer prayers at commencement, gave him printed guidelines for offering prayers at public occasions, and advised him that the prayer must be nonsectarian. Although the rabbi offered prayers that he considered to be nondenominational, they contained references to God and to Hebrew Scripture that had a Jewish character to them. Nonetheless, a Jewish student and

her father filed suit, seeking a permanent injunction that would prevent similar religious expressions at future commencement exercises.

Justice Anthony Kennedy wrote the opinion, holding the commencement
prayers to be unconstitutional because when the school principal selected the
person to give the prayers and offered printed guidelines and advice about
their content, the state was determining the content of the prayer. That had
shades of *Engel;* the state may not determine the content of prayers.

More fundamentally, psychological coercion was inflicted on those who
might not want to participate in the prayers because the audience (students)
were expected to rise and stand in respectful silence while the prayers were
being said. A dissenting student might perceive that acceding to the expected
behavior would be perceived by others as agreeing with the religious exercises,
rather than just showing respect for those who did agree with it. The state may
not use social pressure to enforce orthodoxy, any more than it may use direct
means. Additionally, although students were not required to attend the commencement exercises, nonetheless graduation is a once-in-a-lifetime event for
which students have been aiming during their entire school careers. It is unreasonable to put them into the position of having to miss their graduation in
order not to have to participate in prayers with which they disagree or that
they believe are wrong in relation to the Establishment Clause. Consequently,
the commencement prayers are unconstitutional. Justice Kennedy wrote a dictum that illuminates the Establishment Clause and the importance of the separation of church and state:

> The First Amendment's Religion Clauses mean that religious beliefs
> and religious expression are too precious to be either proscribed or
> prescribed by the State. The design of the Constitution is that preser-
> vation and transmission of religious beliefs and worship is a responsi-
> bility and a choice committed to the private sphere, which itself is
> promised freedom to pursue that mission. It must not be forgotten
> then, that while concern must be given to define the protection
> granted to an objector or a dissenting nonbeliever, these same Clauses
> exist to protect religion from government interference. . . . [T]he
> Establishment Clause is a specific prohibition on forms of state inter-
> vention in religious affairs with no precise counterpart in the [freedom
> of] speech provisions. The explanation lies in the lesson of history that
> was and is the inspiration for the Establishment Clause, the lesson that
> in the hands of government what might begin as a tolerant expression
> of religious views may end in a policy to indoctrinate and coerce. A
> state-created orthodoxy puts at grave risk that freedom of belief and
> conscience which are the sole assurance that religious faith is real, not
> imposed.
>
> The lessons of the First Amendment are as urgent in the modern
> world as in the 18th Century when it was written. One timeless lesson

is that if citizens are subjected to state-sponsored religious exercises, the State disavows its own duty to guard and respect that sphere of inviolable conscience and belief which is the mark of a free people. To compromise that principle today would be to deny our own tradition and forfeit our standing to urge others to secure the protections of that tradition for themselves.[24]

Prayers at Football Games

The reaction to *Lee v. Weisman* led to further litigation. As just noted, *Weisman* declared commencement prayers unconstitutional because school officials directed the person giving the prayer concerning the nature of the prayer. Officials in the Clear Creek School District, in Texas, decided to circumvent *Weisman* by allowing the senior class each year to vote on whether or not they wanted to have prayer at commencement. If the class voted to have an invocation and/or a benediction, it/they would be delivered by a student volunteer. The Fifth Circuit Court of Appeals found the Clear Creek plan constitutional.[25]

The school district at Santa Fe, Texas, apparently inspired by *Clear Creek*, decided to go beyond it in insulating itself from *Weisman*. Instead of having one student election, it would have two. The first would determine whether the students wanted "invocations or benedictions" at commencement. If the answer was affirmative, a second election would follow to choose who, from a list of candidates, would give them. The idea of the two student elections was to distance the school board from the prayer procedure so the board could say the prayers were by student initiative and represented free student speech. Somewhat later the school board applied the same procedure for a "brief invocation and/or message" before home football games. The Supreme Court made a judgment on the constitutionality of that program.

The case was *Santa Fe Independent School District v. Doe*,[26] Justice John Paul Stevens writing for the majority. He found the program unconstitutional on a number of grounds. Santa Fe argued its prayer program promoted free speech by students. But the student who won the second election, that is, the one who gave the invocation or message, was the same student for the entire season. That was a rule of the program. The Court said that this was hardly "free" or diverse student speech. It was also a charade to say the student election divorced the game prayer policy from the school board. The board set up the mechanism of the election. The board in essence said to the students, "You *will* have a two-part election." In light of that, it was inconceivable that the Santa Fe school board could claim to be uninvolved in the prayer process.

The school's policy said the statement before a game could be an "invocation

and/or message." The school's stated purpose for such a statement was to solemnize the event. But Justice Stevens said only a religious message would
accomplish that goal; a football game was difficult to solemnize. The only kind
of message specified in the policy was an invocation, showing the school board
had prayer on its mind. Stevens was sure the students understood the policy to
clear the way for football game prayers.[27] Furthermore, the invocation was to
be said at a school-sponsored event, in a school-owned stadium over a school-
owned public address system, the control of which remained with school officials. In the spirit of hometown loyalty, the school's name would be displayed
on banners, students' and parents' clothing, and perhaps on the stadium or field
itself. It is virtually inconceivable that a person would not think a prayer said in
such a context was "stamped with her school's seal of approval."[28]

> The delivery of such a message—over the school's public address sys-
> tem, by a speaker representing the student body, under the supervi-
> sion of the school faculty, and pursuant to a school policy that
> explicitly and implicitly encourages school prayer—is not properly
> characterized as "private" speech.[29]

Santa Fe school district also argued that the prayers at ball games were different from the commencement prayer discontinued in *Weisman* because they
were not coercive; attendance at games was entirely voluntary. Justice Stevens
acknowledged that students are less likely to go to football games than to miss
a once-in-a-lifetime commencement. But for some students, ball games are
not optional. Players, band members, cheerleaders have to be at the games.
Persons not compelled to attend may be strongly motivated to go by the
excitement of the games, school or community loyalty, or the desire to see
their children perform. For them, attendance may not seem as voluntary as it
would appear on the surface. It is inconsistent with religious freedom to force
a person who attends an event to which they have strong personal commitment to be subjected to a religious ceremony that they may find personally
offensive. But, even if game attendance were absolutely voluntary for everyone and hearing a prayer was not offensive to anyone, saying a prayer prior to
the game would have the effect of coercing those present to take part in an act
of worship. That is inconsistent with the Establishment and Free Exercise
Clauses.[30] Justice Stevens summarized his opinion:

> The District, nevertheless, asks us to pretend that we do not recognize
> what every Santa Fe High School student understands clearly—that
> this policy is about prayer. The District further asks us to accept what
> is obviously untrue: that these messages are necessary to "solemnize" a
> football game and that this single-student, year-long position is essen-
> tial to student speech. We refuse to turn a blind eye to the context in

which this policy arose, and that context quells any doubt that this policy was implemented with the purpose of endorsing school prayer.[31]

Trying unsuccessfully to forestall negative reaction, Justice Stevens affirmed that public schools do not have to be barren of religion. Referring to the Establishment and Free Exercise Clauses, he wrote:

> By no means do these commands impose a prohibition on all religious activity in our public schools. Indeed, the common purpose of the Religion Clauses "is to secure religious liberty." Thus, nothing in the Constitution as interpreted by this Court prohibits any public school student from voluntarily praying at any time, before, during, or after the schoolday. But the religious liberty protected by the Constitution is abridged when the State affirmatively sponsors the particular religious practice of prayer.[32]

The "bottom line" of this decision is that high school football game prayers are unconstitutional under the Establishment Clause for a variety of reasons. By showing that student elections are stalking horses for official school prayer, which effectively stifle free speech by making it virtually impossible for religious minorities to participate, the Court also effectively invalidated *Clear Creek*.

In summary, on the issue of prayer in the public schools, state legislatures or school boards are prohibited from writing and requiring prayers to be said in the classroom, from dictating the nature of prayers or allowing public prayers at commencement exercises or football games, or even expressing a preference for prayer during a minute of silence. They are prohibited from requiring Bible reading as a devotional exercise at the beginning of each school day. But schools are permitted to have a truly neutral minute of silence, which may be used for prayer if a student or teacher chooses to so use it. They may teach religion, in all its dimensions, as part of the regular curriculum of a school, so long as it is *instruction* and not evangelization. Students, furthermore, are permitted to pray at any time, so long as they are not disruptive of the educational environment or process, which usually would mean the prayers would be silent. Public schools are not to be shadow or surrogate churches, but they are not constitutionally required to be insulated from or purged of religion, either. (Other dimensions of this issue are explored in *Board of Education v. Mergens*, later in this chapter.)

TEACHING EVOLUTION AND CREATION SCIENCE

From time to time the debate between evolution and conservative Christianity has been played out in curriculum issues in the public schools. The debate first came to national prominence with the trial of John Thomas Scopes in Dayton, Tennessee, in 1925. Tennessee was one of several states to pass laws prohibiting the teaching of evolution in the public schools. Scopes, a high school biology teacher, was convicted of having violated the law, although the conviction was later overturned by the Tennessee Supreme Court because of a legal technicality.[33]

The first time this issue came to the United States Supreme Court was in 1968 in *Epperson v. Arkansas*.[34] Arkansas law prohibited teaching the theory of evolution in its public schools, including universities. The law also banned the adoption or use of any textbooks in the public schools that contained the concept of evolution. When a high school biology teacher in Little Rock, Susan Epperson, realized that her local school board had adopted a textbook containing evolution, she was in a dilemma. She could either use the adopted book and be in violation of state criminal law and subject to dismissal, or refuse to use the book and face disciplinary action from her local school authorities. She attempted to remove the dilemma by removing the law. She filed suit, seeking a court's declaration that the law was void and an injunction that would prevent the state from enforcing it. (That the Little Rock school board violated the law by initially adopting the book was never an issue in this case.)

When the case reached the Supreme Court in 1968, the Court decided that Arkansas's law violated the Establishment Clause because it was passed to forbid teaching a view opposed by some Christians. That is, the legislature had prohibited teaching one concept about the origin of life because it perceived that concept to be contrary to the book of Genesis as literally interpreted. It had attempted, with this law, to preserve a literal understanding of the Genesis account of creation by forbidding the teaching of evolution. The law was unconstitutional because it violated the secular purpose part of the three-part test for interpreting the Establishment Clause. Justice Abe Fortas wrote for the Court: "There is and can be no doubt that the First Amendment does not permit the State to require that teaching and learning must be tailored to the principles or prohibitions of any religious sect or dogma."[35]

Because of *Epperson*, states were forbidden to prohibit the teaching of evolution in public schools. Those who were opposed to evolution for religious reasons had to devise another strategy for blunting the teaching of evolution in public education.[36]

Simultaneously with this issue came the development of "creation science," also known as "scientific creationism." Although the roots of scientific creationism lie in the religious antievolutionism of the late nineteenth century, its modern momentum began coincidentally with the rise of the Christian fundamentalist movement in the 1920s. Creationism is a more sophisticated approach to the question of origins than a simple rejection of evolution. It tends to undermine evolution by showing that all the alleged evolutionary data actually conform with the creation account and worldview of Genesis. It should come as no surprise, given that its subject matter is the huge one of the origin of life, that there is variety in creationist views. "Young earth creationists" assert that the universe is some six thousand years old and that creation took place in six twenty-four-hour days. "Old earth creationists" believe the earth is millions of years old. Most of them adhere literally to the biblical book of Genesis but believe the "six days" of creation mentioned there were not twenty-four-hour days but rather longer periods, that each "day" could be thousands of years long. Some "old earth creationists" accept a form of development: the various species of life were created as "kinds," and, although there may be some development within a "kind," there is no development in life forms from one "kind" to another. Many in this camp have become advocates of "intelligent design," typically even acknowledging the idea of development of forms, but denying that it happens by "natural selection." Rather, they argue, biological structures are too complex to have arisen naturally and must be the result of some intelligent agent.

This variety of views notwithstanding, in general creation science attempts to offer an alternative view to evolution by showing that the various findings of modern science are consistent with the biblical account of creation, which is generally taken to be literally true.[37]

Advocates of creation science were determined to try to use it to battle the teaching of evolution in the public schools. Because *Epperson* prohibited any laws forbidding the teaching of evolution, the new approach was to pass "balanced treatment" laws. The idea was to require creation science be taught whenever evolution is. Arkansas took the lead in this. In 1981, Act 590 mandated that in all the public schools of the state, whenever evolution was taught or included in a textbook, creation science had to be given "balanced treatment." Balanced treatment did not mean equal time. Classroom presentations did not need to match minute for minute time devoted to evolution and creation science, nor did textbooks or other materials (including library holdings) need to match line for line. But there did have to be balanced coverage of each theory in the course or the literature as a whole.

Several people, including some clergy, sued to have the Arkansas act declared unconstitutional as a violation of the Establishment Clause. The federal district court ruled that, despite its claims to the contrary, creation science was based on religious ideas. To require its inclusion in the public school curriculum every time evolution is taught was unconstitutional.[38] Creation science advocates decided not to appeal this case, because there was another balanced treatment law in Louisiana, and they felt that a case contesting that law had a better chance of gaining approval in the Supreme Court.

Those hopes were dashed, however, when the Supreme Court handed down *Edwards v. Aguillard*,[39] holding that the Louisiana balanced treatment law was unconstitutional. Louisiana claimed the law's purpose was to advance academic freedom by guaranteeing that every time evolution was taught creation science would be also—that is, by presenting students with more than one view of the beginnings of life. But the Court found that Louisiana teachers had the opportunity to present more than one view of origins before the law was passed. So, in reality the act did nothing to advance academic freedom. The actual purpose of the law was to discredit evolution by counterbalancing it with creation science and, furthermore, to give preference to a religious doctrine that rejects the factual basis of evolution in its entirety. It was clear to the Court that the balanced treatment law violated the secular purpose part of the three-part test for interpreting the Establishment Clause:

> [T]he Creationism Act is designed *either* to promote the theory of creation science which embodies a particular religious tenet by requiring that creation science be taught whenever evolution is taught *or* to prohibit the teaching of a scientific theory disfavored by certain religious sects by forbidding the teaching of evolution when creation science is not also taught. The Establishment Clause, however, "forbids *alike* the preference of a religious doctrine or the prohibition of theory which is deemed antagonistic to a particular dogma." Because the primary purpose of the Creationism Act is to advance a particular religious belief, the Act endorses religion in violation of the First Amendment.[40] (first emphasis in original, second emphasis added)

The conclusion of this line of cases is, then, that states may neither forbid the teaching of evolution in public schools nor demand that creation science be taught alongside it. The reason for these prohibitions is because so far both plans have been premised on religious opposition to evolution, and laws passed because of a religious motivation are unconstitutional.

SECULAR HUMANISM

In the early 1960s, the governor of Maryland appointed Roy Torcaso to the position of notary public. When the time came to actually assume the duties of the position, he was refused a commission to serve. The Maryland constitution required that, to hold public office, one had to state "a declaration of belief in the existence of God." Torcaso refused to declare such a personal belief. Furthermore, he filed suit in a state court, claiming the requirement in the state constitution of a declaration of belief in the existence of God as a condition for public office violated both Article VI and the Establishment Clause of the federal Constitution. The case is *Torcaso v. Watkins*.[41]

In an opinion written by Justice Hugo Black, the Court found in favor of Torcaso. Black recalled the words he had written in *Everson v. Board of Education*, that under the Establishment Clause neither a state nor the federal government can force a person "to profess a belief or disbelief in any religion."[42] Maryland did just that to those who would hold public office in the state. The state argued that no one was compelled to hold public office, so the requirement of belief in God was narrow in scope. The Court responded that no one should have to sacrifice a constitutionally guaranteed liberty in order to hold public office. A state may not insist on a religious affirmation as a condition for holding public office any more than may the federal government. Consequently, the Court declared a section of the Maryland state constitution to be unconstitutional under the Establishment Clause.

This is an important case concerning religious activities in public schools because of some of the opinion's dicta. In stating that neither states nor the federal government can impose a test oath on officeholders, the opinion said: "Neither can constitutionally pass laws or impose requirements which aid all religions as against nonbelievers, and neither can aid those religions based on a belief in the existence of God as against those religions founded on different beliefs." As an illustration of the last point, Justice Black added a footnote: "Among religions in this country which do not teach what would generally be considered a belief in the existence of God are Buddhism, Taoism, Ethical Culture, Secular Humanism, and others."[43]

Since the mid-1970s conservatism has grown in American religion, both in number of adherents and in intensity. Adherents of theological and social conservatism are willing, indeed eager, to become involved in the political arena as the "Christian Right." Part of its effort has focused on what conservatives perceive as the dramatic decline in the quality of public school education. They believe that not only are the public schools not educating young people for their future places in society, but that they have abdicated their role of teaching those civic virtues so important to the survival of the nation, the civic values that nourish the soul of the nation. The public schools, they argue, have surrendered this crucially important function because they have become pervaded by secular humanism and pass that on to the students.

The Christian Right claims that the Supreme Court has ruled that traditional, theistic religion cannot be taught or practiced in the public schools. (Actually, as we have seen, the Court did no such thing.) But they insist a religion *is* being taught in the schools: secular humanism. They can say that secular humanism is a religion because the Supreme Court has said that it is. For this argument they go to Justice Black's footnote 11 of *Torcaso v. Watkins*, quoted above. These conservatives contend that if it is unconstitutional to teach traditional religious values, it is equally unconstitutional to teach the religion of secular humanism,[44] which they believe is being taught all the time. To leaders of the Christian Right, the promulgation of secular humanism is the root cause of the disaster the public schools have become. The schools have lost most of their educational quality and become war zones dominated by violence and drug dealing. They point to the massacre at Columbine High School, Littleton, Colorado, April 20, 1999, as only the most dramatic and terrible of many examples. Moreover, they argue, there is no respect for the authority of teachers and administrators. Secular humanism has led to this sad state of affairs, they argue, because it is relativistic. It has no absolute values, because it has no conception of God. Secular humanism is a "do what makes you feel good" ethic, and that sort of ethic can only lead to chaos in the lives of individual students. Certainly it is not an adequate basis for a civic ideology.

The Christian Right has responded to what they perceive as the religion of secular humanism in the public schools in at least two ways: the Christian school movement and the attempt to incorporate the Ten Commandments into the public schools.

The "Christian School" Movement

Although Protestant parochial schools are not new, their number has grown dramatically since the 1950s, when many of them opened in response to the desegregation of public schools after the Court's decision in *Brown v. Board of Education*.[45] Many of those early Christian schools were segregation academies. But in more recent years the principal stimulus for starting these schools has been the perceived decay of the public schools, which is attributed to the pervasiveness of secular humanism in the curriculum. Much of the rationale for such schools, now a major alternative to public schools, is derived from the alleged declaration by the Supreme Court that secular humanism is a religion. It is likely that supporters of the Christian Right would have made their humanism argument without the footnote in *Torcaso v. Watkins*, but they seized on it as a powerful aid in making their point.

It is ironic that the Christian Right, which so often has maligned and reviled the Supreme Court and distorted its decisions, has relied so much on the Court's statement in making this claim. But when it serves their purposes, persons of the Christian Right put aside their usual contempt for the Court and assert that what it has said is certainly true. The footnote, however, is only an illustration of a very different point, that a state may not prefer a religion based on a belief in the existence of God over one that does not have that belief. The state may not impose theism as a condition of employment. It may be that members of the Court thought that secular humanism is a religion. But the footnote is, at most, dictum upon dictum and does not appropriately carry the great weight the Christian Right has placed on it.

The Ten Commandments

In another attempt to deal with the impact of secular humanism, this time in the public schools, the Kentucky legislature passed a law requiring that the Ten Commandments be posted in every public schoolroom in the state. The posters were paid for by private contributions, rather than state funds. Perhaps because they foresaw an Establishment Clause fight over the program, the legislators also required that the following notation appear at the bottom of each poster: "The secular application of the Ten Commandments is clearly seen in its adoption as the fundamental legal code of Western Civilization and the Common Law of the United States."

The legislators predicted correctly. In spite of the disclaimer at the bottom of the posters and the fact that they were paid for from private funds, a lawsuit was filed. The plaintiffs claimed that the posting of the Ten Commandments in the public schools violated the Establishment Clause.

The Supreme Court dealt with the issue in 1980 in a rare unsigned opinion, *Stone v. Graham*.[46] The Court decided the program violated the Establishment Clause under the secular purpose test. Kentucky argued that the purpose articulated by the disclaimer at the bottom of the posters was a secular one. Its purpose was to teach students the influence of the Ten Commandments on the legal structure of Western society. The Court disagreed. To be sure, the Ten Commandments prohibit murder, adultery, lying, stealing, all of which are prohibited by civil law. But they also exhort persons to worship God alone, to avoid idolatry, to observe the Sabbath, and not to blaspheme God. "The pre-eminent purpose for posting the Ten Commandments on schoolroom walls is plainly religious in nature. The Ten Commandments is undeniably a sacred text in the Jewish and Christian faiths, and no legislative recitation of a supposed secular purpose can blind us to that fact."[47] The purchase of the posters by private funds did not save the program. They were in the schoolrooms because Kentucky law required that they be there. It was also not significant that the Ten Commandments were merely positioned on the walls rather than being read aloud, because minor breaches of the principle of separation are just as forbidden as major ones.

EQUAL ACCESS

Primarily as a reaction to what they perceived the school prayer decisions to mean, and because of their resentment of the Ten Commandments decision and their fear of the perceived influence of secular humanism, some people began to wonder if there was any way at all for religion to be included in public schools. (As we have seen, however, the prayer decisions did not sanitize public schools from all aspects of religion—far from it.) There was the additional issue that around the country some courts had prohibited religious organizations or student clubs in public schools, believing that they violated the Establishment Clause and that if a public school permitted religious clubs to meet, it would be impermissibly sponsoring and advancing religion. Some groups began to work in Congress for the passage of an "equal access" bill, which would give religious clubs access to school time and facilities equal to that of nonreligious clubs.

In 1984 Congress passed the Equal Access Act,[48] which said that if a high school received federal funds and if it had a "limited open forum," it would be unlawful to deny students the opportunity to meet on the basis of the religious, political, or philosophical content of their speech at such meetings. A "limited open forum"[49] means the school permits free discussion of ideas and issues, but the forum is open only to its students, as opposed to the public at large. In this law, the limited open forum exists when the school allows secular student groups or clubs to use school facilities in noninstructional time for their activities and when those activities are not related to the normal curriculum of the school. When those conditions are met, the school is required to allow religious clubs the same use of its facilities allowed other noncurriculum-related clubs. It is also required that the religious clubs must be voluntary, student-initiated, and student-run, with no direction from public school employees or nonschool persons.

This law was tested before the Supreme Court in 1990 in *Board of Education v. Mergens*.[50] The case was initiated, not by persons who wanted to challenge the Equal Access Act, but by those who wanted to utilize it. Bridget Mergens and some of her friends wanted to start a Christian club at her high school in Omaha that would meet before the beginning of regular instruction, like many other student clubs. They applied to the principal for permission and were denied, a decision later endorsed by the board of education. School officials based their decision on their belief that a religious club would be in violation of the Establishment Clause. The students however claimed that the school, by denying their request, violated the Equal Access Act. The students brought suit in federal district court to compel the school board to comply with the act. The school board responded by claiming that the Equal Access

Act did not apply to this high school and, if it did, was unconstitutional under the Establishment Clause. This was the form of the case that reached the Supreme Court.

The Court found in favor of the students and against the school board. The first issue addressed was whether the act actually applied to the school. The law is triggered if a school has clubs not related to its curriculum. That is, a school is obligated to accommodate a religious club that would not be related to the school's curriculum only if other student clubs are not curriculum-related. The school in this case claimed that all its clubs were curriculum-related, and thus the act did not apply—it was not required to give permission for the formation of a religious club. The Court, in an opinion written by Justice Sandra Day O'Connor, disagreed. The school wanted to define "curriculum-related" to mean anything at least remotely related to its general educational goals. The Court used a much narrower definition. A student group not directly related to the courses taught in the school is not curriculum-related. Under that definition, the Omaha school had several clubs that were not related to the curriculum.[51] Consequently, the school had a limited open forum and the act did apply to the school. It could not deny the religious club the opportunity to organize and meet in preschool hours.

To the more substantive question of the constitutionality of the act under the Establishment Clause, the Court had a ready answer—the law was constitutional. The act had a secular purpose, because Congress intended for it to prohibit discrimination on the basis of philosophical or political speech, as well as religious speech. That is, because the law did not give religious speech preferential treatment over other kinds of speech, it did not have a religious purpose.

The school board claimed that the act had the primary effect of advancing religion, in that it compelled the school to recognize religious clubs and give them support by providing them time and place to meet. The Court disagreed:

> [T]here is a crucial difference between *government* speech endorsing religion, which the Establishment Clause forbids, and *private* speech endorsing religion, which the Free Speech and Free Exercise Clauses protect. We think that secondary school students are mature enough and are likely to understand that a school does not endorse or support student speech that it merely permits on a nondiscriminatory basis.[52] (emphasis in original)

Finally, the board argued the act created excessive entanglement between the school and religion, in that school officials, particularly teachers, would have to exercise a supervisory role over the religious clubs. The Court simply pointed out that the act forbade school officials to organize, promote, or lead the religious clubs or any particular meeting of the clubs. The act did permit teacher presence at the meetings of the clubs to maintain order and to satisfy school insurance requirements, but they were not allowed to participate in the students' religious meetings. Such custodial surveillance did not excessively entangle the public school in the day-to-day administration of religious activities. The Equal Access Act, according to the Court, passed all three tests and did not violate the Establishment Clause. If the school met the criterion of having a limited open forum and permitted noncurriculum-related student clubs access to that forum, religious clubs initiated and led by students must be permitted equal access to school facilities. The Establishment Clause does not prohibit this government accommodation of religion.

Both *Mergens* and the Equal Access Act of which it was a test relied on a 1981 case at the university level, *Widmar v. Vincent*.[53] The University of Missouri in Kansas City made available meeting rooms in university buildings to a wide variety of student groups. Among those was a group of Christian students calling themselves "Cornerstone," who met for prayer, Bible reading, and discussion of religious topics. But after several years of such meetings, the university withdrew permission for Cornerstone to continue to meet in university facilities, claiming to be enforcing a rule made five years previously, that the university should not allow its facilities to be used "for purposes of religious worship or religious teachings." The university claimed the reason for its rule and its prohibition of Cornerstone's meetings was that it did not want to violate the Establishment Clause and that for it to allow Cornerstone to continue to meet would give state sanction and encouragement to religious activity, a breach of the no-establishment principle. The students responded that they were guaranteed the right to meet in an orderly fashion for religious activity by both the Free Exercise and the Free Speech Clauses of the First Amendment. So this case presented a classic conflict between the establishment and free-exercise principles.

The Court decided in favor of the students. Its opinion, written by Justice Lewis Powell, began with the recognition that the university had created a "limited open forum" by making its facilities available to a multiplicity of student groups for meetings. (The open forum was "limited" because it was available only to students and their invited guests, including speakers, and not to the general public.) Cornerstone must be allowed "equal access" to this limited public forum.[54] The Free Exercise Clause demands that the university not prohibit the religious activity of the students. The Free Speech Clause mandates that the university must not discriminate against the religious content of the students' speech in their meetings, particularly since it allows many other kinds of speech in student meetings. The Court disagreed with the university's Establishment Clause argument that to accommodate the religious group would have the impermissible primary effect of advancing religion. Given the existence of the open forum, the university's allowing the students to meet simply did not have that effect.

> In this context we are unpersuaded that the primary effect of the public forum, open to all forms of discourse, would be to advance religion. . . . First, an open public forum in a public university does not confer any imprimatur of State approval on religious sects or practices. . . . Second, the forum is available to a broad class of non-religious as well as religious speakers. . . . The provision of benefits to so broad a spectrum of groups is an important index of secular effect.[55]

The Court acknowledged that no group has unlimited access to university facilities, and that the university could impose time, place, and manner regulations on religious groups and could exclude groups that were disruptive of the educational environment of the campus. But the university could not deny access of student religious groups to its facilities simply because they were religious. In this case, the Free Exercise/Free Speech argument prevailed over the Establishment Clause. In a dissent, Justice Byron White lamented subsuming the religion clauses under free speech principles.

> A large part of respondents' argument, accepted by the court below and accepted by the majority, is founded on the proposition that because religious worship uses speech, it is protected by the Free Speech Clause of the First Amendment. Not only is it protected, they argue, but religious worship *qua* speech is not different from any other variety of protected speech as a matter of constitutional principle. I believe that proposition is plainly wrong. Were it right, the Religion Clauses would be emptied of any independent meaning in circumstances in which religious practices took the form of speech.[56]

In cases beginning in the early 1990s, Justice White's prediction came true, primarily at the expense of the Establishment Clause.

A somewhat different kind of equal access case was *Lamb's Chapel v. Center Moriches Union Free School District*.[57] The school district, consistent with New York state law, denied a church group access to high school facilities in non-school hours to show a film about family issues, approached from a religious perspective. The church had asked to use the high school auditorium for several evenings to present programs, open to the public, on child rearing and discipline. The centerpiece of the programs would be films that approached the topic from a Christian viewpoint. The request was denied because of a school district policy forbidding school property to be used for any religious purpose. The church claimed that the school's policy violated the Free Speech, Free Exercise, and Establishment Clauses of the First Amendment.

The Court, in an opinion by Justice Byron White, agreed with the church, basing its decision principally on free speech grounds.[58] In prior cases, the Court had ruled that the government may not "regulate speech in ways that favor some viewpoints or ideas at the expense of others."[59] In this specific instance, the school district would have allowed other presentations on the topic of child nurture to be presented in the school but denied Lamb's Chapel because its material had a religious orientation. This was impermissible discrimination on the basis of content. More broadly, the school district had a rule that prohibited school facilities from being used for any religious purpose, even in nonschool hours. But it had ten other, secular purposes for which schools could be used by nonschool groups. The Court ruled that content/viewpoint discrimination was built into the policy itself. That is contrary to the principle of free speech. The school district could not forbid religious groups to use the school facilities so long as it, as a matter of policy, allowed secular groups to use them.

The Court did not directly address the Establishment Clause complaint by Lamb's Chapel. In passing, Justice White said that if the case had been decided on the basis of the no-establishment principle, permitting the religious film to be shown in the public school would have passed the three-part "*Lemon* test." Justices Scalia, Thomas, and Kennedy asserted that they would have decided the case without any reference to the Establishment Clause and criticized the "*Lemon* test."

Must a public school district allow religious instruction and worship for young people in its building after school hours? If the school had created a limited public forum, it must. The question was raised in *Good News Club v. Milford Central School*.[60] The Good News Club was a Christian organization formed to provide religious moral instruction for children ages six through twelve. Some adult leaders in Milford, New York, requested the use of rooms in the city's public schools for weekly club meetings after school hours. The school denied the request, citing the necessity not to violate the Establishment Clause.

The Milford School's community use policy replicated provisions from New York state law. One provision said the school would be available "for social, civic and recreational meetings and entertainment events, and other uses pertaining to the welfare of the community." Under this rule the school allowed religious groups access to the facility to address social issues from religious perspectives. But at Good News Club meetings, children learned Bible verses, sang hymns, said prayers, and were taught that religion was applicable to their lives. School authorities perceived this activity to be equivalent to worship; it went much beyond the normal "religious perspectives." That dimension of the program caused Milford to deny the Club access, fearing that level of religiosity would violate the Establishment Clause.

The Good News Club claimed the school had discriminated against it on the basis of its religious speech. Justice Clarence Thomas began his opinion for the Court at that point. He concluded initially that Milford School had created a forum for speech by the public for those who qualified to use the building. It allowed the expression of religious perspectives on its approved topics. But it would not allow the Good News Club's expression of overt religiosity. That was "viewpoint discrimination," unconstitutional under the Free Speech Clause. That is, any group that promoted the moral and character development of children was able to use the building. The Good News Club taught morals and character development to children, but it was denied access because its particular style of teaching was considered unacceptable. "Thus, the exclusion of the Good News Club's activities . . . constitutes unconstitutional viewpoint discrimination."[61]

The Court rejected Milford's claim that its adherence to the Establishment Clause motivated its actions. It asserted the school had no valid Establishment Clause defense. The Club's meetings would be after school hours, not sponsored by the school, and open to any student of the appropriate age who had parental permission. Also, the school was open to other groups; if admitted, the Club would not have received preferential treatment. To the argument that children would have felt pressured to participate, the Court countered that they needed parental permission to go to meetings. If anything, parents would more likely feel pressure. They could handle it. Furthermore, parents would understand the school was not endorsing religion, but just making its facilities available. In sum:

> When Milford denied the Good News Club access to the school's limited public forum on the ground that the Club was religious in nature, it discriminated against the Club because of its religious viewpoint in violation of the Free Speech Clause of the First Amendment. Because Milford has not raised a valid Establishment Clause claim, we do not address the question whether such a claim could excuse Milford's viewpoint discrimination.[62]

Once again, the freedom of speech principle "trumped" Establishment Clause prohibitions of government supporting religion.

THE PLEDGE OF ALLEGIANCE

In 2004 a court case out of California burst upon the public awareness and touched a raw nerve in a society already on edge about such things as abortion, the war in Iraq, and high unemployment. It was about the constitutionality of the phrase "under God" in the Pledge of Allegiance to the flag. Michael Newdow's daughter attended public school. In accord with California law, children in her school began each day by saying the Pledge of Allegiance. Newdow was an atheist and did not want his daughter taught the theological concept of the existence of God and God's power over the nation. He sued, asserting the required recitation violated both the Establishment and Free Exercise Clauses. The trial court dismissed the complaint, but the Ninth Circuit Court of Appeals reversed that judgment. In a lengthy, careful opinion, it declared the phrase "under God," as a part of a required exercise in a public school, was indeed unconstitutional.

The Pledge of Allegiance was written in 1892 by Francis Bellamy, a Baptist minister, who was extensively involved in educational matters at the national level. He wrote the Pledge as a way of celebrating Columbus Day in the schools in 1892. It was published in a popular magazine, *The Youth's Companion*, the same year. The original language was: "I pledge allegiance to my Flag and to the Republic for which it stands, one nation, indivisible, with liberty and justice for all." In 1924 the National Flag Conference changed "my Flag" to "the Flag of the United States of America." It was not until 1942 that Congress adopted the Pledge as the official expression of respect for the flag, although, as we saw in chapter 3 in the case of *Minersville School District v. Gobitis*, school districts were requiring students to say the Pledge prior to then. In 1954, as a response to atheistic communism, Congress added the phrase "under God" to the Pledge. The date of that law was June 14, 1954.[63]

The decision of the Ninth Circuit Court of Appeals, declaring "under God" to be unconstitutional, flashed across the nation and had the effect of the proverbial "fingernails on a chalkboard." Many radio and TV stations broke into regular programming with a special report announcing the decision. E-mails flew across the country. Regularly scheduled news broadcasts gave considerable attention to the story. It stimulated grotesque political grandstanding by members of Congress and the president. I say "grotesque" because they denounced the decision instantaneously, that is, within minutes of the news release, without any knowledge whatsoever of the reasoning of the court. Both houses of Congress interrupted their sessions so that members, Republican and Democrat alike, could rage against the ruling. For the hour or so after the decision was made public, one of the most dangerous places in America one could be was between a politician and a TV camera. President George W. Bush joined the frenzy of public statements, declaring indignation against that "liberal court."

The school district in which Newdow's daughter was enrolled appealed the Ninth Circuit's decision to the Supreme Court, *Elk Grove Unified School District v. Newdow*.[64] But this highly anticipated case turned out to be anticlimactic because the Court did not consider the question of the constitutionality of the God language in the Pledge. It disposed of the case by ruling that Newdow did not have standing to bring the suit. Newdow and the mother of his child did not live together, and the mother had legal custody of the little girl. Indeed, a California court had ruled that Newdow and the mother, Sandra Banning, should consult in how to raise their daughter, but where they disagreed, Banning had final say, what the Supreme Court called "veto power." Furthermore, Banning made it known to the Ninth Circuit Court of Appeals, *after* its decision that had caused the furor, that she was a Christian, as was her daughter, and that neither of them had any objection to the daughter's reciting the Pledge of Allegiance with the phrase "under God." Justice John Paul Stevens wrote for the Court that, given those facts and the strong inclination of federal courts to stay out of domestic relations disputes, but rather to defer to state courts in those matters, Newdow did not have standing. Referring to some California custody cases Newdow had cited to support his argument, the Court said:

> The California cases simply do not stand for the proposition that Newdow has the right to dictate to others what they may and may not say to his child respecting religion. . . . There is a vast difference between Newdow's right to communicate with his child—which both California law and the First Amendment recognize—and his claimed right to shield his daughter from influences to which she is exposed in school despite the terms of the custody order. We conclude that, having been deprived under California law of the right to sue as next friend, Newdow lacks prudential standing to bring this suit in federal court.[65]

Chief Justice Rehnquist and Justices O'Connor and Thomas, however, could not let go of the issue. They each wrote opinions in which they addressed the constitutionality of the God language in the Pledge of Allegiance. Rehnquist and O'Connor would have found the statement constitutional. Although they came at it from different angles (Justice O'Connor in her usual meticulous way), they each concluded the God language was not religious. Its purpose was principally historical, to acknowledge the role of religion in American history rather than to inspire faith or to be an expression of worship. Given that the phrase "under God" was not actually religious, it could not violate the Establishment Clause, even if schoolchildren were required to say it.

Justice Thomas thought similarly, but the thrust of his opinion was that the Establishment Clause ought not to be applied to the states. He would abandon the concept of incorporation because of his concept of the intent of the authors of the Constitution. Unlike the Free Exercise Clause, he wrote, the Establishment Clause was not designed to protect individual rights, but rather was simply to keep the national government out of the religious arrangements of the various states. In light of that background, it is a mistake to think the God language in the Pledge of Allegiance violates the Establishment Clause, for that clause does not defend individual rights.

Because the Court "punted" on the substantive question, many believed that someone else would raise the issue; that the Court would be called upon to revisit the controversy in the future.

8

Blue Laws, Bars, Taxes, and Plastic Reindeer

The Complexity of Establishment Clause Issues

Although a large proportion of the Supreme Court's Establishment Clause cases have focused on school questions, the Court has considered a variety of other issues as well. The issues are wide-ranging and affect American life in significant ways.

SUNDAY CLOSING LAWS

The idea of rest on the day of worship is as old as the Judeo-Christian tradition. One of the Ten Commandments concerns the Sabbath:

> Remember the sabbath day, and keep it holy. Six days you shall labor and do all your work. But the seventh day is a sabbath to the LORD your God; you shall not do any work. . . . For in six days the LORD made heaven and earth, the sea, and all that is in them, but rested the seventh day; therefore the LORD blessed the sabbath day and consecrated it.[1]

Christianity changed the day of worship and rest to Sunday, in honor of Jesus' resurrection, and as one step toward Christianity's becoming the established religion of the Roman Empire, Sunday observance became mandated by law, on March 7, 321, by decree of the Emperor Constantine:

> All judges, city-people and craftsmen shall rest on the venerable day of the Sun. But countrymen may without hindrance attend to agriculture, since it often happens that this is the most suitable day for sowing grain or planting vines, so that the opportunity afforded by divine providence may not be lost, for the right season is of short duration.[2]

Notice that an exception to the prohibition accommodated activity essential to human welfare.

The observance of Sunday as a day of rest and worship continued throughout medieval times and was brought to the New World. The first Sunday law of America, promulgated in Virginia in 1610, forbade work on Sunday so that all residents could give attention to preparing for and attending Christian worship. Later, the prohibition of the sale of merchandise on Sunday was added to the laws. All the colonies had such laws, and they were generally retained by the states well after the ratification of the First Amendment.

In 1961 the Supreme Court ruled on the constitutionality of the Sunday laws. In *McGowan v. Maryland*[3] the laws were challenged on Establishment Clause grounds. Maryland's laws were typical of those around the country: businesses were to be closed on Sunday. However, following the precedent set as early as Constantine's law, exceptions were made to the prohibitions against doing business on Sunday. Occupations of necessity and charity were exempted, for example, hospital personnel, firefighters and police officers, and grocery store workers. But exemptions were also extended to businesses that facilitated the enjoyment of the day of rest, such as ice cream stores, swimming pools, spectator sports, amusement parks, and sellers of greases and gasoline, for those who enjoyed a Sunday drive.

McGowan was brought by some employees of a large department store who were indicted for selling a notebook, a can of floor wax, a stapler and staples, and a toy submarine, all prohibited by the law. This list of items shows that the law had begun to target the sale of certain items, rather than just state whether a business could stay open on Sunday. With the advent of the large department store, as opposed to small specialty shops, this kind of refinement of the law happened in many places. The store employees contended in this case that the Sunday law violated the Establishment Clause because it gave state recognition to and compelled at least minimal observance of the Christian day of worship. They had suffered economic injury because the state had forced on them deference to Sunday.

Chief Justice Earl Warren wrote the opinion in this case. The Court reached its decision by employing an argument from history, examining the history of Sunday legislation from medieval times through the colonial period in American history. The Court readily acknowledged that the original Sunday legislation, both in Europe and in the American colonies, was religious in orientation. Just as in Constantine's legislation, the laws were designed to protect the Christian day of worship from profanation and distracting activities, so that people could more faithfully observe it. But, the Court observed, at least as early as the beginning of the eighteenth century, nonreligious arguments were heard in favor of Sunday statutes, and laws themselves began to become more secular. These more secular rationales centered on the desir-ability and the healthfulness of periods of rest and relaxation from the labors by which one made one's living. This line of reasoning continued and became more prevalent in the twentieth century. In short, the Sunday closing laws had become secularized. Their purpose was to benefit individuals and society as a whole by providing a day of rest. Sunday was regarded in the laws as a day when people could rest and recover from the work of the week past and mentally and physically prepare for the workweek that approached. The laws were now no more than social-welfare legislation. In light of the evolution of Sunday clos-ing laws, the laws at issue in this case did not violate the Establishment Clause. That the states' secular rest and relaxation laws happened to correspond with the Christian day of worship was of no constitutional significance. The Court mentioned laws against murder, condemned by both Judaism and Christian-ity, as an example of legitimate secular legislation that incidentally corre-sponded with religious precept:

> Sunday Closing Laws, like those before us, have become part and par-cel of this great governmental concern wholly apart from their origi-nal purposes or connotations. The present purpose and effect of most of them is to provide a uniform day of rest for all citizens; the fact that this day is Sunday, a day of particular significance for the dominant Christian sects, does not bar the State from achieving its secular goals. To say that the States cannot prescribe Sunday as a day of rest for these purposes solely because centuries ago such laws had their genesis in religion would give a constitutional interpretation of hostility to the public welfare rather than one of mere separation of church and State.[4]

The plaintiffs in the case also contended that the state could reach its pub-lic-welfare goal by another means, namely, by mandating that employers pro-vide for their employees one day of rest in every seven. The Court recognized that that would be a plausible plan, but said that states were not obligated to do that. Such a plan would be much more difficult to enforce than a uniform day of rest. Furthermore, a state might want there to be a virtually uniform day of rest in order to promote family solidarity, that is, a day when all family mem-bers could be together. Because Sunday was already regarded by people of all religions and no religion as a traditional day of rest, it was only logical that a state might enforce its use with Sunday closing laws, given that it now had a sec-ular rationale. Sunday closing laws did not violate the Establishment Clause.[5]

In *Braunfeld v. Brown*,[6] also in 1961, the plaintiffs argued that Sunday laws violate the Free Exercise Clause as well as the Establishment Clause. The plaintiffs were Orthodox Jews who operated a business. Their religion required them to cease from work (and thus close their business) for purposes of worship on Saturday; the law compelled them to close on Sunday. They claimed that the law infringed on the exercise of their religion, in that they had to suffer economic loss and competitive disadvantage to businesses operated by non-Sabbatarians; it forced them into competitive disadvantage if they practiced their religion. Furthermore, the law would likely cause the Orthodox Jewish faith to be less attractive to potential converts, knowing that converting to that faith would put them at economic risk.

One might think that this free exercise argument would make this case harder than a purely establishment one. But actually Chief Justice Warren's opinion for the Court made short work of it. He reasserted that the Free Exercise Clause prohibits government from passing any law that compels the acceptance of any creed or the prohibition of any activity of worship. The Sunday closing law, even as applied to Sabbatarians, had neither of those effects. "[T]he statute before us does not make criminal the holding of any religious belief or opinion, nor does it force anyone to embrace any religious belief or to say or believe anything in conflict with his religious tenets."[7] The law did not prohibit the Jews from practicing their faith, it just made it more expensive. Although that is regrettable, it does not prohibit a state from enacting a constitutional (remember *McGowan v. Maryland*) law that has the beneficial effects of enforcing a day of rest for the majority of the population. The Sunday closing law was not unconstitutional under the Free Exercise Clause as it applied to Sabbatarians.

There were dissents from the opinions in the Sunday closing law cases. In the *Braunfeld* case, Justice Potter Stewart summed up what he saw as the flaw in the majority opinion in just five sentences:

> Pennsylvania has passed a law which compels an Orthodox Jew to choose between his religious faith and his economic survival. That is a cruel choice. It is a choice which I think no State can constitutionally demand. For me this is not something that can be swept under the rug and forgotten in the interest of enforced Sunday togetherness. I think the impact of this law upon these appellants grossly violates their constitutional right to the free exercise of their religion.[8]

Some may say these cases are essentially moot these days. The pervasiveness of the large department store makes item-specific sales prohibitions virtually impossible to enforce. Furthermore, item-specific prohibitions are foolish, for they fail to accomplish what has been the secular rationale for Sunday closing laws—a day of rest for employees. When stores are allowed to stay open because some items may be sold, while other items may not, employees still have to work. In addition, as our society has become increasingly materialistic and commercialized, as we have virtually become a 24-7 society, there is not the sentiment in the general population for Sunday closing laws. But the cases are still worth review, if for no other reason than they are a reminder of the religiously pluralistic nature of our society and the need for sensitivity to the beliefs of others, particularly minorities. That is the reason for including both Justice Stewart's dissent and the long quote from Justice Douglas in note 8.

Twenty-four years after *McGowan* and *Braunfeld*, the Court handed down a workplace case that had Sunday-law-like characteristics, *Estate of Thornton v. Caldor.*[9] Connecticut amended its Sunday closing law to say that no one could be required to work on his or her day of worship. One assumes that the law was passed out of free-exercise-of-religion considerations, that is, to avoid the kind of discrimination that had been upheld in *Braunfeld*. Thornton was a Presbyterian who claimed Sunday as his day of worship. His employer, the Caldor Company, opened its stores for Sunday business and expected its managers to work at least one Sunday a month. When Thornton refused, he was demoted in rank and salary. Thereupon Thornton filed a grievance with the state's arbitration service and claimed that the Caldor Company had violated Connecticut law. So far this case sounds very much like *Frazee v. Illinois Department of Employment Security*, described in chapter 4. As in that case, one would expect that Thornton would win on Free Exercise Clause grounds. But Caldor Company responded with the contention that the law violated the Establishment Clause, in that it gave employees the absolute right to impose their day of worship on employers and fellow employees. That controversy worked its way through the state courts to the U.S. Supreme Court.

The Court decided for Caldor. Chief Justice Warren Burger made short work of the case. He began with a pithy and true statement: "Under the Religion Clauses, Government must guard against activity that impinges on religious freedom, and must take pains not to compel people to act in the name of religion."[10] But Connecticut's law forced employers and employees to conform their business practices and their own schedules to the religious practices of any employee who wanted to observe her or his particular day of worship.

> The State thus commands that Sabbath religious concerns automatically control over all secular interests in the workplace; . . . The employer and others must adjust their affairs to the command of the State whenever the statute is invoked by an employee.[11]

Consequently, the law had a primary effect of advancing religion in violation of the Establishment Clause. Workplace laws may not give employees an absolute right to impose their Sabbath requirements on their employers.

LEGISLATIVE CHAPLAINS

There is a longstanding practice in this country, at both state and federal levels, of having state-paid chaplains for legislative bodies. The chaplains perform a variety of functions, such as counseling individual legislators about personal problems, and may even conduct an occasional wedding or funeral for legislative personnel. But their most visible activity is opening legislative sessions with prayer. Such an obviously religious activity conducted at state expense in the very seat of government has caused many to question its constitutionality. In 1983 the issue was raised at the Supreme Court level in *Marsh v. Chambers*.[12]

Marsh came from the state of Nebraska. The challenge was raised by a member of the legislature, and therefore it was clear he had standing. Chambers attacked the chaplaincy program in three ways. First, the state funding of the chaplain violated the Establishment Clause. Second, the legislature had employed the same chaplain, a Presbyterian, for sixteen years, impermissible preferential treatment for one religion over others. Third, the chaplain's prayers were distinctly Judeo-Christian in content, again showing preference for one tradition over others.

The Court, in an opinion by Chief Justice Burger, began its response to the challenges by pointing out the long history of legislative chaplains in the country. Most specifically to the point, the precedent was begun by the Continental Congress. In April and May 1789, the Senate and House elected chaplains, and on September 22, 1789, they passed a law to pay them from federal funds. Just three days later, the Congress finalized the language of the religion clauses of the First Amendment. The Court concluded that if those who wrote the Establishment Clause did not think that providing governmentally paid chaplains for the legislative bodies was a violation, it must not be. There was the further evidence that the national Congress had had chaplains for two hundred years, and many states have a long history of the practice as well. Nebraska had had legislative chaplains for over one hundred years:

> In light of the unambiguous and unbroken history of more than 200 years, there can be no doubt that the practice of opening legislative sessions with prayer has become part of the fabric of our society. To invoke Divine guidance on a public body entrusted with making the laws is not, in these circumstances, an "establishment" or a step toward establishment; it is simply a tolerable acknowledgement of beliefs widely held among the people of this country.[13]

This historical argument was enough to deal with the three challenges to the program. Paying a chaplain with state funds was not unconstitutional. The historical evidence rehearsed in the opinion showed that. That the legislature had hired the same chaplain for sixteen years simply showed that they were satisfied with his work, not that they preferred Presbyterianism. (In fact, the chaplain had invited ministers of other religious groups to give prayers before the legislature.) The content of the prayers, predominantly Judeo-Christian, was not a violation of the Constitution so long as the prayers were not used to proselytize, and there was no evidence of that in this case.

Although the three-part *"Lemon* test" for interpreting the Establishment Clause had been formulated by the time *Marsh v. Chambers* was decided, the test was not used in this case, for at least one possible reason, perhaps two. First, Chief Justice Burger may have believed that an argument from history was sufficient to reach the conclusion he thought was correct and so it was not necessary to apply the three-part test—although this was the first Establishment Clause case since it was formulated in which some aspect of it had not been applied. Second, the Chief Justice may have realized that the program of legislative chaplains could not be affirmed if the three-part test were applied. Both the court of appeals below and two of the three Court dissenters in the case argued that legislative chaplains failed all three parts of the test, and therefore legislative chaplains were clearly unconstitutional under the Establishment Clause. At any rate, the test was not applied.

Marsh v. Chambers marks the beginning of what strict separationists feel has been an erosion of a strict (and correct) interpretation of the Establishment Clause. As the more accommodationist approach to the clause has evolved, both in the nation and on the Court (a process discussed in chapter 9), *Marsh v. Chambers* has been seen as a bellwether and model of what that accommodationism should look like. But its immediate and obvious result was that using state-paid legislative chaplains, even of one denomination year after year, is constitutional.

Other chaplaincy programs are similarly alleged to raise constitutional questions, although the Supreme Court has not dealt with any of them. Many argue that for the federal government to provide chaplains to the military at government expense, and for the federal government or the various state governments to provide chaplains to prisoners in their respective prisons, is a violation of the Establishment Clause. But the counterargument (and this is the position the various governments have taken) is that if a government did not provide chaplains for military personnel or prisoners, they would be denied their Free Exercise Clause rights. The government takes military personnel and prisoners out of their home environments and compels them to go somewhere else. In their new locations the religious among them do not have the opportunity to practice their religion as they did at home. For the government not to provide any religious services to them would be an unconstitutional establishment of secularism and a denial of their free exercise of religion. Of course, the government does not compel the persons to utilize the services. Consequently, although providing chaplains with government funds might appear to violate the Establishment Clause, the Free Exercise Clause requires government to supply the opportunity for religious activity, thus justifying the "violation."[14]

A CHURCH AS GOVERNMENT AGENT

Larkin v. Grendel's Den[15] is a strange case. It deals with a Cambridge, Massachusetts, ordinance prohibiting the licensing of a place of business to sell alcoholic beverages if the business was within five hundred feet of a church or school and if the governing body of the church or school protested its presence. Grendel's Den, a restaurant located ten feet from Holy Cross Armenian Catholic Church, applied for a liquor license. Holy Cross Church protested the granting of the license, as it was entitled to do under the law, and the License Commission voted to deny Grendel's Den's application. The restaurant then sued the License Commission in federal district court, claiming that the statute violated the Establishment Clause.

The Supreme Court, in an opinion written by Chief Justice Warren Burger in 1982, decided in favor of Grendel's Den. The rationale was that the law allowed churches to exercise governmental authority, so that it was the protest of the church that triggered the enforcement of the law. Without church action, the statute would not be activated in reference to the application for a liquor license. Consequently the church functioned in a governmental manner; no greater intermixing of church and state could occur. The ordinance had the primary and principal effect of advancing religion, a violation of the second part of the "*Lemon* test":

> [T]he core rationale underlying the Establishment Clause is preventing "a fusion of governmental and religious functions." The Framers did not set up a system of government in which important, discretionary governmental powers would be delegated to or shared with religious institutions.[16]

The Court emphasized that it had no objection to the intent of the law in question; it is perfectly acceptable to have zoning laws that prohibit the sale of alcoholic beverages close to schools and churches. But the enforcement of such laws must be triggered by a true governmental agency, such as a city council or a zoning commission, not by a church, synagogue, or mosque.

A case similar to *Larkin v. Grendel's Den* was about Hasidic Jews. The Hasidim are ultraorthodox in their observance of Jewish tradition. They are to Judaism what the Amish are to Christianity. They try to live pure, unadulterated religious lives.[17] This means, among other things, that they try to maintain as much separation from "the world" as possible. Among the strictest of the various Hasidic groups are the Satmar. When the Satmar Hasidim came to America in the late 1940s, fleeing from the savagery of the Holocaust and the aftermath of World War II, they settled in Brooklyn, New York. But later, in the attempt to protect themselves physically from society, they moved to a rural area northwest of New York City, where they created a village called Kiryas Joel.

In keeping with their tradition of separation from corrupt society, the Hasidim developed parochial schools to train their children, particularly the boys, in Torah and Talmud. Those schools were not, however, equipped to deal with learning disabled children. So, for a while, the Satmar sent their special needs children to appropriate public schools away from their village. That proved to be highly unsatisfactory, because it did not provide the cultural distinctiveness desired by the Hasidim, and, given their learning disabilities, switching back and forth from Kiryas Joel to a public school was very confusing for the children. At that point, the New York legislature passed a law that enabled Kiryas Joel to create a public school district with a board made up of Hasidim. This allowed Kiryas Joel to have its special needs school in the village, in familiar surroundings for the children, and yet gave them the authority to levy property taxes to finance the school and hire competent staff for special education. In response, the New York State School Boards Association filed suit, claiming that legislation creating a public school district for the purposes of a single religious group violated the Establishment Clause.

The issue came to the Supreme Court in 1994 in *Board of Education of Kiryas Joel v. Grumet*.[18] Justice David Souter, writing for the majority, found against Kiryas Joel. Although the facts of the cases were not exactly parallel, they were close enough for him to use *Larkin v. Grendel's Den* as precedent. In *Grendel's Den* the law gave churches veto power over applications for liquor licenses. In *Kiryas Joel* the law gave an exclusively religious community the authority to operate a public school district. In both cases, the law created a "fusion of governmental and religious functions,"[19] allowing a religious entity to function as a government entity, which had the effect of excessively and impermissibly entangling religion and civil authority. So, just as *Grendel's Den* had declared that program unconstitutional, the Court held the Kiryas Joel arrangement to be unconstitutional:

> The Establishment Clause problem presented by Chapter 748 [the enabling legislation for the Kiryas Joel school district] is more subtle, but it resembles the issue raised in *Larkin* to the extent that the earlier case teaches that a State may not delegate its civic authority to a group chosen according to a religious criterion. . . . In these cases we are clearly constrained to conclude that the statute before us fails the test

of neutrality. It delegates a power this Court has said "ranks at the very apex of the function of a State," to an electorate defined by common religious belief and practice, in a manner that fails to foreclose religious favoritism. It therefore crosses the line from permissible accommodation to impermissible establishment.[20]

UNEQUAL GOVERNMENT TREATMENT

Chapter 4 discussed cases concerning the regulation of solicitation of funds by religious groups. *Larson v. Valente*[21] is a solicitation case with an Establishment Clause dimension. An issue that has risen occasionally since the 1960s has been concern over "cults." A widespread perception exists, sometimes fed by media hunger for sensationalist headlines, that cults are heretical, sinister, fraudulent, and rapacious in their search for money. As a result of this image, governments have sometimes taken measures to try to inhibit controversial religious groups or at least to keep them under close surveillance. That seems to have been Minnesota's motivation when it amended its charitable solicitation law in 1978. Prior to that, the law required organizations soliciting funds in the state to submit forms specifying the percentage of income spent on administrative costs. Organizations with administrative costs above 30 percent were forbidden to solicit funds in the state. Religious groups were exempt from the requirement. In 1978 the state legislature added to the law a provision that a religious group that raised more than 50 percent of its revenue from its own membership would continue to be exempt. If more than 50 percent of its revenue came from nonmembers, however, the organization would have to register with the state, file financial disclosure forms, and be subject to state scrutiny. Right after the change in the law, state officials wrote to the Unification Church, which is led by the Rev. Sun Myung Moon, saying it was now required to register. The church initiated a lawsuit, claiming that the law discriminated among religious organizations, a violation of the Establishment Clause.

The Supreme Court found in favor of the Unification Church. Justice William Brennan's opinion began with the recognition that Minnesota had a significant interest in protecting its citizens from fraudulent charitable organizations. But, he wrote, it is also clear the Establishment Clause commands that the state cannot prefer one denomination over another, and that was what the law did in this case. The law clearly subjected to stricter state scrutiny those religious groups that solicited funds in airports, parks, or shopping centers than those which received most of their funds from the Sunday morning offering plate. The 50 percent rule treated different religious groups differently, and the no-establishment principle would not allow this. The Unification Church could not be compelled to register and report under that provision of the statute.

The larger lesson, of course, is that governments may not pass laws that enable them to inflict greater surveillance and regulation on controversial religious groups.

TAXES

The question of the taxation of religious institutions has been a vexing one over the years. Many have argued that churches should not be exempt from either income or property taxes. Especially during economic hard times, such as in the late 1980s and early 1990s, when governmental units searched frantically for new sources of revenue, some have argued that if the religious institutions were taxed, the economic problems of America would be over. Not only is that too optimistic a statement; it also fails to recognize the strong constitutional arguments for the exemption of religious institutions from taxation. The Supreme Court has dealt with several different dimensions of the question of the taxation of religious institutions.

Property Tax Exemptions

One of the earliest tax issues taken up by the Supreme Court, in 1970, involved property tax exemptions for religious institutions. In *Walz v. Tax Commission of the City of New York*,[22] a taxpayer challenged tax exemptions for buildings used exclusively for worship. The case was a narrow one; it did not involve parsonages, education buildings, camps, or other properties religious institutions might own. The Supreme Court has never dealt with exemptions for those kinds of properties, but on the question of tax exemptions for sanctuaries, the Court spoke clearly in *Walz*. The allegation in that case was that property tax exemptions are a violation of the Establishment Clause, because they amount to government support of religion. Religious institutions are obviously relieved of an expenditure because of the exemptions, which allows them to spend that money for religious programming. Furthermore, those who do pay property taxes indirectly make contributions to religious institutions. That is, church properties are the beneficiaries of government services (for example, police and fire protection) for which they do not pay. Because those services are funded, at least in part, by those who do pay property taxes, those taxpayers are indirectly compelled to make a contribution to religious organizations, in violation of the Establishment Clause. The exemptions also make taxpayers' taxes higher.

The Court, in an opinion written by Chief Justice Burger, decided that property tax exemptions do not violate the Establishment Clause. It used three arguments to support its finding. One, a historical argument, observed that tax exemptions for religious properties are nothing new in American history. The Court found examples in the colonial period and in other times since the Revolutionary War and concluded that despite a long history of such tax exemptions, there is no evidence that the practice has ever created even "the remotest sign of leading to an established church or religion."[23]

A second rationale was what may be called a "charitable class argument," which identified religious properties as part of a larger class of eleemosynary institutions (from the Greek *eleēmosynē*, "mercy") such as schools, museums, libraries, and hospitals, all of which were exempt from property taxes. So religious properties did not receive special government favor.

A third argument raised the issue of "excessive entanglement." The Establishment Clause was designed to minimize interaction between church and state. Were governments allowed to collect property taxes from religious institutions, the effect would be to raise the level of interaction between churches and civil authority. In contrast, continuing to exempt religious properties from taxation would keep the entanglement of church and state at a lower, and acceptable, level:

> Either course, taxation of churches or exemption, occasions some degree of involvement with religion. Elimination of exemption would tend to expand the involvement of government by giving rise to tax valuation of church property; tax liens, tax foreclosures, and the direct confrontations and conflicts that follow in the train of those legal processes. Granting tax exemptions to churches necessarily operates to afford an indirect economic benefit and also gives rise to some, but yet a lesser, involvement than taxing them.[24]

(As described earlier, this argument became the third "prong" of the "*Lemon* test" for interpreting the Establishment Clause.)

These three arguments combined made it very clear that property tax exemptions for places of worship do not violate the Establishment Clause.

The class argument is an effective answer to those who would take away the tax exemptions of religious institutions, whether for property or income taxes. Given that there is a broad class of exempt organizations, to eliminate the exemptions only of religious organizations would single them out for special, negative treatment, and that is arguably a violation of the Establishment Clause. Only the most radical enemy of exemptions would be willing to eliminate all such exemptions for charitable organizations, given the variety of beneficial services those organizations render to society. But that would be the only way to remove the exemptions for religious organizations without running afoul of the Constitution.

Social Security Taxes

Social Security taxes were in 1982 the subject of *United States v. Lee*.[25] The case was about the Old Order Amish and their attitudes toward interaction with government. The Amish have a strong belief in hard work and self-sufficiency and, because of that, prefer to care for their own sick or aged. They regard this as a religious obligation in response to 1 Timothy 5:8: "Whoever does not provide for relatives, and especially for family members, has denied the faith and is worse than an unbeliever." Thus, to pay Social Security taxes and receive benefits therefrom is to acknowledge that the government has a responsibility to care for the aged and infirm—and that is to deny the faith. So the Amish, basing their petition on Free Exercise Clause grounds, petitioned Congress for an exemption from participating in the Social Security program. Congress granted an exemption for the self-employed among the Amish and any other religious groups with theological objections to Social Security from paying the taxes and receiving the benefits of the program.[26]

Lee arose when an Amish employer of Amish employees failed to file required Social Security tax forms for them, withhold the tax from the employees' paychecks, and pay the employer's share of the Social Security tax. Eventually the IRS presented Lee with a bill for back taxes. Instead of paying, Lee sued, claiming his free exercise of religion rights exempted him from making the required payments and submitting the required forms. He argued this was especially true in light of the exemption Congress had granted the Amish from participation in the Social Security program.

Chief Justice Warren Burger wrote the opinion for a unanimous Court. Although the justices accepted the fact that the Amish had religiously based conscientious objection to participation in Social Security, they ruled against Lee for two reasons. First, the exemption from Social Security granted by Congress was only for self-employed Amish, not Amish employers, even when their employees were also Amish. The Court was not willing to, indeed could not, go beyond the narrow exemption provided by the law. Second, although Lee's request was based on sincerely held religious belief, his free exercise argument could not prevail in this circumstance: "Not all burdens on religion are unconstitutional. The state may justify a limitation on religious liberty by showing that it is essential to accomplish an overriding governmental interest."[27] The essential governmental interest in this case was preserving the integrity of the Social Security tax system, a huge system with millions of participants. For the government to have to grant exemptions beyond what Congress had already authorized would put a strain on the system:

> The tax system could not function if denominations were allowed to challenge the tax system because tax payments were spent in a manner that violates their religious belief. Because the broad public interest in maintaining a sound tax system is of such a high order, religious belief in conflict with the payment of taxes affords no basis for resisting the tax.[28]

Congress had earlier provided the Amish a narrow exemption from Social Security taxes. That was all they were to have.

Sales Tax

The Court has also dealt with the question of religious exemptions from sales tax collection. A Texas law exempted from its sales tax periodicals that promoted the teaching of religious faith and books that were writings sacred to a religious faith. Nonreligious periodicals and books were not exempt from the sales tax. A secular magazine, *Texas Monthly*, filed suit, claiming that the exemption for religious publications was discriminatory and a violation of the Establishment Clause, because it gave preferential treatment to the religious publications.

The Supreme Court, in *Texas Monthly v. Bullock*,[29] in 1989 decided against the state of Texas. Justice William Brennan's opinion began with the observation that the Establishment Clause does not forbid government policies or programs that incidentally aid religion, that is, when the secular, nonsectarian aims of government and those of religion overlap. The primary way to tell whether the government aid to religion is actually incidental to religion is to determine whether the aid is widely distributed to nonreligious organizations as well. Texas's tax exemption was not available to publications generally; it was available only to those magazine subscriptions and books that had religious content and, indeed, *promulgated* the teachings of religious faiths. To not require the buyers of such publications to pay sales tax clearly was a government aid to their sale. The Court concluded that the tax exemption was state sponsorship of religious belief and, consequently, banned by the Establishment Clause.

Texas tried to make its case by arguing that if it were not allowed to exempt religious publications, it would be infringing on the Free Exercise Clause rights of their publishers. In making this argument, it relied on *Murdock v. Pennsylvania*,[30] a 1943 Jehovah's Witness case in which the Court had ruled that a city could not impose a flat tax on a religious activity *for the privilege of engaging in that activity*. Texas's theory was the sales tax exemption was necessary to avoid the kind of tax forbidden in *Murdock*. The Court rejected that argument, saying there was no evidence the payment of a sales tax by subscribers would inhibit the religious activity of the publishers. Conversely, Texas also argued that to uphold *Murdock* would suggest that government may never tax religious publications, and that would be a violation of the Establishment Clause. The Court rejected that argument, as well. It said the *Murdock* rule held that while the government may not tax a minister *for the privilege of preaching*, it may tax the income of the minister, just as it taxes the income of people in other professions, as a part of a general taxation program.

Consequently, the Court held that a state may exempt the sale of all books and subscriptions to magazines, including those with religious content, from its sales tax; and it may tax the sale of all books and subscriptions to magazines, including those containing religion. But it may not exempt religious publications only, for that violates the Establishment Clause.

Another case involving sales taxes was *Jimmy Swaggart Ministries v. Board of Equalization of California*.[31] California requires retailers to pay a sales tax on the items they sell. There is also a use tax, which is a sales tax paid by the residents of California for the items they buy from out-of-state retailers. In both cases, the tax is collected by the seller at the time of sale.

Between 1974 and 1981 Jimmy Swaggart Ministries conducted twenty-three evangelistic crusades in California. During those meetings, religious and nonreligious items were sold to those who attended. The Ministries also published a magazine, sold nationwide by subscription. The magazine carried advertisements and order forms for items that could be purchased from the Ministries' headquarters in Baton Rouge, Louisiana. Among those who made mail-order purchases were residents of California.

In 1980 the California Board of Equalization informed Jimmy Swaggart Ministries that its sales were subject to both sales and use taxes. The Board calculated how much had been bought in in-state crusades and through the mail order process and sent the Ministries a bill for back taxes, interest, and a penalty, for a total of $166,145.10. The Swaggart organization did not protest the taxes on merchandise such as T-shirts, mugs, bowls, plates, pen and pencil sets, all with the logo of the Ministries on them, but it did contest the taxes on religious items such as books, tapes of sermons, and Bibles, and on religious music in the form of songbooks, tapes, and records. The Swaggart organization argued that a tax on religious materials violates both the Free Exercise and Establishment Clauses.

The Free Exercise challenge alleged that the taxes inhibited the exercise of the Ministries' religion. Swaggart based his challenge on *Murdock v. Pennsylvania*, claiming that that case forbids a state from imposing a tax on the sale of religious items used for evangelistic purposes by a religious organization.

Justice Sandra Day O'Connor, writing for the Court, rejected that argument. Noting that *Murdock* had held only that a state may not put a tax on a religious activity as a precondition to engaging in that activity (that is, the tax could not be a prior restraint), the Court held California's tax did not have that function. The tax was not restricted to sales of religious items only but, rather, applied to all retail sales made in the state. It in no sense was a prior restraint. It was not collected from the seller as a payment for the privilege of conducting sales in the state, but from the buyer only as the item was sold. Furthermore, there was no evidence the tax violated the religious beliefs of those engaged in the ministry. The Court concluded the Free Exercise Clause did not require the state to grant the Ministries an exemption from its sales and use taxes.

Swaggart Ministries also claimed the taxes violated the Establishment Clause in that they created excessive entanglement between government and the religious organization. The Court disagreed, claiming the collection and payment of sales and use taxes creates hardly any entanglement at all. Indeed, a general tax, which does not exempt sales of religious articles, actually lessens the possibility of entanglement between government officials and religious groups. If religious items were exempt from taxation, government officials would have to determine what is religious, and so qualifies for the exemption, and what is not. That would entangle the activities of government and the religious organization more than a tax that applied to all sales of all items. (This is virtually identical to one of the Court's arguments in the property tax exemption case *Walz v. Tax Commission*.) Consequently, the California sales and use taxes did not create excessive entanglement between church and state and were not unconstitutional as they applied to the sales of religious items.

Federal Income Tax

Finally, there is a line of cases involving religion and federal income taxes. Section 501(c)(3) of the Internal Revenue Code describes the categories of institutions and organizations that are exempt from federal income tax. The law exempts, in pertinent part:

> Corporations, and any community chest, fund, or foundation, organized and operated *exclusively* for religious, charitable, scientific, testing for public safety, literary; or educational purposes, . . . *no part* of the net earnings of which inures to the benefit of any private shareholder or individual, *no substantial part* of the activities of which is carrying on propaganda, or otherwise attempting, to influence legislation . . . , and which does not participate in, or intervene in (including the publishing or distributing of statements), any political campaign on behalf of any candidate for public office.[32] (emphases added)

For a religious organization, either a denomination or a local congregation, to be exempt from federal income tax, it must conform with the restrictions in this section of the law. Furthermore, the law on deductibility, section 170 of the code, contains virtually identical language to section 501(c)(3). So, if an organization loses its tax exemption, it also loses deductibility. That is, those who donate to the now nonexempt organization cannot deduct their contributions from their personal income taxes. Because many people make contributions to religious organizations in order to get the tax deduction, for the organization to lose its tax exemption would be a double blow: it would now have to pay taxes on income, and its donors and potential donors would lose a primary incentive to make donations.

A case that vividly illustrates how this works is *Christian Echoes National Ministry v. United States*.[33] Although this case was not decided by a Supreme Court opinion, it is included because it has such relevance to denominations and local churches. Christian Echoes National Ministry was organized by Dr. Billy James Hargis in 1951 and recognized by the IRS as a 501(c)(3) organization in 1953. The Ministry was fundamentalist in theology and vehemently opposed to Communism. "Its mission [was] a battle against Communism, socialism and political liberalism, all of which [were] considered arch enemies of the Christian faith."[34] In 1964 the IRS revoked the Ministry's tax exemption, and thus its deductibility, because through its publications and radio broadcasts, which were the bulk of its activities, the Ministry had encouraged people to write to their congressional representatives in support of conservative causes. Among these many causes were supporting the Becker and Dirksen amendments (both attempts to amend the Constitution to restore prayer to the public schools after *Abington Township School District v. Schempp*); withdrawing from the United Nations; outlawing the Communist Party in the United States; and stopping federal aid to education, "socialized" medicine, and public housing, among a long list of political concerns. In addition, the Ministry endorsed the candidacy of Barry Goldwater in the 1964 presidential election. In the face of the IRS's action, the Ministry paid the back taxes, interest, and penalty and sued in federal court to recover its money and restore its exemption.

The court of appeals found in favor of the government. The following passage from the opinion spells out the rationale for exempting charitable organizations and also the rationale for removing exemptions because of political activity by charitable organizations:

> The exemption to corporations organized and operated exclusively for charitable, religious, educational or other purposes carried on for charity is granted because of the benefit the public obtains from their

activities and is based on the theory that: ". . . the Government is compensated for the loss of revenue by its relief from financial burden which would otherwise have to be met by appropriations from public funds, and by the benefits resulting from the promotion of the general welfare." H.R. Rep. No. 1860, 75th Cong., 3d Sess. 19 (1939). Tax exemptions are matters of legislative grace and taxpayers have the burden of establishing their entitlement to exemptions. The limitations in Section 501(c)(3) stem from the Congressional policy that the United States Treasury should be neutral in *political affairs and that substantial activities directed to attempts to influence legislation or affect a political campaign should not be subsidized.*[35] (emphasis in original)

The court concluded the IRS was correct in removing the Ministry's exemption, on the ground that a substantial amount of its time and resources had been devoted to legislative initiatives and the support of specific candidates. But Christian Echoes National Ministry vigorously argued that such activity was protected by the Free Exercise Clause because it was religiously motivated. The Ministry and its followers had religious convictions about the welfare of the nation and its citizens, and for that reason it had become involved in the political arena. To remove the tax exemption was an attack on free exercise rights and a discrimination against religion.

The court answered that argument by essentially ignoring it. The IRS and the court explicitly acknowledged that Christian Echoes engaged in the political activities because of religious motivations. They said the Ministry could engage in whatever political activity it wanted, for even religious motivations; it just could not do so *and* have a tax exemption:

> A religious organization that engages in substantial activity aimed at influencing legislation is disqualified from tax exemption, whatever the motivation. . . . The free exercise clause of the First Amendment is restrained only to the extent of denying tax exempt status and then only in keeping with an overwhelming and compelling Governmental interest: That of guarantying [*sic*] that the wall separating church and state remain high and firm. . . . The taxpayer may engage in all such activities without restraint, subject, however, to withholding of the exemption or, in the alternative, the taxpayer may refrain from such activities and obtain the privilege of exemption.[36]

In essence, your religious organization can be political *or* you can have tax exemption and deductibility; but you cannot have the tax benefits if you believe that religion places an obligation on you to be involved in the social/political arena and you use a "substantial" amount of time and resources to do it. The United States Supreme Court subsequently denied certiorari to the *Christian Echoes* case.[37]

Beginning about the off-year election of 2002, advocates of the Christian

Right tried to remove the section 501(c)(3) rule for churches, but not for other tax exempt organizations. Claiming the prohibition against electioneering violated the free exercise and free speech rights of the clergy and of religious institutions, Representative Walter Jones (R-NC) introduced the "Houses of Worship Free Speech Restoration Act" into the House of Representatives. In 2004 it had 130 cosponsors in the House. Congressman Jones articulated the societal importance of removing the rule: "Nothing is more important than our spiritual leaders having the right to name candidates who stand for protecting morality."[38] But the legislation was not enacted. Most members of Congress realized that the proposal carried peril for religious organizations, as one news report explained:

> [O]pponents argue that it would turn houses of worship into campaign vehicles and possibly reshape America's religious and political landscapes in harmful ways. They worry that political endorsements could divide churches, lead to reconfiguring memberships along political lines, adulterate their spiritual purpose and prophetic role as societal consciences, and even perhaps turn their coffers into unregulated channels for campaign financing.[39]

Passage of the bill also would have brought potential Establishment Clause problems. Removing electioneering prohibitions for religious institutions but not for secular tax exempt institutions would have given preferential treatment to the former.

One of the most celebrated and bitterly fought cases of the late 1970s and early 1980s was *Bob Jones University v. United States*.[40] In 1970, based on its interpretation of the Civil Rights Act of 1964, the IRS announced that henceforth institutions that discriminated on the basis of race could no longer be section 501(c)(3) and section 170 institutions. Bob Jones University, a fundamentalist Christian institution, believed the Bible clearly forbids interracial dating and marriage. At that time, the university had a policy of not admitting black students. In 1971 it changed its policy and admitted black people married within their race but continued to exclude unmarried black people. After 1975 it admitted unmarried black students but continued to have strict rules against interracial dating; the penalty for violation was expulsion from the school. After some preliminary notification, in 1975 the IRS revoked the tax exemption of Bob Jones University because it was not in conformity with congressionally established public policy. The school had not violated any of the specific provisions of section 501(c)(3), but its racial policies were not consistent with national policy on that issue. The university responded with a suit in federal court, claiming that the IRS action denied its free exercise of religion and that the IRS had acted improperly, in that it had assumed a role that belonged only to Congress.

The Supreme Court seemed to think that this was not a difficult case. Chief Justice Burger's opinion began with the assertion that there are essentially two dimensions to income-tax exemption. One dimension is the specifications of the law itself. Obviously an institution must conform to those specifications to maintain exempt status. Second, to be exempt, an institution also must be consistent with public policy. The rationale behind exempting organizations is that they perform charitable services the government otherwise would have to perform at taxpayer expense. Thus, an exempt institution must serve a public purpose that is not contrary to public policy established by Congress. Because the Civil Rights Act of 1964 had made racial discrimination contrary to public policy, Bob Jones was not in compliance. Consequently, although the university had not specifically violated any of the provisions of section 501(c)(3), the IRS had acted properly in revoking its tax exemption and deductibility:

> [I]t cannot be said that educational institutions that, for whatever reasons, practice racial discrimination, are institutions exercising "beneficial and stabilizing influences on public life," or should be encouraged by having all taxpayers share in their support by way of special tax status. . . . Whatever may be the rationale for such private schools' policies, and however sincere the rationale may be, racial discrimination in education is contrary to public policy. Racially discriminatory educational institutions cannot be viewed as conferring a public benefit within the "charitable" concept . . . or within the Congressional intent underlying §170 and §501(c)(3).[41]

The Court disagreed with the university's allegation that the IRS had assumed for itself a role appropriate only to Congress, observing that Congress had created the agency to implement and enforce the tax laws and had given the agency the authority to do so. This authority included making the kind of rulings being attacked in this case. Congress can change IRS rules and procedures if it considers either one wrong, but until that happens, the agency has the authority to implement public policy. The Court was unwilling to step in here.

On the more important constitutional question of whether the IRS's action had denied Bob Jones University freedom of religion, the Court's answer was almost curt. It asserted that religious freedom is subject to limitation, if the limitation is necessary for the government to accomplish a major interest. The government interest here—the elimination of racism in America—was compelling. Consequently, the university was not entitled to its tax exemption. The IRS action did not interfere with the university's freedom of religion. The university could still believe, based on sincerely held theology, that racial intermixing was wrong. It just could not implement such a belief *and* have an income-tax exemption:

> Denial of tax benefits will inevitably have a substantial impact on the operation of private religious schools, but will not prevent those schools from observing their religious tenets. . . .The governmental interest at stake here is compelling. . . . [T]he government has a fundamental, overriding interest in eradicating racial discrimination in education. . . . That governmental interest substantially outweighs whatever burden denial of tax benefits places on petitioners' exercise of their religious beliefs.[42]

So, religious groups stand in danger of losing their income-tax exemption and their deductibility, if they become substantially involved in the political arena or maintain beliefs or practices that are contrary to established public policy.

Charitable Contributions

Two cases have dealt with the issue of what *is* a charitable contribution under section 170 of the IRS code. One of those, *Hernandez v. Commissioner of Internal Revenue*,[43] was about the deductibility from personal income taxes of payments made for services received from the Church of Scientology.

Scientology is a psychologically oriented organization, whose members are expected to undergo a procedure known as "auditing." Auditing is designed to identify and eliminate a person's spiritual and/or psychological difficulties. An auditor (counselor) asks a series of probing questions to bring suppressed psychic stress to a person's consciousness in order to discuss the stress, identify it for what it is, and thereby purge it. The goal of Scientology is to help a person to reach the condition of "clear." Roughly equivalent to salvation, clear is the state of being free of all psychological/spiritual malfunctions. Because a person may have a multitude of such problems, accumulated not only from the earlier years of his or her present life but from previous lives, the process of auditing may be long, requiring many sessions.

In addition to auditing, Scientology offers doctrinal courses, known as "training." The primary function of this instruction is to prepare people to become auditors. The training courses, like auditing sessions, are provided in sequential levels. Scientologists believe that spiritual gains result from participation in such courses.

Scientology charges fees for both auditing and training. It calls these charges a "price," a "fixed donation," or a "fixed contribution." Furthermore, there is a schedule with a set price for each level of each service. The payments are based on a central concept of Scientology, the "doctrine of exchange," the idea that anytime one receives something, one must pay something back. Under this doctrine, the revenue generated from auditing and training are Scientology's primary source of income.

The plaintiffs in *Hernandez* had deducted from their federal income tax the payments they had made for auditing and training, claiming that they were a section 170 charitable contribution. The IRS disallowed the contributions, saying because they were payments for specific services and made in response to a specific fee schedule, they were not real *contributions*. The plaintiffs sued to restore the deductibility of their contributions.

The Supreme Court, like the lower courts, denied their request. The Court, in an opinion by Justice Thurgood Marshall, asserted that Congress, in passing the charitable contribution section of the law, said that payments made in return for goods or services are not contributions: "'The *sine qua non* of a charitable contribution is a transfer of money or property *without adequate consideration*'"[44] (emphasis on final phrase added).

The plaintiffs argued they were entitled to the deductions because a quid pro quo analysis is not appropriate when the benefit the taxpayer receives is completely religious in nature. Furthermore, any payment made in order to be able to participate in a religious service should be automatically deductible. The Court was not persuaded by these arguments, concluding that the language of section 170 would not support them. Congress has restricted deductibility to gifts and contributions, and payments to religious organizations are not in a separate category. Furthermore, the Scientologists' theory would increase the entanglement between church and state. That is, the IRS and ultimately the judiciary would have to differentiate between religious benefits and secular ones. That would be impermissible under the Establishment Clause. Accordingly, the Court held that payments for auditing and training, made on the basis of a quid pro quo fee schedule, were not deductible.

The Scientologists argued the law created a denominational preference by erecting a harsher standard of deductibility for religious groups that raise funds by imposing fixed costs for participation in some religious practices. The Court disagreed. The law does not discriminate between denominations. If the payment is a gift or contribution, it is deductible. If it is given with the expectation of a quid pro quo return, it is not deductible. Those provisions of the law are true in reference to all religions. Section 170 bears no animus to religion in general or Scientology in particular. As for entanglement, while it is true that ascertaining whether a payment to a religious institution is a quid pro quo transaction may require the IRS to obtain pertinent information from the religious group, that involves neither inquiry into religious doctrine nor close administrative contact between the IRS and the religious group in question. Also, section 170 does not require the government to put a monetary value on a religious service.

The Scientologists also argued that the denial of deductibility of these payments to the church violated their free exercise rights by deterring adherents from engaging in auditing and training sessions, and that it interfered with the observance of the "doctrine of exchange." The Court responded by saying the doctrine of Scientology does not forbid the payment of taxes generally or, specifically, in connection with auditing or training. At most, the denial of deduction may mean that adherents have less money available to use for auditing and training. The same is true with the doctrine of exchange. But *any* taxing program reduces one's discretionary money; it does not make that tax unconstitutional.

The Scientologists continued their fight with the IRS, however, and on November 1, 1993, the Court's decision became academic for them when the IRS reversed its position and granted tax exemption and deductibility.

In a similar case, *Davis v. United States*,[45] some Mormon parents wanted to deduct the payments they had made to their sons who were engaged in missionary work on behalf of the church. The money was sent to the missionaries, who had discretion over how it was to be spent, rather than to the church. Even though the missionaries were acting on behalf of the church and had used the money for expenses directly related to their missionary work, the IRS would not allow the deductions. The reason was that the contributions were not "for the use of" the church and were not in the control of the exempt organization, as required by the statute. The Supreme Court upheld the IRS's ruling.

The "bottom line" of all this is that no payment to a religious organization, national or local, is deductible from federal income taxes if it is given in expectation of a specific return, or in payment, according to a set price, for goods or services already rendered. If money is given in such a way that the exempt organization does not have control over its use, it likewise is not deductible under section 170.

RELIGIOUS SYMBOLS ON PUBLIC PROPERTY

One of the more interesting problems to come before the Court was the question of the constitutionality of religious symbols, sometimes financed by public funds, on public property. A 1984 case came from Pawtucket, Rhode Island, *Lynch v. Donnelly*.[46] Each Christmas the city erected a display, a nativity scene surrounded with other paraphernalia of Christmas—a wishing well, reindeer, candy-striped poles, a Christmas tree, Santa Claus, and Santa's house. Some residents of the community sued, claiming the display, owned and maintained by the city, which contained the scene of the birth of Jesus, was clearly city sponsorship of religion, a violation of the Establishment Clause.

The Supreme Court disagreed with that contention. Chief Justice Warren

Burger wrote for the Court that the Establishment Clause does not demand strict separation between church and state. In fact, he said, it demands accommodation between the two. In this case, it was clear the city did not intend to—and did not—promote Christianity with its display. Analogous to religious paintings hanging in the National Gallery of Art, the crèche with Jesus, Mary, and Joseph appeared with many secular symbols of Christmas that communicated that it is really just a festive season. "The crèche in the display depicts the historical origins of this traditional event long recognized as a National Holiday."[47] Given the visual impact of the total display, the city had not singled out a specifically religious symbol for display for the winter holiday season, and thus had not violated the Establishment Clause. There was no reason for the city not to continue to use the display.

The key to *Lynch* is that the nativity scene was surrounded by a multitude of secular symbols of the season. This has been referred to as the "plastic reindeer rule." After the decision was handed down, legal scholars wondered what the Court would decide if there were a city-sponsored nativity scene standing alone.

Five years later, *Allegheny County v. ACLU of Pittsburgh*[48] enabled them to find out. Two religious symbols were involved in this case. One was a nativity scene that stood on the "grand staircase" of the Allegheny County courthouse. The staircase was in a prominent place in the courthouse and readily observable by all who came into the building. The crèche included the holy family, some animals, shepherds, wise men, and a manger. Positioned above the scene was an angel bearing a banner with the inscription "Gloria in Excelsis Deo!" Small evergreen trees and poinsettia plants surrounded the display, as well as a sign stating "This Display Donated by the Holy Name Society." The display was essentially a stand-alone nativity scene.

A block away, at a building jointly owned by the city and the county was an eighteen-foot Hanukkah menorah, donated by a group of Lubavitcher Hasidim, an ultraorthodox branch of Judaism. Alongside the menorah was a forty-five-foot Christmas tree, below which was a sign bearing the mayor's name and the motto "Salute to Liberty." Beneath the motto the sign stated: "During this holiday season, the City of Pittsburgh salutes liberty. Let these festive lights remind us that we are the keepers of the flame of liberty and our legacy of freedom."

The Pittsburgh chapter of the ACLU and some local residents filed suit, claiming the displays violated the Establishment Clause because they gave government endorsement to religion. The Supreme Court had to determine whether the crèche and the menorah, in their particular settings, had the effect of endorsing religious beliefs.

The Court, in Justice Harry Blackmun's opinion, declared the nativity scene, standing alone in the courthouse, to be unconstitutional. Unlike the crèche in *Lynch v. Donnelly*, there was nothing to detract from its religious message. Furthermore, it was located on the grand staircase of the county courthouse, which communicated the message of government approval and support:

> Thus, by permitting the display of the crèche in this particular physical setting, the county sends an unmistakable message that it supports and promotes the Christian praise to God that is the crèche's religious message. . . . [T]he Establishment Clause does not limit only the religious content of the government's own communications. It also prohibits the government's support and promotion of religious communications by religious organizations. . . . In sum, *Lynch* teaches that government may celebrate Christmas in some manner and form, but not in a way that endorses Christian doctrine. Here, Allegheny County has transgressed this line. It has chosen to celebrate Christmas in a way that has the effect of endorsing a patently Christian message: Glory to God for the birth of Jesus Christ.[49]

The Court reached a different conclusion on the question of the menorah. The menorah was accompanied by both a Christmas tree and a sign in praise of liberty. Justice Blackmun recognized that the menorah is a religious symbol of Judaism, although it is the symbol of a holiday that has both religious and secular dimensions, as is the Christmas tree. To have the menorah and the Christmas tree in juxtaposition is to recognize that they represent two holidays, not one. That, by itself, would not save them from Establishment Clause stricture. If the city celebrates two religious holidays, it still violates the clause. But if it celebrates them as secular holidays, then the clause is not violated. The Court concluded that the two symbols together showed that the city did not want to endorse either religion, but

> rather simply recognizes that both Christmas and Chanukah are part of the same winter-holiday season, which has attained secular status in our society. . . . [I]t is not "sufficiently likely" that residents of Pittsburgh will perceive the combined display of the tree, the sign, and the menorah as an "endorsement" or "disapproval . . . of their individual religious choices."[50]

Another religious symbols on public land case came from an unexpected direction, the Ku Klux Klan. In Columbus, Ohio, a ten-acre area surrounds the state capitol building. Naturally, the area is called "Capitol Square." The use of the square was governed by the Capitol Square Review and Advisory Board. The Board had, for some time, allowed the square to be used by all sorts of groups for displays, that is, to communicate their messages. In December 1993, the Board approved the erection of a state-owned Christmas tree and a menorah, provided by a local synagogue. With the advent of the menorah, the Board received a request from the local Ku Klux Klan, represented by Vincent Pinette. The Klan group wanted to put up a Christian cross as an answer to the Jewish symbol.

The Board denied Pinette's request, citing its need to adhere to the prohibition of the Establishment Clause against advancing or promoting religion. Pinette sued. A federal district court ruled that Capitol Square was a traditional public forum, open to all, with no policy against freestanding, unattended, displays. Consequently, the court allowed the Klan's cross. Soon the Board received and granted requests from several other Christian groups to put up crosses in the square, crosses competing with the Klan's. The Board appealed the district court's ruling, and the case ultimately in 1995 made it to the Supreme Court, *Capitol Square Review Board v. Pinette*.[51] Justice Antonin Scalia wrote the opinion.

The Court ruled in favor of Pinette. The square was a public forum. Access was widely available. Given that, when the state allowed the expression of a religious message, in this case, in the form of a cross, people would understand that the state simply permitted the symbol, it did not endorse it. Stated differently, "The State did not sponsor [Pinette's] expression, the expression was made on government property that had been opened to the public for speech, and permission was requested through the same application process and on the same terms required of other private groups."[52] Because it was private speech simply permitted by the government through its public forum policy, the cross was permissible. The Establishment Clause applies only to the government's own communication. The cross was private speech, not the government's, so there was no Establishment Clause violation.

So, in the matter of religious symbols either financed with public money or sponsored by the government, the rule seems to be that if the symbol stands alone, it is a violation of the Establishment Clause. But if a display combines the symbols of several religions and is accompanied by some secular object, if it passes the "plastic reindeer rule," or if the holiday clearly has a cultural as well as a religious dimension, the display merits constitutional approval.

Furthermore, if a government has established a public forum, religious symbols can be placed on public property. The symbol is the communication of the entity sponsoring it, not of the government, so the government is not communicating religion in violation of the no-establishment principle.

9

Flash Points and the Future

In the preceding chapters the decisions of the Supreme Court have been described with only occasional notice taken of dissenting opinions and with little commentary. That should not suggest that everything is tranquil, positive, or unanimous in the area of church-state relationships. In fact, the contrary is true. In this area, as in so many other areas of American social and political life, things are in turmoil. The Court itself is deeply divided, especially on the interpretation of the Establishment Clause. In this chapter I note some of the areas of greatest concern to those who, like me, believe the maximum amount of religious liberty is consistent with the Constitution and best for religious groups and American life in general.

THE RISE OF THE CHRISTIAN RIGHT

Since the late 1970s the Christian Right has attracted the attention of the media, religious folk, and observers of church-state relations. The movement began primarily for secular reasons. Several leaders of the secular political right wing recognized that evangelical and fundamentalist Christians, and perhaps conservatives of other religions, were a great, untapped market for their political philosophy. In an attempt to reverse the influence of both moderate and liberal lawmakers at every level of government, particularly national, these political operatives persuaded conservative Christians to become involved in the political arena. One of the earliest of these conservative Christians to make the change from being antipolitical (or at least apolitical) to political activism was Jerry Falwell. Pastor of the Thomas Road Baptist Church in Lynchburg, Virginia, in the late 1970s Falwell founded the Moral

Majority, the first and perhaps most famous of the organizations of the Christian Right. This movement fit into the larger phenomenon of the turn to the right in America. Beginning in the mid-1970s and continuing today, America has experienced a growing nostalgia for earlier, simpler times and much more conservative politics. The results of this include the election of Ronald Reagan to the presidency for two terms and George Bush for one, Republicans' taking control of Congress in 1994, and the election of George W. Bush in 2000 and 2004.

Since its secular political beginnings, the Christian Right has been able to maintain vitality because an increasing number of people have become concerned about what they consider the moral decline in the nation. This issue, the concern for moral corruption in every stratum of society, became the trademark of the Christian Right. Its advocates have performed a service for society by raising the issue of morality—in politics, in personal and family life, and in the media—and by stimulating national discussion. Unfortunately, the discussions have often yielded more heat than light, because Christian Right advocates themselves, and their opponents, have often taken intractable positions that have tended to polarize society. Nonetheless, it is good to have had these issues raised so that people have had to think about them and participate in a national debate. A democratic society is designed to thrive and progress on the basis of robust debate. In many ways, society is the better and stronger for having had the Christian Right in its midst raising issues, some of which are of transcendent importance.

What has been more problematic about the movement, from the perspective of church-state relations, is its political efforts to remake the country in its own image. Not content with simply raising the issues of public morality for public debate, the Christian Right has attempted to correct the problems it identified by trying to vote out of office those who did not share its moral values and to vote into office those who were more acceptable from their point of view. Of course, nothing in the Constitution prevents citizens from acting in the political arena from a religious perspective. Indeed, the Free Exercise Clause guarantees people the right to participate in politics—as candidates, as voters, and as lobbyists—because of religious motivation. As Christian Right leaders are wont to say, "The First Amendment was designed to separate church from state, not religion from government." Although the statement glosses over many complexities, it is essentially correct. So, beginning in the 1980s, adherents of the Christian Right, at both rank-and-file and leadership levels, have tried to effect change by voting their religious convictions at the ballot box. Religion played such an enormous role in the presidential election of 2004 that the phenomenon itself became newsworthy. A student of the movement summarizes their motivation:

The leadership of the movement will always be dedicated toward achieving an effective working relationship between national piety and national patriotism so that the two might function as harmonizing collaborative teammates in the pursuit of the common good. The movement remains committed to synthesizing selected Christian theological judgments with specific conceptions of how a democracy ought to function. In working toward this objective, the New Right believes that it carries the authority of both the Bible and the guiding philosophical principles of the nation's Founding Fathers.[1]

So far, so good. But then there is that very first mention of religion in the Constitution, in Article VI: "[N]o religious Test shall ever be required as a Qualification to any Office or public Trust under the United States." To vote people in or out of office because of their adherence, or lack thereof, to a theological standard is to violate the spirit, if not the letter, of Article VI. Some of the more ardent advocates of the Christian Right argue vociferously for the creation of a "Christian America," which they mistakenly[2] think was the posture of the nation in its first generation. To make this nation Christian, they believe, it is necessary to put into office born-again Christians or those sympathetic to their views. But the Constitution prohibits any sort of religious litmus test for public office.

Furthermore, to try to impose specifically theological ideas on the nation through legislation is contrary to the Establishment Clause, which requires the government to be religiously neutral. But the clause also means that the government must not be hostile to religion. It does not mean religious values may not be injected into the body politic by the religiously concerned. What the concept of separation prohibits is religious groups, singly or in concert, trying to legislate the relation of people to God. Such concepts or procedures would be narrowly theological and inappropriate. But it is entirely legitimate to legislate the social principles of religion, as long as (1) there is a broad public consensus on the desirability of such moral tenets, (2) the laws are grounded on public policy considerations, and (3) they are expressed in secular terms.

The rise of the Christian Right has thus raised interesting issues for the church-state (and the broader moral) debate and, at the same time, placed great stress on the concept of separation. This stress regarding the Supreme Court on church and state was very much apparent in the election of Ronald Reagan and, later, George Bush, to the presidency. While the Christian Right was certainly not wholly responsible for electing either of these men, there is evidence that it contributed significantly to that result. Both candidates courted the Christian Right and identified with it, at least for purposes of being elected. In part to appeal to the Christian Right, both these Presidents adhered to the philosophy that the justices of the Court were to be "strict constructionists" and judicial passivists (not pacifists). This means that they must judge on the basis of the original meaning of the constitutional text. This is also known as judging on the basis of the "original intent" of the authors of the Constitution. This philosophy is especially applicable to adjudicating under the Establishment Clause, and will be discussed shortly. The idea of a passivist as opposed to an activist judiciary is frequently expressed in the saying that judges "are to interpret law, not make law." A judicially passive Court would defer to the other branches of government, especially the legislative branch, as much as possible.

In their appointments to the Court, Presidents Reagan and Bush adhered to this philosophy, with the exception of Justice David Souter, who has written some very separationist opinions.[3] From the viewpoint of their many critics, their philosophy and appointments turned back the cultural and judicial clock. In the area of church-state relationships, the justices appointed by Presidents Reagan and Bush have made a dramatic change in the Court.[4] (President Clinton appointed two justices, but they have made little appreciable difference to church-state law [see note 18]. The decade between 1994 and 2004, with no appointments, was one of the longest periods of membership continuity in Court history. The possibility of up to four appointments in the next term was an issue in the 2004 presidential campaign. President George W. Bush had said if he had the opportunity, he would appoint "strict constructionists" like Justices Scalia and Thomas. If so, that would continue the trend described here.) The Supreme Court has changed direction in its understanding of the Religion Clauses. In what follows, I argue that the approach of the Court has put religious freedom in the greatest peril.

THE FREE EXERCISE CLAUSE

To understand the assault on religious freedom from the free-exercise side, it is necessary to quickly review what was said in chapter 4 about the "compelling state interest test." It is commonly accepted that the Free Exercise Clause is not absolute; the clause does not mean that "anything goes" in the area of religious behavior. From the time of Jefferson's "Bill for Establishing Religious Freedom," through *Reynolds v. United States*, to *Cantwell v. Connecticut*, it was assumed that the government has the right to interfere with religious action. The question was, how much latitude does the government have to prevent or hinder religious freedom? The *"Sherbert* test," a most satisfactory answer to the question, was given in *Sherbert v. Verner*. This "compelling state interest test" says the government may not interfere with religious endeavors *unless* it has a compelling interest the religious action violates. Furthermore, the government may not prevent or inhibit the expression of religious freedom if it has an alternative way to accomplish its legitimate goals without interference with religion. The compelling state interest test has meant that religious freedom is the rule, government interference the exception.

This important principle was seriously undermined by *Employment Division of Oregon v. Smith.*[5] In the opinion, Justice Antonin Scalia wrote that the compelling state interest test was no longer available in most free exercise of religion cases. His reasoning was that the test should not apply to laws of general applicability. The Court held that if a law targets religion specifically, that is, if it bans religious acts or compels acts that religious conviction forbids, then that law can be struck down under the Free Exercise Clause. However, if a law has application across the board, if it does not single out religion, then the compelling state interest test cannot be used to adjudicate the concerns of a religious plaintiff. For example, in *Smith* the law in question was a law prohibiting the use of drugs on the state's list of forbidden drugs. It was a law of general applicability, in that it prohibited a wide range of drugs the legislature perceived as dangerous, including peyote. Consequently, the Court was not willing to apply the Free Exercise Clause to the worship of the Native American Church, which uses peyote as its sacrament. The law of general applicability took precedence over the free exercise of the Native Americans in this case. Justice Scalia was not willing to apply the compelling state interest test to the issue. Furthermore—and this is one of the most important parts of this case—he generalized to say that henceforth the compelling state interest test should never be used on laws of general applicability, except in unemployment compensation cases.

But that was not all. The majority ruled that the Free Exercise Clause itself does not apply to laws aimed at general behavior, except in certain circumstances. The Free Exercise Clause can be used to adjudicate a law of general application considered to be burdensome to religion *if* it is used *in combination with* other constitutional principles such as free speech, freedom of the press, or the rights of parents.[6] This means the Free Exercise Clause is powerless unless it is supported by some other constitutionally guaranteed right. It is no longer a freestanding, independent constitutional freedom. It is no longer one of the principal freedoms that historically have made this country unique—and great.

In some of the cases of the 1940s, religious freedom, guaranteed by the Free Exercise Clause, was called by the justices a "preferred freedom."[7] Now, after the opinion of Justice Scalia, joined by Chief Justice Rehnquist and Justices Kennedy, Stevens, and White in the majority opinion in *Smith*, it was not even a discrete freedom.

As a result of *Smith*, neither the compelling state interest test nor the Free Exercise Clause itself could be used as a defense against laws of general application, no matter how burdensome they may be to practicing religion. In fact, Justice Scalia wrote that the solicitude for religious freedom, which originally was the reason for the compelling state interest test, is a "luxury" which "we cannot afford."[8] This means that government, at whatever level, except in the most narrow of circumstances, no longer had to show that it had a strong interest to justify its burden on religious exercise. Whereas before *Smith*, religious freedom was the rule and government interference was the exception, now just the opposite was true. Whereas before, government was of limited power in reference to religious behavior, now government had virtually unlimited power. Essentially the only limit to that power was a prohibition against passing a law specifically targeting religion for hostile government action. But if the law was one of general applicability, no matter how burdensome it was to religion, government would have its way under the *Smith* doctrine.

The previous paragraph must be nuanced slightly. Justice Scalia pointed out that legislatures could carve out exceptions for religion in their laws of general applicability. (For example, at the time of *Smith*, twenty-three states and the federal government had made exemptions, in their laws prohibiting drugs, for the sacramental use of peyote by the Native American Church.) Although they *could* carve out such exceptions, they were not constitutionally required to. But the possibility of legislative exceptions was small consolation for small, obscure, or unpopular religious groups. Such groups were at a decided disadvantage in trying to win recognition of their religious freedom needs as exceptions to general laws. Legislators are not likely to be supportive of the practices of religious groups that cannot produce many votes or that are thought of as being odd or out of favor with the majority. Justice Scalia acknowledged that fact but said this kind of disadvantage for the minority religious group is just an "unavoidable consequence of democratic government."[9]

Justice Robert Jackson, a generation earlier, was more on target than Justice Scalia. Justice Jackson recognized that certain liberties are not subject to majority rule, as essential as that is to democracy.

> The very purpose of a Bill of Rights was to withdraw certain subjects from the vicissitudes of political controversy, to place them beyond the reach of majorities and officials and to establish them as legal principles to be applied by the courts. One's right to life, liberty, and property, to free speech, a free press, freedom of worship and assembly, and other fundamental rights may not be submitted to vote; they depend on the outcome of no elections.[10]

Having forgotten the sound constitutional principle articulated by Justice Jackson, the Court in *Smith* adopted a position of "majoritarianism" or "statism." That is, it embraced the view of the sovereignty of the majority or of the state. One might ask, "What is wrong with that? In a democratic country, the majority rules. That is what a democracy is all about." That is so, but American government is a system of checks and balances. The very concept of checks and balances recognizes that unfettered power by any branch, or by the majority over the minority, is tyranny. Specifically, the founders of the nation recognized that the state, governed by the majority, might assume to itself unlimited power. James Madison, a principal author of the Constitution, wrote in his famous "Memorial and Remonstrance": "True it is, that no other rule exists, by which any question which may divide a Society, can be ultimately determined, but the will of the majority; but it is also true, that the majority may trespass on the rights of the minority" (see appendix A, ¶ 1).

The power of the state, arrayed against an individual or a minority group, is awesome. Recognizing this potential for raw power and its abuse, the founders created a government in which none of the branches could assume dominant power over the other two. That system is a symbol for the larger concept that the state, the majority, must recognize the rights of the weak; that is, minority groups and individuals. State power must be kept in check. To do that, the founders enacted the Bill of Rights. Those ten amendments to the Constitution are all designed in some way to protect the minority, the powerless, the accused against the power of the majority acting through the mechanisms of the state.[11] To turn specifically to the freedom of religion, Peter Berger argues that

> *Religious freedom is fundamental because it posits the ultimate limit on the power of the state.* . . . [R]eligion limits the power of the state because it refuses to recognize the state's sovereignty as ultimate; religion posits *another* sovereignty beyond and indeed over that of the state. . . . [T]he state that guarantees religious liberty does more than acknowledge another human right: It acknowledges without knowing it, that its power is less than ultimate. . . . [D]emocracy, whose very essence is the limitation of state power, is always in need of firm guarantees of religious liberty.[12] (emphasis in original)

Whether or not the authors of the Constitution were fully aware of this insight, they wrote the First Amendment as a limitation on the power of the state to have its way with the people in the matter of religion. As Justice Sandra Day O'Connor insisted in her strong dissent from the rationale in *Smith*, the First Amendment was

> enacted precisely to protect the rights of those whose religious practices are not shared by the majority and may be viewed with hostility. . . . The compelling interest test reflects the First Amendment's mandate of preserving religious liberty to the fullest extent possible in a

pluralistic society. For the Court to deem this command a "luxury," is to denigrate "[t]he very purpose of a Bill of Rights."[13]

The religion clauses of the First Amendment, particularly the Free Exercise Clause, exist to protect the minority from the tyranny of the majority. The judiciary, particularly the Supreme Court, is the branch of government to best serve that protective role.[14] But the Court, in *Smith*, in the name of judicial passivity, abdicated its role as defender of minority or unpopular religious groups by abandoning the compelling state interest test, relegating the Free Exercise Clause to the extreme margin of constitutionally guaranteed liberties, and exposed minority religions to the vagaries of legislative bodies— majoritarianism with a vengeance.[15]

It would have been bad enough if the Supreme Court had taken this position for itself alone. But, of course, the Supreme Court establishes the ultimate precedents for the adjudication of law by courts, federal and state, all over the country. So all the courts began to interpret free exercise cases along the lines laid down in *Smith*. Within a few months, cases began to appear all over the country in which the free exercise of religion was curtailed, if not prohibited, in ways that never would have been possible when the compelling state interest test was applied.[16] The bottom line of all this is that religious freedom in this country was, for a time, in extreme jeopardy. The majoritarianism/statism of the Reagan-Bush Court's decision in *Smith*, along with the growth of government, put religious freedom at significant risk.

After the *Smith* decision, the sense of alarm about its disastrous effects on religious freedom was shared by so many that, in response, the Religious Freedom Restoration Act (RFRA) was introduced into Congress. Its purpose was to restore the compelling state interest test as a principle of adjudicating laws. The proposed law required courts to compel the government, at whatever level, to demonstrate that it had a legitimate public-good interest of great importance that could be accomplished in no other way before it could curtail or prohibit religious activity by individuals or groups. Who would ever have thought the American people would have to petition Congress to restore what the founders of the country thought they had guaranteed through the Free Exercise Clause? But that was exactly the situation after Justice Scalia and four of his colleagues dismantled the clause in *Smith*. The bill had the support of religious groups from across the theological spectrum, including groups of the Christian Right. Even those who had supported Presidents Reagan and Bush and insisted that they appoint conservative jurists to the federal courts, and especially to the Supreme Court, were having second thoughts in the area of religious liberty, recognizing that the position taken by the Court in *Smith* was devastating to religious liberty in this country.

The Religious Freedom Restoration Act became law in November 1993.[17] Courts, including the Supreme Court, again were obligated to use the compelling state interest test when deciding Free Exercise Clause cases. Religious liberty was presumably secure again, but it was not clear how the Court would implement the mandate of RFRA, since justices who were willing to weaken this freedom were (and are) still on the Court.[18]

As described in chapter 4 and just above, with the passage of RFRA, things were far from settled in the free exercise arena. Some scholars began to write that *Smith* was not such a bad decision, after all, and some broached the theory that RFRA was unconstitutional. The Court took the opportunity to test that proposition in *Boerne v. Archbishop Flores*[19] and, indeed, found it unconstitutional as a violation of the concept of separation of powers. Many interpreters believed *Boerne* found RFRA unconstitutional as it applied to the states, but constitutional as it applied to the federal government.[20] Consequently, several state legislatures passed "state RFRAs" to give themselves the protection of the compelling interest test in free exercise disputes in their states.[21] As a result, free exercise law in the United States was in turmoil: with *Boerne*, the law had reverted to the *Smith* rule in the states, unless they had enacted state RFRAs, but not for the federal government's action in reference to free exercise disputes.

As a way to bring order out of this confusion, the RFRA coalition petitioned Congress to pass the Religious Land Use and Institutionalized Persons Act (RLUIPA).[22] This legislation was thought to be consistent with *Boerne* but still allowed the application of the compelling state interest test in limited areas of American free exercise of religion life by means of the Commerce Clause.[23] For example, in the institutionalized persons side of RLUIPA, Congress asserted its authority to regulate local and state prisons because Congress usually provides federal funding for them. On the land use side, zoning and land use matters often involve shipping building materials through interstate commerce, and the denial of building permits may affect interstate commerce. Consequently, Congress has power to assert its jurisdiction in these types of transactions.

However, as one might guess, RLUIPA was not without its detractors, especially since it relied on such a strained conception of congressional power. The criticism seemed to focus on the dimension of the law concerning institutionalized persons. Specifically, critics charged that RLUIPA violates the Establishment Clause. By lifting the burden on the free exercise of prisoners' religion (although RLUIPA does not exempt prisoners from the security and discipline needs of penal institutions), Congress treated religious prisoners differently from nonreligious prisoners, thus violating the no-establishment principle. Stated differently, by granting prisoners the right to expect prison authorities to show a compelling reason why they cannot accommodate prisoners' religious practices, the law endorses religion, which it may not do under the Establishment Clause. In late 2004 the Supreme Court granted certiorari to a case, *Cutter v. Wilkinson*[24] out of Ohio, to determine whether RLUIPA violates the Establishment Clause. Readers of this book should look at the Court's opinion in that case to see a further permutation on the interpretation of the Free Exercise Clause, all begun because of *Employment Division of Oregon v. Smith* in 1990.

THE ESTABLISHMENT CLAUSE AND ORIGINAL INTENT

The meaning and interpretation of the Establishment Clause is a flash point, as well, with the controversy centering on the "original intent" of the authors of the Constitution. Many strict constructionists believe that later generations can know the minds of those who wrote the Constitution and that judges should use this original intent in their interpretation of that document. Justice William Rehnquist (later chief justice) expressed this belief succinctly in 1985:

> The true meaning of the Establishment Clause can only be seen in its history. As drafters of our Bill of Rights, the Framers inscribed the principles that control today. Any deviation from their intentions frustrates the permanence of that Charter and will only lead to the type of unprincipled decisionmaking that has plagued our Establishment Clauses since *Everson*.[25]

Regarding the Establishment Clause, strict constructionists argue the founders intended only to prohibit the creation of a "national church." That is, all they intended with the no-establishment principle was to prohibit the government from picking one church or denomination to be the established church of the nation. The implication, then, is they did not intend strict separation, but rather wanted to create a system in which nondiscriminatory government aid to religion was permissible. From this it follows that government can aid religion, so long as it does so in an evenhanded way that does not show preference for one religion over another. To use terms mentioned earlier, this approach is "nonpreferentialism" or "accommodationism." In fact, according to this understanding, the government must affirmatively aid religion in order to avoid being hostile to it. This accommodationist view was articulated in 1984 by Chief Justice Burger in *Lynch v. Donnelly*:

> "It has never been thought either possible or desirable to enforce a regime of total separation. . . . " Nor does the Constitution require

complete separation of church and state; it affirmatively mandates accommodation, not merely tolerance, of all religions, and forbids hostility toward any. Anything less would require the "callous indifference" we have said was never intended by the Establishment Clause.[26]

This original intent concept was argued at length in 1985 by then-Justice William Rehnquist in his dissenting opinion in *Wallace v. Jaffree*. He summarized his argument as follows:

> The Framers intended the Establishment Clause to prohibit the designation of any church as a "national" one. The Clause was also designed to stop the Federal Government from asserting a preference for one religious denomination or sect over others. Given the "incorporation" of the Establishment Clause as against the States via the Fourteenth Amendment in *Everson*, States are prohibited as well from establishing a religion or discriminating between sects. As its history abundantly shows, however, nothing in the Establishment Clause requires government to be strictly neutral between religion and irreligion, nor does that Clause prohibit Congress or the States from pursuing legitimate secular ends through nondiscriminatory sectarian means.[27]

Based on this view, the concept of strict separation between church and state, so forcefully stated in *Everson v. Board of Education*, which had been the predominant view of the Court, is wrong. "The 'wall of separation between church and State' is a metaphor based on bad history, a metaphor which has proved useless as a guide to judging. It should be frankly and explicitly abandoned."[28]

I believe, however, that what is *really* "bad history" and wrong is the entire "original intent" viewpoint, with its accommodationist ramification. The attempt to discern the intent of the authors of the First Amendment (to take only the part of the Constitution most relevant to our study) is flawed, if for no other reason than that so many consented to its language. We know that some were enthusiastic supporters of adding the amendments to the Constitution as guarantees of fundamental rights to American citizens. Others, however, were philosophically opposed to a Bill of Rights but went along with the enterprise because otherwise some states might not have ratified the Constitution. Did enthusiastic advocates and reluctant supporters of the First Amendment have the same ideas in mind when they voted for it? We cannot know. Did all the members of the Constitutional Convention understand the terms "establishment" and "free exercise" in the same way? We cannot know.[29] An eminent scholar of the Constitution, Laurence Tribe, speaks directly to such questions:

The nagging doubt prompted by inquiries like these is that no collective body—be it the Congress or the Constitutional Convention or the aggregate of state legislatures—can really be said to have a *single*, ascertainable "purpose" or "intent." And even if such a mythical beast could be captured and examined, how relevant would it be to us today? Should the peculiar opinions held, and the particular applications envisioned, by men who have been dead for two centuries *always* trump contemporary insights into what the living Constitution means and ought to mean? . . . But the constitutional text is not enough—we need to search for, and explain our selection of, the *principles behind* the words.[30] (emphasis in original)

Interpretation of the Constitution cannot proceed on the basis of a slavish, literalistic reading of the text. But that does not mean that judges can decide anything they want. They are, after all, supposed to interpret the Constitution. But, as Professor Tribe says, the interpretation must express "the principles behind the words." What the Court must do is to find and apply the great, living truths of the Constitution.[31] One of those great truths is the idea that government is to be limited government.[32] But the principle of limited government argues against accommodationism. In the words of the constitutional scholar Leonard Levy:

Every bit of evidence goes to prove that the First Amendment, like the others, was intended to restrict Congress to its enumerated powers. Since the Constitutional Convention gave Congress no power to legislate on matters concerning religion, Congress had no such power even in the absence of the First Amendment. It is, therefore, unreasonable to believe that an express prohibition of power—"Congress shall make no law respecting an establishment of religion"—creates the power, previously non-existent, of supporting religion by aid to one or all religious groups. The Bill of Rights, as Madison said, was not framed "to imply powers not meant to be included in the enumeration."[33]

To say we cannot discern the intent of the Founders does not mean we have no clue about what they meant by their constitutional language. Professor Tribe is correct that modern interpretation must look for "the principles behind the words." That means we have to take the words seriously. A bit of historical work gives a good idea what the Founders meant (or did not mean) by the Establishment Clause. That is, we have historical tools that help us understand the words and principles behind them.

In chapter 2 we saw that not only did the founders believe in limited government, but they also were much aware of multiple establishments, because that system existed in several of the colonies. The historical fact is that they were familiar with the very same kind of nonpreferential, nondiscriminatory government aid to religion that Chief Justice Rehnquist and other accommodationists argue for. Indeed, three clearly nonpreferentialist proposals came before the Senate as the Congress hammered out the language of the religion amendment: "Congress shall make no law establishing one religious sect or society in preference to others, nor shall the rights of conscience be infringed." "Congress shall not make any law, infringing the rights of conscience, or establishing any Religious Sect or Society." "Congress shall make no law establishing any particular denomination of religion in preference to another, or prohibiting the free exercise thereof, nor shall the rights of conscience be infringed." They rejected all three of these! Then a conference committee of the Senate and House wrote the language adopted as the First Amendment, "Congress shall make *no law respecting* an establishment of religion. . . ."[34] The word "respecting" means "about," "concerning," or "regarding." They knew of nondiscriminatory aid for religion, but said "no law"! Therefore, based on history, the principle behind the Establishment Clause that must be applied to the present is that the government should refrain from extending itself into religion, neither hindering it *nor aiding it, even if that aid can be given in a nondiscriminatory, evenhanded way.* That is what the separation of church and state, no establishment, means. We cannot know that every person who signed the Constitution understood the words that way, but the history of language rejected and language adopted leads to that conclusion.

Just as there has been a conservative attack on the concept of separation, there has also been an attack on the "*Lemon* test,"[35] the method by which the Establishment Clause has been interpreted. Few doubt that the application of this three-part test has usually led to strict separationist decisions by the Court. It is also clear that these decisions have been opposed by those of a more accommodationist understanding of separation of church and state. Consequently, the conservative justices on the Court have tried to modify or even remove the test for interpreting the Establishment Clause. In *Marsh v. Chambers*, the legislative chaplains case, Chief Justice Burger refused to use the test in order to come down on the accommodationist side. Justice Rehnquist, in the "original intent" argument just reviewed, came to the conclusion that the three-part test should be abandoned.[36]

Justice Sandra Day O'Connor, who I believe has written the most thoughtful and creative church-state opinions of any of the justices during her time on the Court, concurred with the majority in *Lynch v. Donnelly*. She agreed with the constitutionality of the nativity scene, surrounded with secular symbols of the winter holiday season, on public property. In the process, she suggested a modification of the "*Lemon* test," that the function of the "secular purpose" part of the test is to inquire whether the government intends to convey a message of endorsement or disapproval of religion. The "primary effect" part of the test is to determine whether government action does actually communicate a message of endorsement or disapproval of religion. That is, the effects test is the inquiry into whether government has operated in such a way as to make religion relevant to an individual's or a group's status in the political community:

> The purpose prong of the *Lemon* test asks whether government's actual purpose is to endorse or disapprove of religion. The effect prong asks whether, irrespective of government's actual purpose, the practice under review in fact conveys a message of endorsement or disapproval. An affirmative answer to either question should render the challenged practice invalid. . . . Endorsement sends a message to nonadherents that they are outsiders, not full members of the political community, and an accompanying message to adherents that they are insiders, favored members of the political community. Disapproval sends the opposite message.[37]

The third part of the test, "excessive entanglement," tries to determine whether or not government has interfered with the independence of religious institutions, given religious groups access to government or government power to the exclusion of nonadherents to the religion, or created political alignments defined along religious lines.[38]

The effect of this reformulation of the "*Lemon* test" was to move somewhat toward accommodationism. Government could either advance or inhibit religion, so long as it did not intend to or actually endorse it or disapprove of it. Justice O'Connor's modification of the three-part test gained some favor on the Court. In fact, it was referred to with approval in the majority opinions in *Wallace v. Jaffree* and *Allegheny County v. ACLU of Pittsburgh*.[39]

But not all the justices were happy with Justice O'Connor's reformulation of the test.[40] Justice Anthony Kennedy, in a sharply worded dissent *in Allegheny County v. ACLU of Pittsburgh*, denounced both the original "*Lemon* test" and Justice O'Connor's restatement of it, strongly rejecting the latter. In Kennedy's view, both tests, as they had been applied, were too hostile to religion; they did not allow enough government accommodation of religion. The endorsement understanding of the test was totally unacceptable to him because it is too broad. Because it asks whether government practice makes nonadherents to a religion feel like outsiders in the political community, Kennedy said, few government acknowledgments of religions would not have that result. National days of prayer, the phrase "under God" in the Pledge of Allegiance, and the statement "In God We Trust" on our currency could surely make some feel like outsiders in the political community, yet all those are acceptable accommodations of religion.

What did Justice Kennedy propose as a proper test for interpreting the Establishment Clause to allow for the proper government accommodation of religion? One should look to American history. Since the founding of the nation, government has recognized the religious inclinations of the people in a variety of ways, such as those mentioned in the previous paragraph. The Establishment Clause must be interpreted to be sympathetic to that tradition:

> Whatever test we choose to apply must permit not only legitimate practices two centuries old but also any other practices with no greater potential for an establishment of religion. . . . A test for implementing the protections of the Establishment Clause that, if applied with consistency, would invalidate longstanding traditions cannot be a proper reading of the Clause.[41]

The test Justice Kennedy recommended to accomplish the proper government accommodation of religion has come to be called the "coercion test." Government may interact with religion in whatever way it chooses, so long as it does not coerce people to be religious or to adopt religious practices. The government may not tax the population to benefit a state-sponsored faith, exert direct compulsion to religious practice, or conduct "exhortation to religiosity that amounts in fact to proselytizing." The "bottom line" is, for Justice Kennedy,[42] that the only forbidden government actions are coercion to observance and direct benefits. Any other sort of government aid or abetment of religion is permitted. This is accommodationism with a vengeance.

Putting aside whether the Establishment Clause ought to be interpreted by the "*Lemon* test," its variation "endorsement test," or the completely separate "coercion test"—although this is a very important debate among the justices—let us return to the more fundamental problem of its original intent. After Justice Rehnquist articulated the basic accommodationist, nonpreferentialist position in his dissent in *Wallace v. Jaffree*, he seemed to lay it aside. That is not to suggest he changed his mind, but that he simply assumed its truth in the decisions he wrote or supported and did not feel the need to argue the point. Then Justice Clarence Thomas took up the cause. More than any other accommodationist justice since Justice Rehnquist's statement in 1985, Justice Thomas wrote in support of that position. In sometimes quite articulate ways he argued[43] that the founders intended the Establishment Clause to mean government should not favor one religion over another, should not establish a "national church." That means it is acceptable for government to aid religion with either money or favorable actions, so long as the aid can be distributed in a nondiscriminatory, evenhanded way, giving none preferential treatment (so, "nonpreferentialism"). This he described as "neutrality" in *Mitchell v. Helms*, his most accommodationist opinion. However, not even his accommodationist colleagues went so far as Justice Thomas's argument that the Establishment Clause should not apply to the states.[44] He believed the clause is a "federalism principle," that is, it was designed *only* to keep the national government out of the religious affairs of the states, but that it does not protect individual rights. Aside from that extreme view, however, Chief Justice Rehnquist and Justices Scalia, Kennedy, and O'Connor (usually) agreed with his general accommodationist position.

Justice Thomas's intellectual and conceptual sparring partner was Justice David Souter, who wrote equally powerful and persuasive opinions from the separationist perspective.[45] Justice Souter's understanding of the intent of the founders was essentially the same as I have argued in this chapter and consistent with Justice Hugo Black's famous comment in *Everson v. Board of Education* (see page 73). He believed "separation" meant just that: religion and civil authority should be separated as much as possible. This attitude was not motivated by hostility to religion, but because he believed separation of church and state stimulates the vitality of each. Because he was usually joined in his opinions by Justices Breyer, Ginsburg, and Stevens, the Court was deeply divided over the issue of the meaning and application of the Establishment Clause. Readers who want to get a sense of the debate between Justices Thomas and Souter should read their respective opinions in *Rosenberger v. University of Virginia*, where each states his position in considerable detail.

As I noted in chapters 7 and 8, the right of free speech has gobbled up the no-establishment principle. As Justice Byron White warned in his *Widmar v. Vincent* dissent, the Court has adopted the position that "religious worship *qua* speech is not different from any other variety of protected speech as a matter of constitutional principle." He predicted that if this were to happen, "the Religion Clauses would be emptied of any independent meaning in circumstances in which religious practice took the form of speech."[46] His prediction has come true.

Growing out of the concept of the "public forum," the Court has ruled that state entities must accommodate religious speech even if it means that government facilities must be used for religious purposes. Examples are *Capitol Square Review Board v. Pinette* (erecting a cross on public land) and *Good News Club v. Milford School District* (public school allowing religious club to meet in its rooms). Or government money must support religion, as in *Rosenberger v. University of Virginia* (university student activity fees must pay expenses of an evangelical Christian paper). In the legitimate desire to avoid viewpoint discrimination, the Court has not even balanced free speech against the no-establishment principle, but has simply ruled the former trumps the latter. To use Justice White's words, the Establishment Clause has been "emptied of any independent meaning": it is a mere shadow of its former self, and the state has become much more intrusive into religion, in the sense that it has become religion's patron when religious speech is involved. How this cozy relationship can be harmful to religion is suggested by the analogy of John Leland, an eighteenth-century Baptist minister:

> Experience . . . has informed us, that the fondness of magistrates to foster Christianity, has done it more harm than all the persecutions ever did. Persecution, like a lion, tears the saints to death, but leaves Christianity pure: state establishment of religion, like a bear, hugs the saints, but corrupts Christianity.[47]

Of course, the same principle is true for any religion, not just Christianity.

In reference to the Establishment Clause, *Zelman v. Simmons-Harris* seems to encapsulate the Court's different approaches. The majority opinion by Chief Justice Rehnquist was built on formalism rather than substance. That is, he decided the case in terms of how many different kinds of schools were included in the program and the fact that private choice dictated where the government money would go. But he never addressed the issue that the Establishment Clause is to prevent government from either promoting or hindering religion, a particularly important concern in reference to parochial schools.

What is a parochial school other than an institution that exists to teach religion? Although it teaches reading, writing, and arithmetic, it also teaches religion—and from a denominational or sectarian perspective. (It also may teach the secular subjects from a religious perspective. See Justice William O. Douglas's dissent in *Board of Education v. Allen*.[48]) Public schools may teach religion,[49] so long as it is taught as part of the regular curriculum and is not designed to elicit faith judgments on the part of students or to disparage any religion. But parochial schools are rightly not under any such restrictions. They may teach the theology of their sponsoring religious organization and do so to nurture faith, and the Court has formally recognized that. For example, in *Lemon v. Kurtzman*, the Court in 1971 said of the Catholic schools at issue in that government aid case:

> The schools are governed by the standards set forth in a "Handbook of School Regulations," which has the force of synodal law in the diocese. It emphasizes the role and importance of the teacher in the parochial schools: "The prime factor for the success or failure of the school is the spirit and personality, as well as the professional competency, of the teacher. . . ." The Handbook also states that: "Religious formation is not confined to formal courses; nor is it restricted to a single subject area." Finally, the Handbook advises teachers to stimulate interest in religious vocations and missionary work. Given the mission of the church school, these instructions are consistent and logical. . . .

> The teacher is employed by a religious organization, subject to the
> direction and discipline of religious authorities, and works in a system
> *dedicated to rearing children in a particular faith.*[50] (emphasis added)

Without denying the right of such schools to exist or disparaging the contribution they make in children's lives or to the society as a whole, government money ought not be paying for, undergirding, supporting that kind of instruction. The Court has been able to find such programs constitutional in cases like *Zelman* and *Mitchell v. Helms* only by focusing on the formal or procedural issues.

But the dissenters in *Zelman* in 2002 seemed to be returning to first principles of the Establishment Clause. Justice John Paul Stevens, for example, made just the point of the previous paragraph, observing that parochial schools are sectarian schools, and government money that enables students to go there facilitates sectarian education.[51] Justice Stephen Breyer similarly noted that parochial schools are about the business of nurturing faith and teaching theological truth as the sponsoring church understands it; and the Establishment Clause demands that the state should not fund religious education. But Justice Breyer took his argument in a different direction and challenged one of the basic assumptions of accommodationism, the idea that government aid to religion must be available in an evenhanded, nonpreferential way. He argued that the founders believed the no-establishment principle would minimize religious contentiousness in American society. When government aided religion, the various groups would compete with each other to get the government's attention and to make sure they got their fair share (if not more). Consequently, there was the potential for religious conflict.[52] But the religious diversity of the late eighteenth century was nothing like the dizzying array of religions in contemporary society. This extreme religious pluralism makes it virtually impossible for government to give equal treatment to all in the distribution of government resources. Some groups may be more aggressive or effective advocates in their appeals for funding. Government officials dispensing the largesse may be more favorably disposed toward some religions than others, in spite of official policy. Justice Breyer concluded:

> The upshot is the development of constitutional doctrine that reads
> the Establishment Clause as avoiding religious strife, *not* by providing
> every religion with an *equal opportunity* (say, to secure state funding or
> to pray in the public schools), but by drawing fairly clear lines of *separation* between church and state—at least where the heartland of religious belief, such as primary religious education, is at issue.[53]
> (emphasis in original)

Parental choice, the centerpiece of most of the aid decisions, does not help avoid uneven treatment or religious conflict:

> Parental choice cannot help the taxpayer who does not want to finance the religious education of children. It will not always help the parent who may see little real choice between inadequate nonsectarian public education and adequate education at a school whose religious teachings are contrary to his own. It will not satisfy religious minorities unable to participate because they are too few in number to support the creation of their own private schools. It will not satisfy groups whose religious beliefs preclude them from participating in a government-sponsored program, and who may well feel ignored as government funds primarily support the education of children in the doctrines of the dominant religions. And it does little to ameliorate the entanglement problems or the related problems of social division. . . . Consequently, the fact that the parent may choose which school can cash the government's voucher check does not alleviate the Establishment Clause concerns associated with voucher programs.[54]

Justice Breyer's recitation of the flaws in the concept of individual, private choice did not mention the most basic one, namely, that its possibility is created by government. When programs were created so that government money was available to secular and religious recipients alike, without any government payment to any entity except individuals, such as parents or disabled persons, government money flowed to religious entities because of private, independent choice. The Court said that result could not be attributed to the government. That is just wrong. In every one of the cases that hinges on individual choice, legislation made the choice possible. When a legislative body creates a program where secular and religious entities alike receive government funds, government creates the situation that allows free choice to have that consequence.

The decision of the Court in *Santa Fe Independent School District v. Doe* (chapter 7) helps make the point. The school board, in order to create the impression the football game prayers were at the initiative of students, established an election policy. The board said to the students, "You *will* have elections." The government created student choice.[55] So also with legislative programs that purport to distribute government funds to secular and religious recipients alike. They say to students and/or parents, "You *will* have a choice." *Witters v. Washington Department of Services for the Blind* and *Zobrest v. Catalina School District* concerned situations where the state had created a program for vocational rehabilitation for the disabled. The state was as surprised as anyone when Witters chose to use his money for ministerial education or Zobrest's parents requested the sign language interpreter in a Catholic school. But in educational aid programs such as those at issue in *Mueller v. Allen, Mitchell v. Helms*, and *Zelman v. Simmons-Harris*, by stipulating that government money will go to both public and private schools, the legislative body knows full well that money will go to sectarian institutions. The government is a player in that result, in spite of the fiction in the cases just mentioned that it is not. That is contrary to the intent of the no-establishment principle.

In the 1990s and early 2000s, church-state issues permeated American society. While many of these did not relate to Supreme Court decisions, they were ripe for attention from the Court. Principal among these was the idea of "charitable choice" or "faith-based initiatives," which involved government money supporting the charitable activities of religious institutions.

The idea of government money, federal, state, or local, supporting the charitable activities of religiously related organizations is not new. For years organizations such as Catholic Charities and United Jewish Communities have received government funds. But they were required to be legally separate from the sponsoring religious organization, and they could not impose religion on their clients. They could say to clients, "We are Catholic Charities (for example), and we have a religiously motivated desire to help you," but they could not go beyond that in exposing their clients to theology or worship.

In 1994, when the Republicans gained control of Congress, two of their goals were to downsize the federal government and reduce the number of people on welfare. The Welfare Reform Act of 1996 accomplished the latter and contributed to the former. Embedded within this huge law was a section that changed the rules for how religious, "faith-based" organizations could receive government money. To oversimplify considerably, they no longer had to be legal entities separate from a religious group or denomination, and they no longer had to sacrifice their religious identity. That is, the charitable services, financed by government money, could be offered in buildings with religious symbols and operate as religious ministries with conversion on their minds. Although the law specified that religious charities receiving government funds were not supposed to proselytize or deny clients of a different faith or no religious faith, the language was ambiguous enough that many were not sure of the boundaries.

When George W. Bush became president, he continued at the national level what he had started while governor of Texas. He established an office of faith-based initiatives, with a full-time director, in the White House and later extended satellite offices in most of the cabinet-level departments of the government. The idea was that religious organizations that had some experience in providing charitable services could apply to the office for funding; if they were approved, they would receive government money (there was not supposed to be a theological litmus test, but many wondered if conservative Christian groups from the President's "political base" would receive preferential treatment). Congress refused to pass legislation to fund the enterprise for a variety of reasons, not least of which was that many members believed it crossed the line of church-state separation. One could hardly think of a more glaring example of "excessive entanglement," which the Court for many years said violated the Establishment Clause, than this government support of religious charities. When Congress refused to appropriate money, the president released money for the program through executive order. He was dedicated to the concept, for in many ways it was the centerpiece of the "compassionate conservatism" by which he characterized his administration.[56]

Some in Congress believed the plan violated the Establishment Clause. This apprehension was shared by many in the religious communities—but not all. Many are interested in this commingling of church and state because of the allure of money. Many clergy supported charitable choice because of its inherent appeal, expressed in Cuba Gooding Jr.'s famous words, "Show me the money."[57] Forgetting the admonition of 1 Timothy 6:10, "For the love of money is a root of all kinds of evil," many support charitable choice because they have been seduced by the idea of receiving government money to do their charitable activities.

In addition to the general unease by separationists that the faith-based charitable program violated the separation of church and state, a more specific problem bothered some both in government and out. In chapter 5 I described how the law allows religious groups to discriminate in hiring on the basis of religion, for both religious and nonreligious jobs. The Court saw no constitutional problem with that in *Church of Jesus Christ of Latter-day Saints v. Amos.* But in those circumstances, the discriminating institutions were explicitly private, and no government money was involved. With charitable choice, that scenario changed. Religious organizations were still discriminating in employment on the basis of religion (which they must have the right to do), but now they were getting government money. It was the first time programs receiving government money were allowed to discriminate in hiring. Many argued this was a clear violation of Title VII of the Civil Rights Act of 1964, not to mention the Establishment Clause (nonreligious groups are generally not allowed to discriminate in hiring). Of course, the easiest and most obvious answer to this dilemma is to not give government money to religious organizations, except under the rules that existed prior to 1996.

Finally, an obvious problem among the many that inhere in the faith-based initiative enterprise is that the program has the practical effect of muzzling religious groups in their relation to the society. In a meeting I attended about charitable choice,

> a Presbyterian minister said, "It surely will compromise the churches' will and courage to criticize the government." And I thought, "That's it. That is the basic problem. That is the fundamental difficulty with this and with any other way the churches get too cozy with the government." Whenever the church comes under the influence of the

state, when it becomes an extension of the state, when it becomes a
tool of the state, its prophetic ministry is compromised. It no longer
has the independence to "speak truth to power."[58]

At the time this is being written in November 2004, none of the problems
mentioned here has been resolved. Furthermore, it is not clear that any cases
are in progress so the Supreme Court can someday test the constitutionality
of charitable choice.

In chapter 7 I noted that the Court, in 1980, declared the posting of the Ten
Commandments in public school classrooms to be unconstitutional in *Stone v.
Graham*. That issue lay relatively dormant for a while, but as the nation seemed
to become more concerned about immorality in society, some began to think
that displaying the Ten Commandments, not only in public schools, but in all
sorts of public buildings and spaces, would improve morality. In one notable
incident, Judge Roy Moore of Alabama insisted on displaying the Ten Commandments in his courtroom. Although his action was legally challenged,
Judge Moore persisted. He ran for the position of Chief Justice of the Alabama
Supreme Court as the "Ten Commandments candidate" and was elected in a
landslide. Shortly thereafter he had a 5,200-pound stone monument with the
Ten Commandments etched on it placed in the lobby of the Alabama Judicial
Building. A federal district court, on Establishment Clause grounds, ordered
him to remove the monument. He refused—and the story made national headlines. When the court had the monument removed, earnest believers (in both
the Ten Commandments and Roy Moore) rallied on his behalf. Finally, Judge
Moore was removed by Alabama legal authority from his position on the state
Supreme Court. He asked the U.S. Supreme Court to review his case. It did
not. The Roy Moore affair gave huge visibility, in a bizarre sort of way, to the
idea of positioning the Ten Commandments on public property.

The strongest impetus to put the Ten Commandments in government
spaces was born of tragedy. On April 20, 1999, two students at Columbine High
School in Colorado took an arsenal of weapons into the school and murdered
or wounded many students and teachers. The nation was shocked and bewil-
dered. What could be done to prevent this in the future? One reaction was the
"Ten Commandments Defense Act," rooted in the idea that the public display
of the Ten Commandments would improve morality in the country.[59]

After that, state legislatures and city councils engaged in a frenzy of legislation authorizing posting the Commandments, in a variety of forms, in courthouses, city halls, public schools, and public parks. In late 2004 the Supreme
Court agreed to hear two Ten Commandments cases, to be argued and decided
in 2005. One is *Van Orden v. Perry*,[60] about whether having a Ten Command-

ments monument, surrounded by several secular monuments, on the Texas state capitol grounds is constitutional. The other is *McCreary County v. ACLU*,[61] about Ten Commandments displays in two Kentucky county courthouses. Readers of this book should look at the Court's opinion in those cases to see if the decisions of this more accommodationist Court are consistent with its Ten Commandments decision of 1980.

Also not directly related to a Supreme Court decision, but very much part of the church-state scene in the early twenty-first century, is an attack on "Blaine amendments" in the various states. The term comes from the nineteenth century. Two of the dominant social movements of that century were immigration and the growth of the public school. As described in chapter 6, these two movements coalesced over the issue of government aid for Catholic schools. Believing the public schools were teaching a kind of generic Protestantism, Catholics began their own schools. But because they believed their schools contributed to society and because of their huge expense, many Catholics agitated for government aid. Many states resisted that appeal; some legislators were anti-Catholic, some believed in strict separation of church and state, and some simply thought it would be too expensive for the state to begin supporting more schools.

In 1875 President Ulysses S. Grant advocated a constitutional amendment that would prohibit government money from supporting sectarian schools and would remove all sectarianism from public schools. There is evidence that even some Catholics approved the proposal. An amendment, introduced into the House of Representatives by James G. Blaine of Maine, included only half of Grant's proposal, a ban on tax aid to religious schools. Some accused Blaine of anti-Catholicism, but apparently he believed the Establishment Clause prohibited government aid to parochial schools. He wanted to extend this to the states, which was the real thrust of the language of his proposal. He also seems to have had the political motive of giving Republicans some luster again after the scandals of the Grant administration.[62] At any rate, the proposed amendment never made it out of Congress.

Many state legislatures, however, passed their own versions of the Blaine amendment, although Representative Blaine never took part in any of these actions. In fact, he died before some of the states amended their constitutions. All of these amendments contained the language prohibiting tax aid to religious schools. Some of them also embraced the ban on sectarian religion in public schools, from which Catholics and minority religions have benefited.[63]

Currently thirty-seven states have Blaine amendments in their constitutions. Now that the Supreme Court has emasculated the Establishment Clause through its nonpreferentialism and concepts of private choice, the enemies of separation of church and state hope to remove the Blaine amendments in those states that have them. This effort has become a high priority among those who support vouchers as a way to allow government money to support parochial schools. After the Supreme Court held vouchers to be constitutional in *Zelman v. Simmons-Harris*, the battlegrounds shifted to Blaine amendment states, because as long as these amendments stand, they blunt the effect of *Zelman*. That is, *Zelman* notwithstanding, if a state constitution blocks voucher-type programs, they cannot proceed. Opponents of the Blaine amendments have couched their attack in terms of their anti-Catholic origins. Although some "Blaine legislators" may have been motivated by prejudice, that was then. This is now. The anti-Catholic claim is diversionary, a way to mask the efforts to undo these state constitutional provisions so Americans will have to support religious schools with their tax money. The Blaine amendments stand for the good truth the Establishment Clause enacted before the Court began to dismantle it in the 1980s. Long may they endure! The assault on them may have been somewhat arrested by the rather surprising decision of *Locke v. Davey* (chapter 6), in which the Court upheld the Blaine amendment in Washington state by holding that government money could not be used for college programs in "devotional theology."

IMPLICATIONS

Readers at this point are likely asking themselves, "Who cares?" or, "All this is just lawyer squabbles, or the bloviations of a grumpy scholar. What difference does it make?" It makes considerable difference. From both the free-exercise and establishment sides, religious freedom is under serious attack; it is in grave danger. Presidents Reagan and George H. W. Bush encouraged the Christian Right, appointed Supreme Court justices who placed religious freedom at risk by relegating the Free Exercise Clause virtually to the ash heap and by eviscerating the separation of church and state with various accommodationist schemes. What is so wrong with the government's aiding religion? Surely religion is a good thing for the welfare of the American people, and for the government to give it aid and comfort cannot hurt and might help. There are several answers why government aid to religion is a bad idea.

The phrase "aid and comfort" can help elucidate the problems with government aid to religion. The Constitution mandates that government should and must give comfort to religion. The Free Exercise Clause requires that government must allow religion the maximum amount of freedom. This freedom does not include the right to act contrary to the public good, in ways that would be harmful to persons, groups, or the society as a whole. But freedom of religion means that religious individuals or groups have the right to worship, evangelize, try to influence public opinion on matters of civic importance, aid the hurting, comfort the sorrowing, and so on, in ways consistent with their theology. How can the government best give "comfort" to these religious activities? By keeping its distance from religion. By not trying to aid religion. When government sets out to accommodate[64] religion, religion usually suffers, in a variety of ways.

First, when government gives money, government control is not far behind. That is the way it should be. Government at whatever level should expect some accountability in the use of its resources. But if government money is given to religious institutions, even in a nondiscriminatory way to agencies sponsored by a variety of religious groups, then the religious institutions find themselves under government supervision. Since World War II, one of the facts of life in America has been the expansion of government. Government is big and getting bigger, both in terms of the regulations it imposes on Americans and in the number of government employees enforcing the regulations. Consequently, there is likely to be rather significant government intrusiveness into those programs in which government money is involved, including religious programs. Those who support the idea of government aid for religion invite that government involvement. They should ask themselves whether they really want government telling them how to operate their religious enterprises.

An example of such government intervention is found in *Zelman v. Simmons-Harris*. The law that created the voucher program to give students opportunities different from those in public schools prohibits participating private schools from discriminating on the basis of religion. In order to get government money, parochial schools have to obey the government about the composition of their student bodies. Suppose a school wants to be an exclusively Jewish (or Muslim, Catholic, Wiccan, or Lutheran) school? It cannot, if it is to participate in the program. The government says so![65] Are churches and related institutions willing to submit to the government regulation that is always appended to government aid?

A second result when a faith-based group seeks government aid or sponsorship is the trivialization of religion. Under our system, government may not sponsor sectarian or denominational religion. Consequently, when groups seek public funds, they have to divest themselves of sectarian or even distinctively religious characteristics.[66] This has the effect of compromising their religion for the purpose of gaining the public aid and/or sponsorship they desire. Five examples come to mind.

In *McGowan v. Maryland* and *Braunfeld v. Brown* (chapter 8) Christians might have considered it a victory when the Court decided it was constitutional for states to have Sunday closing laws if they chose. But one should remember the Court was able to reach that decision only by declaring the laws were now devoid of religious meaning, in spite of their clearly theological content at the time of their origin. That is, the laws could stand only because they were completely secularized! This was no victory for Christian theology, even though churches did and do indirectly benefit from the fact that some of their members do not have to be at work on Sunday mornings.

Similarly, one thinks of the issues of religious symbols on public property, litigated in *Lynch v. Donnelly* and *Allegheny County v. ACLU of Pittsburgh* (chapter 8). The Court decided that religious symbols on public property did not violate the Establishment Clause, but only because they were surrounded by other paraphernalia that were not distinctively religious—the "plastic reindeer rule." Furthermore, Christmas, the holiday that caused the religious symbols to be placed on public ground, was described as a festive season, a winter holiday season devoid of any specifically religious content. The problem with that was rather flamboyantly expressed by Russell H. Dilday Jr., then president of Southwestern Baptist Theological Seminary, in a speech to the Southern Baptist Convention.

> Call on Big Brother in Washington to help you witness and worship, and Big Brother will trivialize your Lord, sanctioning his sacred birth as nothing more than a folk festival, giving Bethlehem's manger no more significance than Rudolf's red nose. Ask the Supreme Court to endorse your Christian faith, and they will relegate the virgin-born Jesus, the only begotten of the Father, the King of Kings and Lord of Lords, to the company of Santa Claus, Frosty the Snowman and Alvin the Caroling Chipmunk.[67]

Western Maryland College, a Methodist school, was one of the colleges involved in *Roemer v. Board of Public Works of Maryland*,[68] a case about state aid to church-related colleges. Apparently the college thought it might lose its state funds if the state lost this case, so it completely withdrew from Methodist sponsorship, that is, it completely secularized itself, so that it would be eligible for state funds, no matter how the case came out.[69] The majority opinion upheld the constitutionality of the law granting state funds to the church schools consistently with *Tilton v. Richardson* (chapter 6). Justice John Paul Stevens wrote a short dissent, one sentence of which is particularly pertinent: "I would add emphasis to the pernicious tendency of a state subsidy to tempt religious schools to compromise their religious mission without wholly abandoning it."[70] Western Maryland College *did* wholly abandon its religious identity in its desire to receive state funds.

Another example of this same phenomenon is the change of policy by Liberty University, founded and headed by Jerry Falwell. From its inception, the university was clearly based on conservative theology and was pervasively religious. As part of that distinctively Christian character, both students and faculty had to adhere to explicitly fundamentalist doctrine, faculty were not allowed to publish anything that did not meet the approval of the school's administration, and students were required to attend chapel or church six times a week. But those charged with administering Virginia's Tuition Aids Grant Program, which provided state aid to students attending Liberty, threatened to withdraw those funds on the grounds that a program that discriminated on the basis of religion did not fit the state's college aid law. At that point, Liberty changed its policy and discontinued basing the admission of students and the hiring of faculty on their adherence to a theological position, agreed to grant academic freedom to professors, and ended mandatory chapel for students.[71] Once again, the desire and need for state funds diluted the religious mission and distinctiveness of an institution.

In the heyday of the Christian Right's efforts to get "balanced treatment" laws passed so "creation science" would be taught in public schools any time evolution was taught, it introduced such a law in Arkansas. (See the discussion of *McLean v. Arkansas* in chapter 7.) When the law was challenged in court, Arkansas submitted a pretrial brief to the court, laying out its case. A passage from the brief shows how much the traditional Christian concept of God had been disposed of in order to try to make creationism winnable in court:

> There is nothing inherently religious about the terms "creator" or "creation," as used in the context of Act 590. Act 590 is concerned with a non-religious conception of "creation" and "creator," not the religious concepts dealt with in the Bible or religious writings. . . . Assuming *arguendo* that a "creator" and "creation" are consistent with some religions, this does not make them inherently religious. The entity which caused the creation hypothesized in creation-science is far, far away from any conception of a god or deity. All that creation-science requires is that the entity which caused creation have power, intelligence, and a sense of design. There are no attributes of the personality generally associated with a deity, nor is there necessarily present in the creator any love, compassion, sense of justice, or concern for any individuals. Indeed, under creation-science as defined in Act 590, there is no requirement that the entity which caused creation still be in existence.[72]

Christians, Jews, and Muslims with any sense of what their religion is about should be offended by that. One wonders how many fundamentalist Christians are aware of how much had to be given up to try to defend the inclusion of creation science into the public schools by law.

A third problem with asking the government to aid religion is that every taxpayer is consequently required to pay for what he or she does not believe. One may respond that this happens all the time. Taxpayers may not believe in public education, or air traffic controllers, or a public highway system, or standing armies, but they still have to pay for them. But the difference is that in the area of religion, constitutional principles are involved. The Establishment Clause guarantees Americans freedom of conscience to believe or disbelieve as they choose and to be free from government-mandated funding of the advancement of religion different from their own or of any religion. Thomas Jefferson said it best, in his famous "Bill for Establishing Religious Freedom," which became law in Virginia in 1786 and was one of the principal influences on the writing of the First Amendment:

> [T]o compel a man to furnish contributions of money for the propagation of opinions which he disbelieves, is sinful and tyrannical; that even the forcing him to support this or that teacher of his own religious persuasion, is depriving him of the comfortable liberty of giving his contributions to the particular pastor whose morals he would make his pattern, and whose powers he feels most persuasive to righteousness.[73]

Requiring a person to support a minister (or religious institution) with whom (or which) that person agrees, much less one with which he or she disagrees, is to deprive that person of the freedom to support religion as conscience guides. An example, of course, of requiring someone to pay for that which they disbelieve is government aid to parochial schools. The Court has repeatedly made the observation that what distinguishes a church-related school from a public school is its religious content and mission. Why do religious schools exist, particularly at the elementary and secondary level? They exist primarily to propagate the religious views of the sponsoring church. They have the constitutional right to do that (*Pierce v. Society of Sisters*; see chapter 6). But to require taxpayers of any or no religion to pay for the propagating of those religious beliefs through programs of government aid is "sinful and tyrannical," in Jefferson's words, because the program demands that they pay for what they disbelieve. So, programs of government aid, accommodation, deprive the religious institutions receiving the aid of freedom from government supervision and deprive the taxpayers of the constitutionally guaranteed right to be free from coercion in matters of religion.

Fourth, accommodation leads to the irrelevance of the church—or synagogue, mosque, or shrine. What happens if government promotes religion in public life? Government may well take over some of the functions of religious institutions. Charitable choice, President George W. Bush's faith-based initiative, comes to mind immediately. The more government does the work of the church, the less relevant the church is in our society. Of course, the classic example is prayer in the public schools. Not only does the requirement of nonsectarian prayer trivialize religion in the manner of the "To whom it may concern" prayer of *Engel v. Vitale*, but it requires the public school to assume one of the principal activities of the church: prayer and worship. That clearly is a violation of the Establishment Clause, as the Court said in *Abington Township School District v. Schempp*. But more to the point here, it makes the church increasingly irrelevant as an institution. I do not understand why many church leaders, not to mention innumerable laypeople, particularly among the Christian Right, insist on a constitutional amendment to require "voluntary" group prayer in public schools.[74] Many of them wonder why the church is not so important in people's lives as it used to be, why secularism seems to be invading the church itself. Yet in the next breath they will ask the government to take over the work of the church in terms of prayer, government-financed religious education, or government-supported charitable activity, thereby marginalizing the church. Government accommodation and promotion of religion is the enemy of a vibrant, creative church.

What is wrong with government aid to religion? I have tried to argue that several things are wrong with it. All of this has been from the Establishment Clause side of the religious freedom issue. Those justices of the Supreme Court who argue the accommodationist position, either from the "original intent," the "result of individual choice," or from the "practices of history" perspective, apparently are doing so out of sympathy for the role of religion in American life. I believe that if this accommodationism is successful, it will not help religion; it will have the opposite effect. One thinks of the question, "If one has friends like this, who needs enemies?" Religious freedom in our time is in great peril.

From the Free Exercise Clause side, the decision in *Employment Division of Oregon v. Smith*, eliminating the "compelling state interest test" and shunting the Free Exercise Clause to the position of being the most minimal of constitutional freedoms, has seriously endangered religious freedom. In free-exercise disputes between government and religious individuals or groups, no level of government has to show any longer that it has a legitimate interest of great importance before it can interfere with the religious behavior at issue. The Free Exercise Clause cannot be used to adjudicate laws of general application unless it is used in tandem with some other First Amendment principle or if a law targets religious behavior only. This great freedom, which has contributed mightily to make this nation so attractive to residents and foreigners alike, was eviscerated by the Supreme Court of the United States. The exceptions to these generalizations are in zoning and the rights of prisoners cases, protected by the Religious Land Use and Institutionalized Persons Act, designed to blunt the impact of *Smith* in those two areas.[75] They are indicative of an attitude abroad in the land (and among some justices still on the Court), which should remind those who cherish religious freedom of the wisdom of the maxim that "eternal vigilance is the price of liberty."

The claim is often made by accommodationists, especially those from the Christian Right, that separation of church and state is hostile to religion. Just the opposite is true. Strict separation is not hostile to religion; strict separation is necessary for religious freedom. The religion clauses of the Constitution demand that government remain distant from religion so religion may flourish. Separation prevents government from meddling in matters of religion. It guarantees the free exercise of religion. Separation is better for the government and better for religion. It is better for government because it prevents government from assuming roles it was not intended to serve, such as involving itself in matters of conscience, persons' relationship with what they perceive as the Divine, and finding meaning for life. It is better for government because it reminds government of its limited nature. Separation is better for religion because it allows religion to grow and prosper as it will, dependent only on its own vitality and persuasiveness.

To those who insist that accommodationism is the best way to understand the relationship between church and state in this country, I close with three statements, two of which echo each other. The first is from James Madison, when he was arguing against the bill that would support the Christian religion in Virginia through a government tax:

> It [the bill] is moreover to weaken in those who profess this Religion a pious confidence in its innate excellence and the patronage of its Author; and to foster in those who still reject it, a suspicion that its friends are too conscious of its fallacies, to trust it to its own merits.[76]

The second statement is from Justice Robert Jackson:

> It is possible to hold a faith with enough confidence to believe that what should be rendered to God does not need to be decided and collected by Caesar.[77]

The third is from Justice John Paul Stevens's dissent in *Zelman v. Simmons-Harris*:

> Whenever we remove a brick from the wall that was designed to separate religion and government, we increase the risk of religious strife and weaken the foundation of our democracy.[78]

Epilogue

For the last several years the Court has handed down at least one church-state case a year, sometimes as many as three or four. Given the heat of this topic, I anticipate this activity by the Court will continue. The church-state relationship, even if confined to Supreme Court decisions, is a moving target and a "growth industry." By having read this far, you have been exposed to most of the major issues and the procedures the Court uses to arrive at its decisions. You are better equipped to understand decisions that may come down from the Court in the future. Search out the best information available to you, and keep up with what the Court does. Some of the journals listed in the bibliography may be helpful. I hope you have become a better-informed consumer of information about the Court and the decisions it makes. I also hope this book has given you greater appreciation for our great heritage of religious liberty.

Is the Supreme Court godless or not? As in so many things in life, even important things, the answer must be that it depends on to whom you talk. Multitudes, particularly those on the political and theological right, believe it is a godless Court. They see its decisions upholding a strict separation between church and state as being somehow harmful to religion. Those with this view have been encouraged by the accommodationist tendencies of the Court in the last twenty years. I believe there is much to fear in this trend. I argued in chapter 9 that in its accommodationist decisions, the Court has put religion in the greatest danger, the danger of being either corrupted by too close association with the state or destroyed by too much deference to the state.

Of course, neither answer to the question is completely true. The Court, by its very nature, is neither godly nor godless. It is, rather, an institution of a secular state. To say the American system of government is secular is not to slander it, even from a conservative Christian perspective. It is instead to argue that the founders showed the greatest respect for religion by mandating that it should be neither an enemy of the state nor a servant of the state. Believing in the inalienable rights of human beings, they created a system of government by which those rights could be actualized. Among those was the right to respond to what one perceived to be the Divine if one chose to and as one chose to, without interference from the powers of government. The Supreme Court has the responsibility to maintain that relationship between church and state, a relationship by which the state maintains the most benevolent attitude toward religion by keeping its distance from it. That may appear to some to be "godlessness," but in reality it is the best for religion in all the forms it has taken in the fertile minds of men and women. As Justice Hugo Black wrote in *Engel v. Vitale*, the separation of church and state

> stands as an expression of principle on the part of the Founders of our Constitution that religion is too personal, too sacred, too holy, to permit its "unhallowed perversion" by a civil magistrate.[1]

Amen and Amen.

Appendix A

Memorial and Remonstrance against Religious Assessments / (1785) To the Honorable the General Assembly of the Commonwealth of Virginia, A Memorial and Remonstrance*

We, the subscribers, citizens of the said Commonwealth, having taken into serious consideration, a Bill printed by order of the last Session of General Assembly, entitled "A Bill establishing a provision for Teachers of the Christian Religion" and conceiving that the same, if finally armed with the sanctions of a law, will be a dangerous abuse of power, are bound as faithful members of a free State, to remonstrate against it, and to declare the reasons by which we are determined. We remonstrate against the said Bill,

1. Because we hold it for a fundamental and undeniable truth, "that Religion or the duty which we owe to our Creator and the Manner of discharging it, can be directed only by reason and conviction, not by force or violence." The Religion then of every man must be left to the conviction and conscience of every man; and it is the right of every man to exercise it as these may dictate. This right is in its nature an unalienable right. It is unalienable; because the opinions, of men, depending only on the evidence contemplated by their own minds, cannot follow the dictates of other men: It is unalienable also; because what is here a right towards men, is a duty towards the Creator. It is the duty of every man to render to the Creator such homage, and such only, as he believes to be acceptable to him. This duty is precedent both in order of time and degree of obligation, to the claims of Civil Society. Before any man can be considered as a member of Civil Society, he must be considered as a subject of the Governor of the Universe: And if a member of Civil Society, who enters into any subordinate Association, must always do it with a

---

*Written by James Madison. Quoted in *Everson v. Board of Education* 330 U.S. 1 at 63–72 (footnotes omitted).

reservation of his duty to the general authority; much more must every man who becomes a member of any particular Civil Society, do it with a saving of his allegiance to the Universal Sovereign. We maintain therefore that in matters of Religion, no man's right is abridged by the institution of Civil Society, and that Religion is wholly exempt from its cognizance. True it is, that no other rule exists, by which any question which may divide a Society, can be ultimately determined, but the will of the majority; but it is also true, that the majority may trespass on the rights of the minority.

2. Because if religion be exempt from the authority of the Society at large, still less can it be subject to that of the Legislative Body. The latter are but the creatures and vicegerents of the former. Their jurisdiction is both derivative and limited: it is limited with regard to the coordinate departments, more necessarily is it limited with regard to the constituents. The preservation of a free government requires not merely, that the metes and bounds which separate each department of power may be invariably maintained; but more especially, that neither of them be suffered to overleap the great Barrier which defends the rights of the people. The Rulers who are guilty of such an encroachment, exceed the commission from which they derive their authority, and are Tyrants. The People who submit to it are governed by laws made neither by themselves, nor by an authority derived from them, and are slaves.

3. Because, it is proper to take alarm at the first experiment on our liberties. We hold this prudent jealousy to be the first duty of citizens, and one of [the] noblest characteristics of the late Revolution. The freemen of America did not wait till usurped power had strengthened itself by exercise, and entangled the question in precedents. They saw all the consequences in the principle, and they avoided the consequences by denying the principle. We revere this lesson too much, soon to forget it. Who does not see that the same authority which can establish Christianity, in exclusion of all other Religions, may establish with the same ease any particular sect of Christians in exclusion of all other Sects? That the same authority which can force a citizen to contribute three pence only of his property for the support of any one establishment, may force him to conform to any other establishment in all cases whatsoever?

4. Because, the bill violates that equality which ought to be the basis of every law, and which is more indispensable, in proportion as the validity or expediency of any law is more liable to be impeached. If "all men are by nature equally free and independent," all men are to be considered as entering into society on equal conditions; as relinquishing no more, and therefore retaining no less, one than another, of their natural rights. Above all are they to be considered as retaining an "*equal* title to the free exercise of Religion according to the dictates of conscience." Whilst we assert for ourselves a free-

dom to embrace, to profess and to observe the Religion which we believe to be of divine origin, we cannot deny an equal freedom to those whose minds have not yet yielded to the evidence which has convinced us. If this freedom be abused, it is an offence against God, not against man: To God, therefore, not to men, must an account of it be rendered. As the Bill violates equality by subjecting some to peculiar burdens; so it violates the same principle, by granting to others peculiar exemptions. Are the Quakers and Menonists the only sects who think a compulsive support of their religions unnecessary and unwarrantable? Can their piety alone be intrusted with the care of public worship? Ought their Religions to be endowed above all others, with extraordinary privileges, by which proselytes may be enticed from all others? We think too favorably of the justice and good sense of these denominations, to believe that they either covet preeminencies over their fellow citizens, or that they will be seduced by them, from the common opposition to the measure.

5. Because the bill implies either that the Civil Magistrate is a competent Judge of Religious truth; or that he may employ Religion as an engine of Civil Policy. The first is an arrogant pretension falsified by the contradictory opinions of Rulers in all ages, and throughout the world: The second an unhallowed perversion of the means of salvation.

6. Because the establishment proposed by the Bill is not requisite for the support of the Christian Religion. To say that it is, is a contradiction to the Christian Religion itself; for every page of it disavows a dependence on the powers of this world: it is a contradiction to fact; for it is known that this Religion both existed and flourished, not only without the support of human laws, but in spite of every opposition from them; and not only during the period of miraculous aid, but long after it had been left to its own evidence, and the ordinary care of Providence: Nay, it is a contradiction in terms; for a Religion not invented by human policy, must have pre-existed and been supported, before it was established by human policy. It is moreover to weaken in those who profess this Religion a pious confidence in its innate excellence, and the patronage of its Author; and to foster in those who still reject it, a suspicion that its friends are too conscious of its fallacies, to trust it to its own merits.

7. Because experience witnesseth that ecclesiastical establishments, instead of maintaining the purity and efficacy of Religion, have had a contrary operation. During almost fifteen centuries, has the legal establishment of Christianity been on trial. What have been its fruits? More or less in all places, pride and indolence in the Clergy; ignorance and servility in the laity; in both, superstition, bigotry and persecution. Enquire of the Teachers of Christianity for the ages in which it appeared in its greatest lustre; those of every sect, point to the ages prior to its incorporation with Civil policy.

Propose a restoration of this primitive state in which its Teachers depended on the voluntary rewards of their flocks; many of them predict its downfall. On which side ought their testimony to have greatest weight, when for or when against their interest?

8. Because the establishment in question is not necessary for the support of Civil Government. If it be urged as necessary for the support of Civil Government only as it is a means of supporting Religion, and it be not necessary for the latter purpose, it cannot be necessary for the former. If Religion be not within [the] cognizance of Civil Government, how can its legal establishment be said to be necessary to Civil Government? What influence in fact have ecclesiastical establishments had on Civil Society? In some instances they have been seen to erect a spiritual tyranny on the ruins of Civil authority; in many instances they have been seen upholding the thrones of political tyranny; in no instance have they been seen the guardians of the liberties of the people. Rulers who wished to subvert the public liberty, may have found an established clergy convenient auxiliaries. A just government, instituted to secure and perpetuate it, needs them not. Such a government will be best supported by protecting every citizen in the enjoyment of his Religion with the same equal hand which protects his person and his property; by neither invading the equal rights of any Sect, nor suffering any Sect to invade those of another.

9. Because the proposed establishment is a departure from that generous policy, which, offering an asylum to the persecuted and oppressed of every Nation and Religion, promised a lustre to our country, and an accession to the number of its citizens. What a melancholy mark is the Bill of sudden degeneracy? Instead of holding forth an asylum to the persecuted, it is itself a signal of persecution. It degrades from the equal rank of Citizens all those whose opinions in Religion do not bend to those of the Legislative authority. Distant as it may be, in its present form, from the Inquisition it differs from it only in degree. The one is the first step, the other the last in the career of intolerance. The magnanimous sufferer under this cruel scourge in foreign Regions, must view the Bill as a Beacon on our Coast, warning him to seek some other haven, where liberty and philanthropy in their due extent may offer a more certain repose from his troubles.

10. Because, it will have a like tendency to banish our Citizens. The allurements presented by other situations are every day thinning their number. To superadd a fresh motive to emigration, by revoking the liberty which they now enjoy, would be the same species of folly which has dishonored and depopulated flourishing kingdoms.

11. Because, it will destroy that moderation and harmony which the forbearance of our laws to intermeddle with Religion, has produced amongst its

several sects. Torrents of blood have been spilt in the old world, by vain attempts of the secular arm to extinguish Religious discord, by proscribing all difference in Religious opinions. Time has at length revealed the true remedy. Every relaxation of narrow and rigorous policy, wherever it has been tried, has been found to assuage the disease. The American Theatre has exhibited proofs, that equal and compleat liberty, if it does not wholly eradicate it, sufficiently destroys its malignant influence on the health and prosperity of the State. If with the salutary effects of this system under our own eyes, we begin to contract the bonds of Religious freedom, we know no name that will too severely reproach our folly. At least let warning be taken at the first fruits of the threatened innovation. The very appearance of the Bill has transformed that "Christian forbearance, love and charity," which of late mutually prevailed, into animosities and jealousies, which may not soon be appeased. What mischiefs may not be dreaded should this enemy to the public quiet be armed with the force of a law?

12. Because, the policy of the bill is adverse to the diffusion of the light of Christianity. The first wish of those who enjoy this precious gift, ought to be that it may be imparted to the whole race of mankind. Compare the number of those who have as yet received it with the number still remaining under the dominion of false Religions; and how small is the former! Does the policy of the Bill tend to lessen the disproportion? No; it at once discourages those who are strangers to the light of [revelation] from coming into the Region of it; and countenances by example the nations who continue in darkness in shutting out those who might convey it to them. Instead of levelling as far as possible, every obstacle to the victorious progress of truth, the Bill with an ignoble and unchristian timidity would circumscribe it, with a wall of defence, against the encroachments of error.

13. Because attempts to enforce by legal sanctions, acts obnoxious to so great a proportion of Citizens, tend to enervate the laws in general, and to slacken the bands of Society. If it be difficult to execute any law which is not generally deemed necessary or salutary, what must be the case where it is deemed invalid and dangerous? and what may be the effect of so striking an example of impotency in the Government, on its general authority?

14. Because a measure of such singular magnitude and delicacy ought not to be imposed, without the clearest evidence that it is called for by a majority of citizens: and no satisfactory method is yet proposed by which the voice of the majority in this case may be determined, or its influence secured. "The people of the respective counties are indeed requested to signify their opinion respecting the adoption of the Bill to the next session of Assembly." But the representation must be made equal, before the voice either of the Representatives or of the Counties, will be that of the people. Our hope is that

neither of the former will, after due consideration espouse the dangerous principle of the Bill. Should the event disappoint us, it will still leave us in full confidence, that a fair appeal to the latter will reverse the sentence against our liberties.

15. Because, finally, "the equal right of every citizen to the free exercise of his Religion according to the dictates of conscience" is held by the same tenure with all our other rights. If we recur to its origin, it is equally the gift of nature; if we weigh its importance, it cannot be less dear to us; if we consult the Declaration of those rights which pertain to the good people of Virginia, as the "basis and foundation of Government," it is enumerated with equal solemnity, or rather studied emphasis. Either then, we must say, that the will of the Legislature is the only measure of their authority; and that in the plentitude of this authority, they may sweep away all our fundamental rights; or, that they are bound to leave this particular right untouched and sacred: Either we must say, that they may control the freedom of the press, may abolish the trial by jury, may swallow up the Executive and Judiciary Powers of the State; nay that they may despoil us of our very right of suffrage, and erect themselves into an independent and hereditary assembly: or we must say that they have no authority to enact into law the Bill under consideration. We the subscribers say, that the General Assembly of this Commonwealth have no such authority: And that no effort may be omitted on our part against so dangerous an usurpation, we oppose to it, this remonstrance; earnestly praying, as we are in duty bound, that the Supreme Lawgiver of the Universe, by illuminating those to whom it is addressed, may on the one hand, turn their councils from every act which would affront his holy prerogative, or violate the trust committed to them: and on the other, guide them into every measure which may be worthy of his blessing, may redound to their own praise, and may establish more firmly the liberties, the prosperity, and the Happiness of the Commonwealth.

Appendix B

An Act for Establishing Religious Freedom, Passed in the Assembly of Virginia in the Beginning of the Year 1786[*]

Well aware that Almighty God hath created the mind free; that all attempts to influence it by temporal punishments or burdens, or by civil incapacitation, tend only to beget habits of hypocrisy and meanness, and are a departure from the plan of the Holy Author of our religion, who being Lord both of body and mind, yet chose not to propagate it by coercions on either, as was in his Almighty power to do; that the impious presumption of legislators and rulers, civil as well as ecclesiastical, who, being themselves but fallible and uninspired men have assumed dominion over the faith of others, setting up their own opinions and modes of thinking as the only true and infallible, and as such endeavoring to impose them on others, hath established and maintained false religions over the greatest part of the world, and through all time; that to compel a man to furnish contributions of money for the propagation of opinions which he disbelieves, is sinful and tyrannical; that even the forcing him to support this or that teacher of his own religious persuasion, is depriving him of the comfortable liberty of giving his contributions to the particular pastor whose morals he would make his pattern, and whose powers he feels most persuasive to righteousness, and is withdrawing from the ministry those temporal rewards, which proceeding from an approbation of their personal conduct, are an additional incitement to earnest and unremitting labors for the instruction of mankind; that our civil rights have no dependence on our religious opinions, more than our opinions in physics or geometry; that, therefore, the proscribing any citizen as unworthy the public confidence

---

*Written by Thomas Jefferson. Quoted in *The Writings of Thomas Jefferson*, ed. Andrew A. Lipscomb (Washington, DC: The Thomas Jefferson Memorial Association, 1904), 300–303. Sometimes referred to as Jefferson's "Bill for Establishing Religious Freedom."

by laying upon him an incapacity of being called to the offices of trust and emolument, unless he profess or renounce this or that religious opinion, is depriving him injuriously of those privileges and advantages to which in common with his fellow citizens he has a natural right; that it tends also to corrupt the principles of that very religion it is meant to encourage, by bribing, with a monopoly of worldly honors and emoluments, those who will externally profess and conform to it; that though indeed these are criminal who do not withstand such temptation, yet neither are those innocent who lay the bait in their way; that to suffer the civil magistrate to intrude his powers into the field of opinion and to restrain the profession or propagation of principles, on the supposition of their ill tendency, is a dangerous fallacy, which at once destroys all religious liberty, because he being of course judge of that tendency, will make his opinions the rule of judgment, and approve or condemn the sentiments of others only as they shall square with or differ from his own; that it is time enough for the rightful purposes of civil government, for its offices to interfere when principles break out into overt acts against peace and good order; and finally, that truth is great and will prevail if left to herself, that she is the proper and sufficient antagonist to error, and has nothing to fear from the conflict, unless by human interposition disarmed of her natural weapons, free argument and debate, errors ceasing to be dangerous when it is permitted freely to contradict them.

Be it therefore enacted by the General Assembly, That no man shall be compelled to frequent or support any religious worship, place or ministry whatsoever, nor shall be enforced, restrained, molested, or burthened in his body or goods, nor shall otherwise suffer on account of his religious opinions or belief; but that all men shall be free to profess, and by argument to maintain, their opinions in matters of religion, and that the same shall in nowise diminish, enlarge, or affect their civil capacities.

And though we well know this Assembly, elected by the people for the ordinary purposes of legislation only, have no power to restrain the acts of succeeding assemblies, constituted with the powers equal to our own, and that therefore to declare this act irrevocable, would be of no effect in law, yet we are free to declare, and do declare, that the rights hereby asserted are of the natural rights of mankind, and that if any act shall be hereafter passed to repeal the present or to narrow its operation, such act will be an infringement of natural right.

Appendix C

Chronological Table of Cases

Because the cases are discussed thematically, it seems helpful to provide a chronological table of cases, in order to provide a sense of the sequence with which the Court has dealt with the issues. A few lower court cases are listed, including three the Court agreed to hear as the book was going to press.

1872   *Watson v. Jones* 13 Wallace 679

1879   *Reynolds v. United States* 98 U.S. 145

1890   *Davis v. Beason* 133 U.S. 333

1923   *Frothingham v. Mellon* 262 U.S. 447

1925   *Pierce v. Society of Sisters* 268 U.S. 510

1929   *United States v. Schwimmer* 279 U.S. 644

1930   *Cochran v. Louisiana State Board of Education* 281 U.S. 370

1931   *United States v. Macintosh* 283 U.S. 605

1931   *United States v. Bland* 283 U.S. 636

1940   *Cantwell v. Connecticut* 310 U.S. 296

1940   *Minersville School District v. Gobitis* 310 U.S. 586

1941   *Cox v. New Hampshire* 312 U.S. 569

1943   *West Virginia Board of Education v. Barnette* 319 U.S. 624

1943   *Murdock v. Pennsylvania* 319 U.S. 105

1944   *Prince v. Massachusetts* 321 U.S. 158

1944   *United States v. Ballard* 322 U.S. 78

1946   *Girouard v. United States* 328 U.S. 61

1947   *Everson v. Board of Education* 330 U.S. 1

1948   *McCollum v. Board of Education* 333 U.S. 203

1952	*Zorach v. Clauson* 343 U.S. 306
1952	*Kedroff v. St. Nicholas Cathedral* 344 U.S. 94
1961	*McGowan v. Maryland* 366 U.S. 420
1961	*Braunfeld v. Brown* 366 U.S. 599
1961	*Torcaso v. Watkins* 367 U.S. 488
1962	*Engel v. Vitale* 370 U.S. 421
1963	*Sherbert v. Verner* 374 U.S. 398
1963	*Abington Township School District v. Schempp* 374 U.S. 203
1965	*United States v. Seeger* 380 U.S. 163
1967	*Jehovah's Witnesses v. King County Hospital* 278 F.Supp. 488, affirmed 390 U.S. 598
1968	*Board of Education v. Allen* 392 U.S. 236
1968	*Epperson v. Arkansas* 393 U.S. 97
1968	*Flast v. Cohen* 392 U.S. 83
1969	*Presbyterian Church v. Hull Memorial Presbyterian Church* 393 U.S. 440
1970	*Walz v. Tax Commission of the City of New York* 397 U.S. 664
1970	*Welsh v. United States* 398 U.S. 333
1971	*Gillette v. United States* 401 U.S. 437
1971	*Lemon v. Kurtzman* 403 U.S. 602
1971	*Tilton v. Richardson* 403 U.S. 672
1972	*Wisconsin v. Yoder* 406 U.S. 205
1972	*Christian Echoes National Ministry v. U. S.* 470 F.2d 849, cert. den. 404 U.S. 561
1973	*Committee for Public Education and Religious Liberty v. Nyquist* 413 U.S. 756
1973	*Hunt v. McNair* 413 U.S. 734
1973	*Levitt v. Committee for Public Education and Religious Liberty* 413 U.S. 472
1975	*Meek v. Pittenger* 421 U.S. 349
1976	*Serbian Eastern Orthodox Diocese v. Milivojevich* 426 U.S. 696
1976	*Roemer v. Board of Public Works of Maryland* 426 U.S. 736
1977	*Trans World Airlines v. Hardison* 432 U.S. 63
1977	*Wolman v. Walter* 433 U.S. 229
1978	*McDaniel v. Paty* 435 U.S. 618
1979	*Jones v. Wolf* 443 U.S. 595
1979	*National Labor Relations Board v. Catholic Bishop of Chicago* 440 U.S. 490
1980	*Stone v. Graham* 449 U.S. 39
1980	*Committee for Public Education and Religious Liberty v. Regan* 444 U.S. 646

1981   *Thomas v. Review Board of Indiana Employment Commission* 450 U.S. 707

1981   *Widmar v. Vincent* 454 U.S. 263

1981   *Heffron v. International Society for Krishna Consciousness* 452 U.S. 640

1982   *United States v. Lee* 455 U.S. 252

1982   *Larkin v. Grendel's Den* 459 U.S. 116

1982   *Valley Forge Christian College v. Americans United for Separation of Church and State* 454 U.S. 464

1982   *Larson v. Valente* 456 U.S. 228

1983   *Mueller v. Allen* 463 U.S. 388

1983   *Marsh v. Chambers* 463 U.S. 783

1983   *Bob Jones University v. United States* 461 U.S. 574

1984   *Lynch v. Donnelly* 465 U.S. 668

1985   *Wallace v. Jaffree* 472 U.S. 38

1985   *Estate of Thornton v. Caldor* 472 U.S. 703

1985   *Aguilar v. Felton* 473 U.S. 402

1985   *Grand Rapids School District v. Ball* 473 U.S. 373

1986   *Bowen v. Roy* 476 U.S. 693

1986   *Goldman v. Weinberger* 475 U.S. 503

1986   *Witters v. Washington Department of Services for the Blind* 474 U.S. 481

1986   *Ansonia Board of Education v. Philbrook* 479 U.S. 60

1987   *Hobbie v. Unemployment Appeals Commission of Florida* 480 U.S. 136

1987   *O'Lone v. Estate of Shabazz* 482 U.S. 342

1987   *Church of Jesus Christ of Latter-day Saints v. Amos* 483 U.S. 327

1987   *Airport Commissioners of Los Angeles v. Jews for Jesus* 482 U.S. 569

1987   *Edwards v. Aguillard* 482 U.S. 578

1988   *Lyng v. Northwest Indian Cemetery Protective Association* 485 U.S. 439

1989   *Frazee v. Illinois Department of Employment Security* 489 U.S. 829

1989   *Hernandez v. Commissioner of Internal Revenue* 490 U.S. 680

1989   *Allegheny County v. ACLU of Pittsburgh* 492 U.S. 573

1989   *Texas Monthly v. Bullock* 489 U.S. 1

1990   *Employment Division of Oregon v. Smith* 494 U.S. 872

1990   *Board of Education of Westside Community Schools v. Mergens* 496 U.S. 226

1990   *Jimmy Swaggart Ministries v. Board of Equalization of California* 493 U.S. 378

1990   *Davis v. United States* 495 U.S. 472

1992   *International Society for Krishna Consciousness v. Lee* 505 U.S. 672

1992   *Lee v. Weisman* 505 U.S. 577

1993   *Church of Lukumi Babalu Aye v. City of Hialeah* 508 U.S. 520

1993   *Lamb's Chapel v. Center Moriches School District* 508 U.S. 384

1993   *Zobrest v. Catalina Foothills School District* 509 U.S. 1

1994   *Board of Education of Kiryas Joel v. Grumet* 512 U.S. 687

1995   *Capitol Square Advisory Board v. Pinette* 515 U.S. 753

1995   *Rosenberger v. University of Virginia* 515 U.S. 819

1997   *Agostini v. Felton* 521 U.S. 203

1997   *City of Boerne v. Archbishop Flores* 521 U.S. 507

2000   *Mitchell v. Helms* 530 U.S. 793

2000   *Santa Fe School District v. Doe* 530 U.S. 290

2001   *Good News Club v. Milford Central School* 533 U.S. 98

2002   *Watchtower Bible and Tract Society v. Village of Stratton* 536 U.S. 150

2002   *Zelman v. Simmons-Harris* 536 U.S. 639

2003   *Cutter v. Wilkinson* 349 F.3d 257

2003   *Van Orden v. Perry* 351 F.3d 173

2003   *McCreary County v. ACLU* 354 F.3d 438

2004   *Locke v. Davey* 540 U.S. 712

2004   *Elk Grove School District v. Newdow* 542 U.S. 1

Notes

1. The Court and Its Procedures

1. "Statistical Recap of Supreme Court's Workload during Last Three Terms," *United States Law Week* 62 (August 17, 1993): 3124; ibid. 73 (July 13, 2004): 3044.
2. Max Radin, *Radin Law Dictionary* (Dobbs Ferry, NY: Oceana Publications, 1970), 50.
3. William Howard Taft, testimony, in *Hearings before the Committee on the Judiciary: House of Representatives, on H.R. 10479*, "Jurisdiction of Circuit Courts of Appeals and United States Supreme Court," 67th Congress, 2nd session, March 30, 1922, 2.
4. Harry W. Jones, "Church-State Relations: Our Constitutional Heritage," in *Religion and Contemporary Society*, ed. Harold Stahmer (New York: Macmillan Co., 1963), 168. Unfortunately, Jones does not identify the justice or when and where he made this statement.
5. An extreme example, but one illustrative of the use of amicus curiae briefs, is the Missouri abortion case *Webster v. Reproductive Health Services* 492 U.S. 490 (1989). In that case there were twenty amicus briefs urging reversal of the lower court opinion, twenty-one urging affirmance, and thirty-four other amici arguing some aspect of the case, for a total of seventy-five different briefs. Because organizations often share in the responsibility and cost of preparing an amicus brief, those seventy-five briefs represented hundreds of different interest groups and individuals.
6. Occasionally the Court considers a case so important that it *must* achieve unanimity and will take extra time to do so. An example is *Brown v. Board of Education* 347 U.S. 483 (1954), the case declaring "separate but equal" education to be unconstitutional.
7. David M. O'Brien, *Storm Center: The Supreme Court in American Politics*, 6th ed. (New York: W. W. Norton & Co., 2003), 133–43. A leading scholar of the Court, Bernard Schwartz, is not so sanguine. Calling the clerks a "Junior Supreme Court," he goes so far as to say, at p. 261, "The development of the law clerk corps as a crucial factor in the Court's decision process has had a baneful effect that may ultimately result in the loss of public confidence in the Supreme Court itself." See Bernard Schwartz, *Decision: How the Supreme Court Decides Cases* (New York: Oxford University Press, 1996), 256–62.
8. 310 U.S. 586 (1940).
9. 319 U.S. 624 (1943).

199

2. Background of Constitutional Principles

1. "Dale's Laws," in *American Christianity: An Historical Interpretation with Representative Documents*, ed. H. Shelton Smith, Robert T. Handy, and Lefferts A. Loetscher (New York: Charles Scribner's Sons, 1960), 1:41–44.
2. John Winthrop, "A Model of Christian Charity," in *American Christianity*, 1:100.
3. Nathaniel Ward, "The Simple Cobbler of Aggawam," in *American Christianity*, 1:127.
4. Among those were Anne Hutchinson and Roger Williams.
5. There is a statue of Mary Dyer in front of the state capitol in Boston, bearing this inscription: "Mary Dyer, Quaker; Witness for Religious Freedom; Hanged on Boston Commons 1660; 'My Life Not Availeth Me in Comparison to the Liberty of the Truth.' Sylvia Shaw Judson—Sculptor."
6. Edwin S. Gaustad and Leigh E. Schmidt, *The Religious History of America*, rev. ed. (San Francisco: HarperSanFrancisco, 2002), 54.
7. For a description of this pluralism with wonderful maps, see Edwin Scott Gaustad and Philip L. Barlow, *The New Historical Atlas of Religion in America* (New York: Oxford University Press, 2001), 1–54.
8. Sidney E. Mead, *The Lively Experiment: The Shaping of Christianity in America* (New York: Harper & Row, 1963), 62.
9. Quoted in Leo Pfeffer, *Church, State, and Freedom*, rev. ed. (Boston: Beacon Press, 1967), 122. See pp. 121–24.
10. Isaac Kramnick and R. Laurence Moore, *The Godless Constitution: The Case against Religious Correctness* (New York: W. W. Norton, 1997), 44. See also Edwin S. Gaustad, *Faith of the Fathers: Religion and the New Nation* (San Francisco: Harper & Row, 1987). A revised edition of this book under the title *Neither King nor Prelate: Religion and the New Nation 1776–1826* was published in 1993 by Wm. B. Eerdmans Publishing Co.
11. Leonard W. Levy, "The Original Meaning of the Establishment Clause of the First Amendment," in *Religion and the State: Essays in Honor of Leo Pfeffer*, ed. James E. Wood Jr. (Waco, TX: Baylor University Press, 1985), 61.

3. Defining the Scope of Religious Freedom Prior to 1963

1. 98 U.S. 145 (1879).
2. 98 U.S. 145 at 164.
3. See Edwin B. Firmage, "Mormon Free Exercise in Nineteenth-Century America," in *Religion and American Law: An Encyclopedia*, ed. Paul Finkelman (New York: Garland Publishing, 2000), 317–25.
4. The Court subsequently handed down decisions in two other cases in which the offense was not practicing polygamy, but advocating a religious belief in polygamy. Even here what was prohibited was the proclamation of the belief, not the belief itself, although the laws affirmed by the Court criminalized membership in an organization that taught polygamy. So, in essence, to be a Mormon was a crime (*Davis v. Beason* 133 U.S. 333 [1890] and *Church of Jesus Christ of Latter-day Saints v. United States* 136 U.S. 1 [1890]. However, the criminalization of belief has never had the same weight as precedent as the belief/action distinction of *Reynolds*. In 1890 the church blunted the government's campaign against it by discontinuing the practice of plural marriage. See Leo Pfeffer, *Church, State, and Freedom* (Boston: Beacon Press, 1967), 645–50.
5. One scholar has made this important point this way: "It is the nuts, or those so

regarded by the rest of us, on whom government restraint or censorship are brought to bear. When they resolutely defend their constitutional liberties, the nuts are surrogates for the freedom of us all" (Harry W. Jones, "Church-State Relations: Our Constitutional Heritage," in *Religion and Contemporary Society*, ed. Harold Stahmer [New York: Macmillan Co., 1963], 178).

6. 310 U.S. 296 (1940).
7. 310 U.S. 296 at 303–4.
8. 310 U.S. 296 at 307.
9. 319 U.S. 105 (1943).
10. 312 U.S. 569 (1941).
11. See *Niemotko v. Maryland* 340 U.S. 268 (1951) and *Fowler v. Rhode Island* 345 U.S. 67 (1953).
12. 321 U.S. 158 (1944).
13. This is known as the *parens patriae*, literally "parent of the country," power of the state. The state has the power to legislate for the public welfare of citizens, especially those less likely to be able to care for themselves, such as the aged, the mentally incompetent, and children.
14. 321 U.S. 158 at 170.
15. See Genesis 9:3–4; Leviticus 17:10–12; Acts 15:19–21. Although these passages refer only to eating blood, the Witnesses make the point that in the ancient world consuming blood was the only way to take it into the body. Modern technology has made ingesting blood possible through transfusion, and that is equally prohibited by God's law. Ingesting blood, that is, life, is the issue, not the methodology.
16. See *Jehovah's Witnesses v. King County Hospital* 278 F.Supp. 488 (1967), affirmed without argument 390 U.S. 598 (1968). (The "F.Supp." in the first citation refers to the *Federal Supplement*, the series of volumes used to report decisions of the U.S. District Courts since 1932.)
17. Of course, this principle has even more impact on those groups, like the Christian Science Church, that refuse medical care altogether.

I thank my colleague Professor John J. Hedl Jr., chair of the Department of Health Services Administration at the University of Texas Southwestern Medical Center at Dallas, for his suggestions and review of this paragraph.
18. See Exodus 20:3–6; Luke 4:8; 1 John 5:21.
19. 310 U.S. 586 (1940). For an interesting and readable biographical sketch of Lillian Gobitis and an explanation of her case, see Peter Irons, *The Courage of Their Convictions* (New York: Free Press, 1988), 13–35.
20. 310 U.S. 586 at 595–96.
21. 319 U.S. 624 (1943).
22. 319 U.S. 624 at 641.
23. 319 U.S. 624 at 642. This case played an indirect role in the 1988 presidential campaign. Governor Michael Dukakis of Massachusetts, the Democratic candidate, had been asked to get the opinion of the Massachusetts attorney general about whether that state's public schools could require the Pledge of Allegiance to the flag. The attorney general responded in the negative, citing *Barnette*. Dukakis made this report public. During the campaign then Vice President George H. W. Bush shamefully impugned Dukakis's patriotism, claiming that he was against the Pledge of Allegiance, never once mentioning that this was not Dukakis's position or that it was the law of the land that one cannot be compelled to salute the American flag.

24. 322 U.S. 78 (1944).
25. Jones, "Church-State Relations: Our Constitutional Heritage," 182. Professor Jones expands on this concept in words worth remembering:

> When we get down to the hard cases, we are forced, however unwillingly, to the conclusion that the free exercise of religion means and must mean both "true" and "untrue" religion, must include the extravagances of the false prophet as well as the witness of the genuinely inspired.
>
> The best test of truth, for constitutional purposes if for no other, is the power of an idea to get accepted. . . . We may choose the "truth," as God gives us to see the truth, but government and the officials of government must not be empowered to pass on questions concerning the truth or sincerity of religious professions. In a genuinely free society, the forum of choice is in the intellect and conscience of the individual, not in the jurisdiction of a judge, jury, postmaster, or licensing official. The American prophet, however venal or misguided, is not without freedom in his own country. (184)

26. 322 U.S. 78 at 86–87.
27. As it did, disastrously, in the Branch Davidian episode near Waco, Texas, in 1993.
28. 322 U.S. 78 at 94–95. Justice Jackson was dissenting, not because he disagreed with the majority opinion, but because he thought that the Court should not have taken the case at all, given the potential of judicial intrusion into religious belief.

4. The Uncertain Status of Religious Freedom: 1963–2004

1. 374 U.S. 398 (1963).
2. Actually, sundown Friday until sundown Saturday.
3. See Genesis 2:1–3; Exodus 20:8–11.
4. 374 U.S. 398 at 406. The Court quoted *Thomas v. Collins* 323 U.S. 516 at 530 (1945).
5. 374 U.S. 398 at 406.
6. 406 U.S. 205 (1972).
7. 406 U.S. 205 at 215.
8. Jehovah's Witnesses have, more often than not, been conscientious objectors to war, primarily in obedience to God's commandment, "You shall not murder" (Exod. 20:13). However, as this case shows, not all members understand this to extend to a prohibition against manufacturing munitions.
9. 450 U.S. 707 (1981).
10. 450 U.S. 707 at 715–16.
11. 450 U.S. 707 at 717–18.
12. 480 U.S. 136 (1987).
13. 480 U.S. 136 at 144.
14. 489 U.S. 829 (1989).
15. 435 U.S. 618 (1978).
16. 435 U.S. 618 at 626, quoting *Sherbert v. Verner* 374 U.S. 398 at 406.
17. 475 U.S. 503 (1986).
18. Actually, the regulation had not been enforced against Dr. Goldman for several years. But after he testified for the defense in a court-martial, wearing his yarmulke but not his service cap, his commanding officer, apparently in retribution for his testimony, began to enforce the regulation.
19. 475 U.S. 503 at 507.

20. 482 U.S. 342 (1987).
21. As noted earlier, *Smith* involved Native Americans, too. But it was actually an unemployment compensation case. The cases now under review focused more centrally on behavior characteristic of Native American religion.
22. 476 U.S. 693 (1986).
23. 476 U.S. 693 at 699.
24. 476 U.S. 693 at 700.
25. 485 U.S. 439 (1988).
26. 485 U.S. 439 at 452–53.
27. 452 U.S. 640 (1981).
28. 482 U.S. 569 (1987).
29. 505 U.S. 672 (1992).
30. As its name implies, the Native American Church is a transtribal religious group organized by and for American Indians. Although it was first legally incorporated in 1918 in Oklahoma, it originated in the nineteenth century. However, at the time of its beginning it incorporated a practice of Indians of North America that seems to go back some 400 or 500 years—the use of peyote as an inducer of spiritual experience. The use of peyote is the central, but not the only, characteristic of Native American Church worship. Its role is to heighten the spiritual sensitivity of the worshipper, to help him or her experience God. The church teaches that peyote itself is a sacred substance and must be properly used, which means that it should never be abused. Consequently, believers are never to use peyote outside worship. Some congregations will expel members who use it improperly, that is, as a "recreational drug." Virtually all states include peyote on their lists of prohibited drugs. But because of the discipline on its use imposed by the Native American Church, at the time the issue came before the Supreme Court in 1990 in the *Smith* case, twenty-three states and the federal government had exempted peyote from prosecution when it is used in worship. Texas, the only place in the United States where the peyote cactus grows naturally, has laws that permit, but regulate, its growth, harvesting, and distribution for religious purposes. Also, going into the *Smith* litigation, there was some case law that permitted the use of peyote for worship purposes. The leading case was decided by the California Supreme Court, *People v. Woody* 394 P.2d 813 (1964). (The "P.2d" in the citation refers to the *Pacific Reporter*, second series, which is the official reporting document for cases of the California Supreme Court and other courts of that region.)
31. 494 U.S. 872 (1990).
32. 494 U.S. 872 at 879, quoting Justice John Paul Stevens, dissenting in *United States v. Lee* 455 U.S. 252 at 263, note 3.
33. 494 U.S. 872 at 885. The first quotation is from *Lyng v. Northwest Indian Cemetery Protective Association* 485 U.S. 439 at 451. The quote from *Reynolds* is 98 U.S. 145 at 167.
34. She believed the Court could have reached the same result by using the compelling state interest test, rather than abandoning it. That is, Oregon had a compelling interest in prohibiting the use of dangerous drugs.
35. 494 U.S. 872 at 891, 899–900, 901–2. The compelling interest test is often called "strict scrutiny" in judicial language.
36. 508 U.S. 520 (1993).
37. 508 U.S. 520 at 531, quoting *Thomas v. Review Board of Indiana* 450 U.S. 707 at 714 (1981).

38. 508 U.S. 520 at 524.
39. 508 U.S. 520 at 547.
40. 42 *United States Code* § 2000bb. (The *United States Code* is the laws of the United States.)
41. Douglas Laycock and Oliver S. Thomas, "Interpreting the Religious Freedom Restoration Act," *Texas Law Review* 73 (December 1994): 244–45.
42. 521 U.S. 507 (1997).
43. Richard B. Saphire, "Religious Freedom Restoration Act of 1993," in *Religion and American Law: An Encyclopedia*, ed. Paul Finkelman (New York: Garland Publishing, 2000), 411.
44. Christopher L. Eisgruber and Lawrence G. Sager, "Congressional Power and Religious Liberty after *City of Boerne v. Flores,*" in *The Supreme Court Review 1997*, ed. Dennis J. Hutchinson, David A. Strauss, and Geoffrey R. Stone (Chicago: University of Chicago Press, 1998), 88.
45. 42 *United States Code* § 2000cc.
46. For a clear and nontechnical explanation of RLUIPA, see Melissa Rogers, "Protecting the Right to Worship," *Liberty: A Magazine of Religious Freedom* 96 (May/June 2001): 24–27.
47. 536 U.S. 150 (2002).
48. 536 U.S. 150 at 166.
49. After *Smith*, courts all across the country began deciding cases in such a way as to restrict religious freedom, a decidedly different trend from decisions before the *Smith* decision. For an article that disagrees with the cautionary tone of this paragraph and my general interpretation of *Smith*, see Eisgruber and Sager, "Congressional Power and Religious Liberty after *City of Boerne v. Flores.*"

5. From Congregational Fights to Pacifism

1. 13 Wallace (80 U.S.) 679 (1872). Before *United States Reports* became the official record of Supreme Court decisions in 1874, the Court reports were named after the court reporter who compiled them, thus the "Wallace" in the citation of this case. See Francis Helminski, "Reporters, Supreme Court" and "Reporting of Opinions," and Morris L. Cohen, "United States Reports," all in *The Oxford Companion to the Supreme Court of the United States*, ed. Kermit L. Hall (New York: Oxford University Press, 1992), 727–29, 889.
2. 13 Wallace (80 U.S.) 679 at 728. In fact, the last sentence of this statement was quoted seventy-two years later in *United States v. Ballard* 322 U.S. 78 at 86.
3. 13 Wallace (80 U.S.) 679 at 727.
4. 280 U.S. 1 (1929).
5. 344 U.S. 94 (1952).
6. For a similar, later case, see *Serbian Eastern Orthodox Diocese v. Milivojevich* 426 U.S. 696 (1976).
7. 393 U.S. 440 (1969).
8. 393 U.S. 440 at 449.
9. 443 U.S. 595 (1979).
10. 443 U.S. 595 at 604. The Court quoted from *Presbyterian Church in the U.S. v. Mary Elizabeth Blue Hull Memorial Presbyterian Church* 393 U.S. 440 at 449.
11. 432 U.S. 63 (1977).
12. 432 U.S. 63 at 84.
13. 479 U.S. 60 (1986).
14. 479 U.S. 60 at 68.

15. A lawyer who practices workplace/religion law described the hardship rule after *Hardison* and *Philbrook:* "Undue hardship is anything that violates a union contract or other seniority agreement, anything resulting in more than a very minor cost or the diminishment of efficiency or productivity, or anything that violates the rights of other workers. Congress built a substantial protective fence around religious observance in the workplace, but the Court cut the fence down to a height so low that most employers can step over it with ease" (e-mail from Mitchell A. Tyner, associate general counsel, General Conference of Seventh-day Adventists, to Ronald B. Flowers, October 12, 2004).

16. 483 U.S. 327 (1987).

17. 483 U.S. 327 at 337. *Lemon* in this quote refers to *Lemon v. Kurtzman* 403 U.S. 602 (1971). *Lemon* articulated a three-part test for interpreting the Establishment Clause. To be constitutional, a law must have a secular purpose, have a primary effect that neither advances nor hinders religion, and not create excessive entanglement between government and religion. A fuller explanation is given in chapter 6.

18. Hiring on the basis of religion has become a principal issue in the dispute about the constitutionality of "charitable choice" or government funding of "faith-based initiatives," covered in chapter 9.

19. 440 U.S. 490 (1979).

20. Exodus 20:13.

21. Matthew 5:9, 39; see also verses 21–22.

22. 279 U.S. 644 (1929).

23. 283 U.S. 636 (1931).

24. 283 U.S. 605 (1931).

25. 8 *United States Code* § 382. *Schwimmer* and *Macintosh* were cited as precedents in a case in which the Court denied the request of Methodist conscientious objector students to be exempted from the requirement of a state university to take R.O.T.C. courses; *Hamilton v. Regents of the University of California* 293 U.S. 245 (1934).

26. These laws are reviewed later in the chapter.

27. 283 U.S. 605 at 623–24.

28. 283 U.S. 605 at 618. Macintosh had been a chaplain in the Canadian army in World War I and served in areas of combat.

29. 283 U.S. 605 at 625. For an earlier expression by the Court of the Christian nation idea, see *Church of the Holy Trinity v. United States* 143 U.S. 457 at 470 (1892).

30. 328 U.S. 61 (1946).

31. 328 U.S. 61 at 64–65.

32. 66 *Statutes at Large* 163 (1952). This law, commonly called the McCarran-Walter Act, was influenced by *Girouard*. (*Statutes at Large* is the official source for the laws and resolutions passed by Congress. It contains every law ever enacted by Congress in order of the date of its passage.)

33. 328 U.S. 61 at 68.

34. For an elaboration of the issues and cases discussed in this section, see Ronald B. Flowers, *To Defend the Constitution: Religion, Conscientious Objection, Naturalization, and the Supreme Court* (Lanham, MD: Scarecrow Press, 2003).

35. Some have argued the Establishment Clause contains the right to conscientious objection exemptions from military service. In fact, in 1917 the Selective Service Act was attacked as a violation of that clause. The Supreme Court brushed

aside that argument as "unsound" and not worthy of discussion (Selective Draft Law Cases [*Arver v. United States* 245 U.S. 366 at 389 {1918}]). Then there was the Court's emphatic statement in *Macintosh*. Since that time, the Establishment argument has been mentioned occasionally, but with no success.

36. 40 *Statutes at Large* 76 at 78 § 4 (1917).
37. Selective Service Act of 1940, 54 *Statutes at Large* 885 at 889 § 5(g).
38. Selective Service Act of 1948, 62 *Statutes at Large* 604 at 612–13 § 6(j).
39. 380 U.S. 163 (1965). For an interesting and readable biographical sketch of Daniel Seeger and an explanation of his case, see Peter Irons, *The Courage of Their Convictions* (New York: Free Press, 1988), 153–78.
40. 380 U.S. 163 at 166 (Seeger), 168 (Jakobson), 169 (Peter).
41. 380 U.S. 163 at 176.
42. 398 U.S. 333 (1970).
43. 398 U.S. 333 at 341.
44. 398 U.S. 333 at 342–43.
45. See the Military Selective Service Act of 1967, 81 *Statutes at Large* 100 at 104 § (7). This law still required that conscientious objector status be based on "religious training and belief," but left out "belief in a relation to a Supreme Being" altogether.
46. 401 U.S. 437 (1971).

6. Aid to Church-Related Schools

1. "New England's First Fruits," in *American Christianity: An Historical Interpretation with Representative Documents*, ed. H. Shelton Smith, Robert T. Handy, and Lefferts A. Loetscher (New York: Charles Scribner's Sons, 1960), 1:124.
2. Ibid.
3. Lawrence A. Cremin, *American Education: The Colonial Experience, 1607–1783* (New York: Harper & Row, 1970), 181.
4. A good, brief biography of Bishop Hughes, including his attitude about schools, is in Andrew M. Greeley, *The Catholic Experience: An Interpretation of the History of American Catholicism* (Garden City, NY: Doubleday, 1967), 101–25.
5. 268 U.S. 510 (1925).
6. 281 U.S. 370 (1930).
7. 281 U.S. 370 at 375.
8. 330 U.S. 1 (1947).
9. Although *Cantwell v. Connecticut* (1940) mentioned the Establishment Clause, it really was only a Free Exercise Clause case and applied that clause only to the states through the Fourteenth Amendment.
10. 330 U.S. 1 at 15–16. The quote comes from Thomas Jefferson's "Letter to the Danbury Baptists," written in 1802, found in a number of sources, including *Church and State in American History: Key Documents, Decisions, and Commentary from the Past Three Centuries*, ed. John F. Wilson and Donald L. Drakeman, 3rd ed. (Boulder, CO: Westview Press, 2003), 74.
11. 330 U.S. 1 at 18.
12. Ibid.
13. 374 U.S. 203 (1963).
14. 397 U.S. 664 (1970).
15. 403 U.S. 602 (1971).
16. *Lemon v. Kurtzman* 403 U.S. 602 at 612–13, quoting *Walz v. Tax Commission of the City of New York* 397 U.S. 664 at 668, 674.

17. *Hunt v. McNair* 413 U.S. 734 at 741.
18. 262 U.S. 447 (1923).
19. 392 U.S. 83 (1968).
20. "The Congress shall have Power To lay and collect Taxes, Duties, Imposts and Excises, to pay the Debts and provide for the common Defence and general Welfare of the United States; but all Duties, Imposts and Excises shall be uniform throughout the United States."
21. 454 U.S. 464 (1982).
22. 421 U.S. 349 at 366.
23. 392 U.S. 236 (1968).
24. 421 U.S. 349 (1975).
25. 433 U.S. 229 (1977).
26. 444 U.S. 646 (1980).
27. 433 U.S. 229 at 248.
28. 403 U.S. 602 (1971).
29. 413 U.S. 756 (1973).
30. 413 U.S. 756 at 777.
31. 413 U.S. 472 (1973).
32. *Meek v. Pittenger* 421 U.S. 349 at 366, quoting *Hunt v. McNair* 413 U.S. 734 at 743. Interestingly, this is exactly contrary to the argument made in *Board of Education v. Allen* 392 U.S. 236 (1968). There the Court held the religious and secular parts of parochial education are easily separable, so it is possible to guarantee that schoolbooks loaned to parochial school students are really used for secular instruction. That was a major rationale for approving the loan of schoolbooks to students in church-related schools, which was done in *Allen* and two subsequent cases.
33. 473 U.S. 373 (1985).
34. 473 U.S. 402 (1985).
35. 413 U.S. 756 (1973).
36. The dollar amounts in this case make more sense if one remembers that the legislation was passed in 1972.
37. 413 U.S. 756 at 791, 793.
38. 403 U.S. 602 at 625.
39. 463 U.S. 388 (1983).
40. 474 U.S. 481 (1986).
41. 474 U.S. 481 at 488.
42. 474 U.S. 481 at 488–89.
43. 509 U.S. 1 (1993).
44. 509 U.S. 1 at 10, quoting *Witters* 474 U.S. 481 at 488.
45. 403 U.S. 672 (1971).
46. In the words of the Court: "This 20-year period is termed by the statute as 'the period of Federal interest' and reflects Congress' finding that after 20 years 'the public benefit accruing to the United States' from the use of the federally financed facility 'will equal or exceed in value' the amount of the federal grant" (403 U.S. 672 at 683).
47. 413 U.S. 734 (1973).
48. 426 U.S. 736 (1976).
49. 515 U.S. 819 (1995).
50. 515 U.S. 819 at 825. The court quoted university policy.
51. "[I]n determining whether the State is acting to preserve the limits of the forum

it has created so that the exclusion of a class of speech is legitimate, we have observed a distinction between, on the one hand, content discrimination, which may be permissible if it preserves the purposes of the limited forum, and, on the other hand, viewpoint discrimination, which is presumed impermissible when directed against speech otherwise within the forum's limitations" (515 U.S. 819 at 829–30).

52. 515 U.S. 819 at 833–35.
53. 515 U.S. 819 at 845–46.
54. 540 U.S. 712 (2004).
55. 540 U.S. 712 at 721, 725.
56. 521 U.S. 203 (1997).
57. 521 U.S. 203 at 234–35.
58. 530 U.S. 793 (2000).
59. A plurality opinion is not joined by a majority of the Court. In *Mitchell*, three justices joined Justice Thomas for a total of four. Two others joined in an opinion concurring in the result, but disagreeing with the reasoning of the main opinion. So, a "plurality," in this case, six, not a majority, announced a result, but arriving at it in very different ways. Because they represent a fragmented Court, plurality opinions are often regarded as not having the precedential authority a true majority opinion does.
60. 530 U.S. 793 at 809–10.
61. 530 U.S. 793 at 813–14.
62. 530 U.S. 793 at 816–19.
63. 530 U.S. 793 at 820.
64. 530 U.S. 793 at 822.
65. See *Lemon v. Kurtzman* 403 U.S. 602 at 636–37 and *Bowen v. Kendrick* 487 U.S. 589 at 621–22.
66. 530 U.S. 793 at 826–28.
67. 530 U.S. 793 at 835.
68. 536 U.S. 639 (2002).
69. 536 U.S. 639 at 654–56.
70. 536 U.S. 639 at 646. The fact that attendance was based on private choice and there was no direct payment of money to religious schools left *Committee for Public Education and Religious Liberty v. Nyquist* 413 U.S. 756 (1973) intact. That is, *Nyquist* forbade direct aid that went to religious schools only. That neither of those happened in *Zelman* left the *Nyquist* rule intact. *Nyquist* had also held it unconstitutional for the state to provide an incentive for parents to send their children to parochial school. The broad range of options available to parents in *Zelman* mitigated any incentive provided by the government to choose a religious school. *Zelman* explicitly acknowledged all this, 536 U.S. 639 at 661–62.
71. 536 U.S. 639 at 662–63.

7. Religion in Public Schools

1. Sidney E. Mead, *The Lively Experiment: The Shaping of Christianity in America* (New York: Harper & Row, 1963), 68.
2. 333 U.S. 203 (1948).
3. 333 U.S. 203 at 209–10.
4. 343 U.S. 306 (1952).
5. 343 U.S. 306 at 313–14.
6. 343 U.S. 306 at 323.

7. 343 U.S. 306 at 325.
8. 370 U.S. 421 (1962).
9. 370 U.S. 421 at 422.
10. 370 U.S. 421 at 425.
11. 370 U.S. 421 at 431–32, quoting James Madison, "Memorial and Remonstrance," ¶5.
12. 370 U.S. 421 at 435.
13. *New York Times*, July 1, 1962, quoted in Leo Pfeffer, *Church, State, and Freedom*, rev. ed. (Boston: Beacon Press, 1967), 466. See Pfeffer, pp. 466–69, for a brief description of the variety of reactions to *Engel*.
14. 374 U.S. 203 (1963).
15. 374 U.S. 203 at 211.
16. For a short history of the Schempp family's involvement in initiating this case, and its aftermath, see Rob Boston, "Forever and Ever Amen: The 30 Years' War over Prayer and Bible Reading in the Public Schools," *Church and State* 46 (June 1993): 7–10.
17. 374 U.S. 203 at 225, quoting *Zorach v. Clauson* 343 U.S. 306 at 314.
18. The Court actually expanded on the language of *Schempp* in a dictum in *Stone v. Graham*, mentioned later in this chapter. "This is not a case in which the Ten Commandments are integrated into *the school curriculum, where the Bible may constitutionally be used in an appropriate study of history, civilization, ethics, comparative religion, or the like*" (449 U.S. 39 at 42, emphasis added).
19. 333 U.S. 203 at 235–36.
20. See Steven K. Green, "Evangelicals and the Becker Amendment: A Lesson in Church-State Moderation," *Journal of Church and State* 33 (Summer 1991): 541–67.
21. 472 U.S. 38 (1985).
22. For an interesting and readable biographical sketch of Ishmael Jaffree and an explanation of his case, see Peter Irons, *The Courage of Their Convictions* (New York: Free Press, 1988), 355–78.
23. 505 U.S. 577 (1992).
24. 505 U.S. 577 at 589, 591–92. In his dissent, Justice Antonin Scalia railed against Justice Kennedy's concept of "psychological coercion." One of his more memorable statements was: "But interior decorating is a rock-hard science compared to psychology practiced by amateurs" (505 U.S. 577 at 636). (Scalia borrowed from a lower court judge who asserted the Supreme Court's Establishment Clause jurisprudence "requir[es] scrutiny more commonly associated with interior decorators than the judiciary.")
25. *Jones v. Clear Creek Independent School District* 977 F.2d 963 (1992), certiorari denied 508 U.S. 967 (1993).
26. 530 U.S. 290 (2000). The defendants, who had originally been the plaintiffs, were designated as "Doe" for their protection. The Court identified them simply as two sets of students and their mothers, one Catholic family and one Mormon. When news of the lawsuit became public, the community's reaction was so hateful, virulent, and threatening, the District Court tried to protect their identities. See 530 U.S. 290 at 294 and note 1.
27. 530 U.S. 290 at 306–7.
28. 530 U.S. 290 at 307–8.
29. 530 U.S. 290 at 310.
30. 530 U.S. 290 at 310–12.

31. 530 U.S. 290 at 315.
32. 530 U.S. 290 at 313, quoting *Engel v. Vitale* 370 U.S. 421 at 430.
33. *Scopes v. Tennessee* 289 S.W. 363 (1927). "S.W" represents the *Southwestern Reporter,* the reporting service in which Tennessee cases are reported.
34. 393 U.S. 97 (1968).
35. 393 U.S. 97 at 106. For an interesting and readable biographical sketch of Susan Epperson and an explanation of her case, see Irons, *The Courage of Their Convictions,* 205–30.
36. Fundamentalists expended much energy to formulate a new strategy in the late 1960s and early 1970s. When *Epperson* came to the Court in 1968, only Arkansas and Mississippi had laws prohibiting the teaching of evolution in public schools, and there was no evidence that Arkansas had made any attempt to enforce its law since it had been passed in 1928. But the decision in *Epperson* corresponded with a dramatic rise of religious and political conservatism. Consequently, antievolutionists used the decision as a rallying cry for greater efforts to discredit evolution and to minimize the impact of teaching evolution on public education.
37. My thanks to Professor C. David Grant, who teaches religion and science at Texas Christian University, for reviewing and making suggestions for this paragraph.
38. See *McLean v. Arkansas Board of Education* 529 F.Supp. 1255 (1982). The opinion of Judge Overton is the best articulation of the idea that creation science is actually a religious concept and thus fails all three parts of the *"Lemon* test"— better than the opinion in the Supreme Court case that came later.
39. 482 U.S. 578 (1987).
40. 482 U.S. 578 at 593, quoting *Epperson v. Arkansas* 393 U.S. 97 at 106–7.
41. 367 U.S. 488 (1961). Article VI states that "no religious Test shall ever be required as a Qualification to any Office or public Trust under the United States." The Court decided the case on the Establishment Clause only and did not have to decide whether Article VI applied to state as well as federal offices.
42. 330 U.S. 1 at 15.
43. 367 U.S. 488 at 495 and note 11.
44. This point was forcefully made and litigated in *Smith v. Board of School Commissioners of Mobile County* 655 F.Supp. 939 (1986). For a commentary on that and a related case, see Ronald B. Flowers, "They Got Our Attention, Didn't They? The Tennessee and Alabama Schoolbook Cases," *Religion and Public Education* 15 (Summer 1988): 262–85.
45. 347 U.S. 483 (1954).
46. 449 U.S. 39 (1980).
47. 449 U.S. 39 at 41.
48. 20 *United States Code* §§ 4071–74.
49. A phrase and concept derived from *Widmar v. Vincent* 454 U.S. 263 (1981), which is discussed later in this chapter.
50. 496 U.S. 226 (1990).
51. An example is the chess club. The school argued it was curriculum-related because chess requires the same kind of logical thinking as mathematics. The Court held that that relationship was entirely too tenuous. The chess club was not curriculum-related because the school did not teach chess or anything like it.
52. 496 U.S. 226 at 250.

53. 454 U.S. 263 (1981).

54. As noted earlier, the concepts of "limited open forum" (at least in reference to disputes about religion) and "equal access," which are so important in the Equal Access Act and *Board of Education v. Mergens*, originated in this case.

55. 454 U.S. 263 at 273–74.

56. 454 U.S. 263 at 284.

57. 508 U.S. 384 (1993).

58. Remarkably, given his reservations about the ascendancy of free speech in religion cases, expressed in *Widmar v. Vincent*, 454 U.S. 263 at 284.

59. *City of Los Angeles v. Taxpayers for Vincent* 466 U.S. 789 at 804 (1984). Cf. also *Cornelius v. NAACP Legal Defense and Educational Fund* 473 U.S. 788 at 806 (1985).

60. 533 U.S. 98 (2001).

61. 533 U.S. 98 at 110.

62. 533 U.S. 98 at 120.

63. It was surely not coincidence that the Court handed down *Newdow* on June 14, 2004, exactly fifty years after "under God" was added to the Pledge. See John Baer, *The Pledge of Allegiance, A Centennial History, 1892–1992* (Annapolis, MD: Free State Press, 1992). Justice Stevens and Chief Justice Rehnquist also have some historical material in *Elk Grove School District v. Newdow* 542 U.S. 1 at 6–9 and 40–42.

64. 542 U.S. 1 (2004). Sometime after the Ninth Circuit decision, Justice Antonin Scalia made a speech in which he disagreed with the ruling. So, when the Court granted certiorari, he recused himself and took no part in the consideration or decision of the case.

65. 542 U.S. 1 at 25–27.

8. Blue Laws, Bars, Taxes, and Plastic Reindeer: The Complexity of Establishment Clause Issues

1. Exodus 20:8–11.

2. *Code of Justinian*, III.xii.3, quoted in *Documents of the Christian Church*, ed. Henry Bettenson and Chris Maunder, 3rd ed. (New York: Oxford University Press, 1999), 20.

3. 366 U.S. 420 (1961).

4. 366 U.S. 420 at 445.

5. See also *Two Guys from Harrison Allentown, Inc. v. McGinley* 366 U.S. 582 (1961), which reached essentially the same result.

6. 366 U.S. 599 (1961). See also *Gallagher v. Crown Kosher Super Market* 366 U.S. 617 (1961).

7. 366 U.S. 599 at 603.

8. 366 U.S. 599 at 616. Justice William O. Douglas wrote a long dissent, which applied to all the Sunday law cases. He ended it by quoting a letter from a pastor, saying that the pastor "has stated my views":

> We forget that, though Sunday-worshiping Christians are in the majority in this country among religious people, we do not have the right to force our practice on the minority. Only a Church which deems itself without error and intolerant of error can justify its intolerance of the minority.
>
> A Jewish friend of mine runs a small business establishment. Because my friend is a Jew his business is closed each Saturday. He respects my right to worship on Sunday and I respect his right to worship on Saturday. But there is a difference. As

a Jew he closes his door voluntarily so that he will be able to worship his God in his fashion. Fine! But, as a Jew living under Christian inspired Sunday closing laws, he is required to close his store on Sunday so that I will be able to worship my God in my fashion.

Around the corner from my church there is a small Seventh Day Baptist Church. I disagree with the Seventh Day Baptists on many points of doctrine. Among the tenets of their faith with which I disagree is the "seventh day worship." But they are good neighbors and fellow Christians, and while we disagree we respect one another. The good people of my congregation set aside their jobs on the first day of the week and gather in God's house for worship. Of course, it is easy for them to set aside their jobs since Sunday closing laws—inspired by the Church—keep them from their work. At the Seventh Day Baptist Church the people set aside their jobs on Saturday to worship God. This takes real sacrifice because Saturday is a good day for business. But that is not all—they are required by law to set aside their jobs on Sunday while more orthodox Christians worship.

. . . I do not believe that because I have set aside Sunday as a holy day I have the right to force all men to set aside that day also. Why should my faith be favored by the State over any other man's faith?

At the end of that quotation, Justice Douglas ended his dissent by saying, "With all deference, none of the opinions filed today in support of the Sunday laws has answered that question" (366 U.S. 420 at 580–81).

9. 472 U.S. 703 (1985).

10. 472 U.S. 703 at 708.

11. 472 U.S. 703 at 709.

12. 463 U.S. 783 (1983).

13. 463 U.S. 783 at 792.

14. See *Katkoff v. Marsh* 755 F.2d 223 (1985), a federal court of appeals case, which upheld the constitutionality of military chaplains on the grounds contained in the preceding paragraph, and clearly expresses that principle. (The "F.2d" in the citation refers to the *Federal Reporter,* second series, which is the official reporting document for cases in federal courts of appeals.)

15. 459 U.S. 116 (1982).

16. 459 U.S. 116 at 126–27, quoting *Abington Township School District v. Schempp* 374 U.S. 203 at 222.

17. Justice David Souter, in the case under discussion, called the Hasidim "vigorously religious people" (*Board of Education of Kiryas Joel v. Grumet* 512 U.S. 687 at 691).

18. 512 U.S. 687 (1994).

19. *Larkin v. Grendel's Den* 459 U.S. 116 at 126.

20. 512 U.S. 687 at 698, 709–10, quoting *Wisconsin v. Yoder* 406 U.S. 205 at 213.

21. 456 U.S. 228 (1982).

22. 397 U.S. 664 (1970).

23. 397 U.S. 664 at 678.

24. 397 U.S. 664 at 674–75.

25. 455 U.S. 252 (1982).

26. 26 *United States Code* § 1402(g).

27. 455 U.S. 252 at 257–58. No more concise statement of the "*Sherbert* test" could be found than this one. This was clearly before the Court's disastrous decision in *Employment Division of Oregon v. Smith.*

28. 455 U.S. 252 at 260. Notice this language could be applied to conscientious objection to taxes beyond the narrow Amish objection to Social Security, for

example, the nonpayment of income taxes because of objections to the government's expenditures for armaments and the waging of war.

29. 489 U.S. 1 (1989).
30. 319 U.S. 105 (1943).
31. 493 U.S. 378 (1990).
32. 26 *United States Code* § 501(c)(3).
33. 470 F.2d 849 (1972).
34. 470 F.2d 849 at 852. Past tense verbs replace present because Christian Echoes National Ministry no longer exists.
35. 470 F.2d 849 at 853–54.
36. 470 F.2d 849 at 854, 857.
37. Certiorari denied, 404 U.S. 561 (1972). Remember denial of certiorari does not mean the Court endorses or agrees with the opinion of the lower court, but it does mean the opinion is the law in that part of the country covered by the lower court's jurisdiction.
38. Jane Lampman, "Does US Law Mute Voices of Churches?" *Christian Science Monitor*, September 23, 2004, 11.
39. Lampman, "Does US Law Mute Voices of Churches?" 11.
40. 461 U.S. 574 (1983). Another case was decided with *Bob Jones*, *Goldsboro Christian Schools v. United States*. The facts in the two cases were essentially the same, except Goldsboro Schools were elementary and secondary, rather than at the collegiate level.
41. 461 U.S. 574 at 595–96, quoting *Walz v. Tax Commission* 397 U.S. 664 at 673.
42. 461 U.S. 574 at 603–4.
43. 490 U.S. 680 (1989).
44. 490 U.S. 680 at 691, quoting *United States v. American Bar Endowment* 477 U.S. 105 at 118 (1986).
45. 495 U.S. 472 (1990).
46. 465 U.S. 668 (1984).
47. 465 U.S. 668 at 680.
48. 492 U.S. 573 (1989).
49. 492 U.S. 573 at 600–601.
50. 492 U.S. 573 at 616, 620, quoting *Grand Rapids School District v. Ball* 473 U.S. 373 at 390.
51. 515 U.S. 753 (1995).
52. 515 U.S. 753 at 763.

9. Flash Points and the Future

1. Walter H. Capps, *The New Religious Right: Piety, Patriotism, and Politics* (Columbia: University of South Carolina Press, 1990), 3.
2. For a brief article on why the Christian nation idea is wrong, see Ronald B. Flowers, "In Search of a Christian Nation," *Liberty: A Magazine of Religious Freedom* 99 (July/August 2004): 16–21. See also Mark A. Noll, Nathan O. Hatch, and George M. Marsden, *The Search for Christian America*, exp. ed. (Colorado Springs, CO: Helmers & Howard, 1989); Isaac Kramnick and R. Laurence Moore, *The Godless Constitution: The Case against Religious Correctness* (New York: W. W. Norton, 1997).
3. See Justice Souter's concurring opinions in *Lee v. Weisman* and *Church of the Lukumi Babalu Aye v. City of Hialeah* and his dissenting opinions in *Agostini v. Felton*, *Good News Club v. Milford*, *Mitchell v. Helms*, and *Rosenberger v. University*

of Virginia. That Souter has felt the need to write so many separationist opinions in recent Establishment Clause cases illustrates the tendency of the Court in an accommodationist direction.

4. But not just in the area of church-state relations. See David G. Savage, *Turning Right: The Making of the Rehnquist Supreme Court* (New York: John Wiley & Sons, 1992).

5. 494 U.S. 872 (1990). The paragraphs on *Smith* that follow here are similar to those in my article "The Reagan Court Is In," *Liberty: A Magazine of Religious Freedom* 87 (May/June 1992): 14, 28.

6. In *Smith* Justice Scalia gave examples of such "hybrid cases." Some are cases mentioned in this book: *Cantwell v. Connecticut* (which had a free-speech component), *Murdock v. Pennsylvania* (free speech), *West Virginia Board of Education v. Barnette* (which Scalia incorrectly said was decided "exclusively upon free speech grounds"), and *Pierce v. Society of Sisters* (right of parents to direct the education of their children—which is *not* a constitutionally enumerated right). See *Smith* 494 U.S. 872.

7. See *Jones v. Opelika* 315 U.S. 584 at 608 (1942); *Murdock v. Pennsylvania* 319 U.S. 105 at 115 (1943); *United States v. Ballard* 332 U.S. 78 at 87 (1944). It must be acknowledged that, in some of these quotes, freedom of speech, press, and others are mentioned as preferred freedoms along with religion. But there is never even a hint that the others take precedence over religion or that freedom of religion receives life only because of its affiliation with the others. Just the contrary is expressed in Justice Frank Murphy's dissent in *Jones v. Opelika* at 621, joined by three others: "Important as free speech and a free press are to a free government and a free citizenry, there is a right even more dear to many individuals—the right to worship their Maker according to their needs and the dictates of their souls and to carry their message or their gospel to every living creature."

8. 494 U.S. 872 at 888.

9. 494 U.S. 872 at 890.

10. *West Virginia Board of Education v. Barnette* 319 U.S. 624 at 638.

11. A wonderful statement on the purpose of the Bill of Rights, American liberty in general, and the cost of obtaining these was written by Chief Judge Ryder of the District Court of Appeal of Florida, Second Circuit, in *Collins v. Florida* 465 So.2d 1266 at 1268–69 (1985):

> We fought a war to obtain these rights. This Nation pledged its wealth, its goods, its lives and many, many lives were, in fact, lost fighting that war against a then autocratic, dictatorial government to gain those rights. These rights were not easily won or wrestled away from that government across the sea whose agents here did their will at their whim in violating their own citizens' homes, papers, and persons by searches without cause, much less probable cause, but on mere suspicion or personal whim. The then continentals were often treated as merely chattels without rights. It was not merely because of a tea tax that this Nation fought the sovereign across the sea—it was not merely [because of] taxation without representation that this Nation undertook a cruel and lengthy war—it was more than that. It was to secure freedom for all peoples of this Nation, all citizens—not just a preferred few. And because of the abuses of power of the government across the sea, abuses directly against our pioneering predecessors, our founding fathers correctly believed that it was right, meet and proper that those abuses should not ever again be given a chance to be inflicted upon the citizenry under its new government; so much so, that inhibitions against the new government in the form of a Bill of Rights

and other amendments to the Constitution were written down and passed into law, to be a permanent and basic, fundamental law of the land, forever protecting the citizens from despotism and the threat of its reappearance in this land.

(The "So.2d" in the citation refers to the *Southern Reporter,* second series, which is the official reporting document for state courts in Florida and other states in that region.)

12. Peter Berger, "Religious Liberty and the Paradox of Relevance," *The Religion and Society Report* 5 (January 1988): 1; Berger spells this out in somewhat more detail in his essay "The Serendipity of Liberties," in *The Structure of Freedom: Correlations, Causes, and Cautions,* ed. Richard John Neuhaus (Grand Rapids: Wm. B. Eerdmans Publishing Co., 1991), 14–16.

13. 494 U.S. 872 at 902–3.

14. I quote with appreciation the words of Judge Goldberg of the U.S. Court of Appeals for the Fifth Circuit:

> [W]e do not labor within a majoritarian jurisprudence. Our responsibility is to apply not the majority ethos, but the Constitution. That great document enforces no religious orthodoxy; it permits no compelled religious expression. Its provisions protect not just the popular, but also the un-; not just the sensible, but also the (seemingly) silly. In return, the Constitution repays our investment of tolerance with a dividend of individual autonomy and social freedom—freedom, in great measure, from the religious hostilities and petty oppressions that have rent nations throughout history and across the globe. (*Society of Separationists v. Herman* 939 F.2d 1207 at 1220 [1991])

15. In describing the impact of *Smith,* professor of constitutional law Douglas Laycock says:

> This is in fact a move to majoritarianism; the Court is getting out of the business of enforcing the religion clauses. Legislatures and enforcement agencies choose when to provide only formal neutrality and when to grant exceptions. Favored religions can be exempted from the rules that burden them, while disfavored religions are denied exemptions from the rules that burden them. ("The Remnants of Free Exercise," *Supreme Court Review* 1990 [Chicago: University of Chicago Press, 1991]: 12)

> Church-state authority Dean M. Kelley observed:

> "Some of [the Court's] members seem to feel that individuals should not have many rights that are judicially enforceable against the government. Apparently, individuals, minorities and courts should get out of the way and let the government—in its infinite wisdom—govern. That view, of course, would put the courts on the side of the strong against the weak and nullify the whole purpose of the Bill of Rights, which is to protect individual rights against government powers." ("Statism, Not Separationism, Is the Problem," *Christian Century* 106 [January 18, 1989]: 49)

16. One example, of many that could be cited, was the situation of a family of Hmongs whose son suffered a seizure while he was sleeping and was rushed to the hospital, where he died. Because the physicians did not know the cause of death, the medical examiner, pursuant to Rhode Island law, which requires an autopsy in those situations in which death occurs "in any suspicious or unusual manner," performed an autopsy on the young man without consulting his parents. Hmong religion prohibits any mutilation of a body, including autopsies and the removal of organs during autopsies. Such mutilation means that the spirit of the dead is not free, and thus would come back to take another person

in the decedent's family. In a long and careful opinion in which it relied on the "compelling state interest test," the U.S. District Court for Rhode Island found that the Hmong family had a religion-based cause of damages against the medical examiner. However, it postponed the determination and awarding of damages until a later hearing. During the time the court was researching the case law in order to fix damages, the Supreme Court issued *Smith*. Subsequently the district court took the highly unusual step of issuing a second decision in the case—rescinding the earlier decision. Expressing "deep regret" because of his profound sympathy for the Hmong family, the judge noted that the *Smith* doctrine would not allow him to find for them, because the state law concerning autopsies was a law of general applicability (*You Van Yang v. Sturner* 750 F.Supp. 558 [1990]; at 559 the judge said: "While I feel constrained to apply the majority's opinion [in *Smith*] to the instant case, I cannot do this without expressing my profound regret and my own agreement with Justice Blackmun's forceful dissent."). So, because of *Smith*, the state needed not make any accommodation for religious objections to autopsies, so long as the law authorizing them is not aimed specifically at religious objections.

17. 42 *United States Code* § 2000bb.
18. Justice Byron White, who voted with Justice Scalia and the majority in *Smith*, retired in June 1993, when the Court's term ended. He was replaced by Justice Ruth Bader Ginsburg. At the time of her appointment by President Clinton, her views on church-state relationships were not clear. Up to the time of the revision of this book, she had not written a church-state opinion, so her views on the subject are not explicit. But she has joined Justice Souter's very separationist dissents in *Agostini v. Felton, Good News Club v. Milford, Mitchell v. Helms*, and *Rosenberger v. University of Virginia*. So it is probably safe to assume that she is more on the separationist than the accommodationist side of the dispute. Justice Stephen Breyer, appointed by President Clinton in 1994, after the first edition of this book had gone to the publisher, is also a rather unknown quantity on the church-state issue. He joined Justice Souter's separationist dissents in *Agostini v. Felton* and *Rosenberger v. University of Virginia*. He also joined Justice O'Connor's "concurring in the judgment" opinion in *Mitchell v. Helms*. Most recently, he wrote a separationist dissent in *Zelman v. Simmons-Harris*.
19. 521 U.S. 507 (1997).
20. See, for example, *Julia Christians v. Crystal Evangelical Free Church* 141 F.3d 854 (1998).
21. As of November 2004, thirteen states had passed RFRA legislation: Alabama, Arizona, Connecticut, Florida, Indiana, Illinois, Missouri, New Mexico, Oklahoma, Pennsylvania, Rhode Island, South Carolina, and Texas.
22. 42 *United States Code* § 2000cc.
23. Article 1, section 8, part 3: "The Congress shall have Power . . . To regulate Commerce with foreign Nations, and among the several States, and with the Indian Tribes."
24. 349 F.3d 257 (2003).
25. *Wallace v. Jaffree* 472 U.S. 38 at 113 (1985).
26. 465 U.S. 668 at 673, quoting first *Committee for Public Education and Religious Liberty v. Nyquist* 413 U.S. 756 at 760, and then *Zorach v. Clauson* 343 U.S. 306 at 314.
27. 472 U.S. 38 at 113.
28. 472 U.S. 38 at 107.

29. Ironically, Justice Antonin Scalia, an "intentionalist" justice, has argued in support of the point being made here. See his dissent in *Edwards v. Aguillard* 482 U.S. 578 at 636–37.

30. Laurence H. Tribe, *God Save This Honorable Court: How the Choice of Supreme Court Justices Shapes Our History* (New York: New American Library, Mentor Book, 1985), 55, 51. Professor of jurisprudence Harry Jones approaches the question of original intent this way: "To consider constitutional law as if it were a mere attempted reconstruction of the intention of the founding fathers is about as helpful as the old query: 'If I had had an uncle, would he have liked prunes?' Nowhere is this more true than in the constitutional law of church-state relations. *It is the task of the Supreme Court in this area to keep the historic purpose of the First Amendment a living influence in contemporary society*" ("Church-State Relations: Our Constitutional Heritage," in *Religion and Contemporary Society*, ed. Harold Stahmer [New York: Macmillan Co., 1963], 173, emphasis added).

31. That the Constitution is dynamic, as opposed to static, and should be interpreted as such, was expressed well by Chief Justice Charles Evans Hughes in *Home Building and Loan Association v. Blaisdell* 290 U.S. 398 at 442–43 (1934) in which he invoked two other greats of the Court, Chief Justice John Marshall and Justice Oliver Wendell Holmes Jr.:

> If by the statement that what the Constitution meant at the time of its adoption it means to-day [*sic*], it is intended to say that the great clauses of the Constitution must be confined to the interpretation which the framers, with the conditions and outlook of their time, would have placed upon them, the statement carries its own refutation. It was to guard against such a narrow conception that Chief Justice Marshall uttered the memorable warning—"We must never forget that it is a *constitution* we are expounding" (*McColloch v. Maryland*, 4 Wheat. 316, 407)—"a constitution intended to endure for ages to come, and consequently, to be adapted to the various *crises* of human affairs." *Id.*, p. 415. When we are dealing with the words of the Constitution, said this Court in *Missouri v. Holland*, 252 U.S. 416, 433, "we must realize that they have called into life a being the development of which could not have been foreseen completely by the most gifted of its begetters. . . . The case before us must be considered in the light of our whole experience and not merely in that of what was said a hundred years ago."

32. Another of those great principles is equality. But how do we achieve maximum equality before government for citizens of an increasingly diverse society? To do so, must we not insist that atheists or adherents to a wide variety of religions, most of them historically not related to Western culture, have equal rights? Does that not, in itself, preclude nonpreferentialism? That is, how does government treat all these religions the same, in an evenhanded way? And if government does manage to promote all these religions in a nondiscriminatory way, how does it manage, at the same time, to treat the nonreligious with equality?

33. Leonard W. Levy, "The Original Meaning of the Establishment Clause of the First Amendment," in *Religion and the State: Essays in Honor of Leo Pfeffer*, ed. James E. Wood Jr. (Waco, TX: Baylor University Press, 1985), 61. The quote from Madison is from a letter to Jefferson, 17 October 1788 (*The Papers of James Madison*, ed. Robert A. Rutland et al. [Charlottesville: University of Virginia Press, 1976], 11: 295).

34. Douglas Laycock, "'Nonpreferential' Aid to Religion: A False Claim about Original Intent," *William and Mary Law Review* 27 (1985): 880–81. Laycock's

long article is rich in reference notes to documents of the time.

35. The test is named after *Lemon v. Kurtzman.* See chapter 6.

36. See *Wallace v. Jaffree* 472 U.S. 38 at 110–12.

37. 465 U.S. 668 at 690, 688.

38. 465 U.S. 668 at 687–88.

39. Justice O'Connor has continued to argue for the utility of her "endorsement/disapproval" test. See her concurring opinion in 2004 in *Elk Grove School District v. Newdow* 542 U.S. 1 at 52–56.

40. A shorter version of the next three paragraphs appears in my article "The Reagan Court Is In," *Liberty: A Magazine of Religious Freedom* 87 (May/June 1992): 13.

41. 492 U.S. 573 at 670 (1989).

42. And Chief Justice Rehnquist and Justices White and Scalia, who joined Justice Kennedy's dissent in *Allegheny.*

43. In *Rosenberger v. University of Virginia* (concurring), *Mitchell v. Helms* (plurality), *Zelman v. Simmons-Harris* (concurring), and *Elk Grove School District v. Newdow* (concurring).

44. See his concurring opinions in *Zelman v. Simmons-Harris* and *Elk Grove School District v. Newdow.*

45. In *Kiryas Joel School District v. Grumet* (majority), *Rosenberger v. University of Virginia* (dissenting), *Mitchell v. Helms* (dissenting), and *Zelman v. Simmons-Harris* (dissenting).

46. 454 U.S. 263 at 284. The entire statement appears in chapter 7.

47. L. F. Greene, ed., *The Writings of the Late Elder John Leland* (New York: G. W. Wood, 1845; reprint, New York: Arno Press, 1970), 278.

48. 392 U.S. 236 at 254–66.

49. *Abington Township School District v. Schempp* 374 U.S. 203 at 225.

50. 403 U.S. 602 at 618.

51. 536 U.S. 639 at 684–86. See also Justice Souter's dissent in *Rosenberger v. University of Virginia* 515 U.S. 819 at 863–99, where he makes the same point in a very different case fact situation.

52. Justice Breyer quoted Justice Wiley Rutledge, dissenting in *Everson v. Board of Education*: "Public money devoted to payment of religious costs, educational or other, brings the quest for more. It brings too the struggle of sect against sect for the larger share or for any. Here one [religious sect] by numbers [of adherents] alone will benefit most, there another. This is precisely the history of societies which have had an established religion and dissident groups" (330 U.S. 1 at 53–54).

He could have just as easily quoted Justice William O. Douglas's dissent in *Board of Education v. Allen* 392 U.S. 236 at 262–66 or Chief Justice Warren Burger's majority opinion in *Lemon v. Kurtzman* 403 U.S. 602 at 622–23, both of which make the same point, both in government aid to parochial school cases. Chief Justice Burger warned against "political divisiveness" resulting from religious groups' competition for public funding and said, at 622: "Ordinarily political debate and division, however vigorous and even partisan, are normal and healthy manifestations of our democratic system of government, but political division along religious lines *was one of the principal evils against which the First Amendment was intended to protect*" (emphasis added).

53. 536 U.S. 639 at 722–23.

54. 536 U.S. 639 at 728.

55. "Contrary to the District's repeated assertions that it has adopted a 'hands-off' approach to the pregame invocation, the realities of the situation plainly reveal that its policy involves both perceived and actual endorsement of religion. . . . The District has attempted to disentangle itself from the religious messages by developing the two-step student election process. The text of the October policy, however, exposes the extent of the school's entanglement. The elections take place at all only because the school 'board *has chosen to permit* students to deliver a brief invocation and/or message'" (*Santa Fe Independent School District v. Doe* 530 U.S. 290 at 305–6, emphasis in original).

56. It is common knowledge from President Bush's biography that at a crisis point in his life he was converted to take Christianity seriously. It made a huge difference, by helping him get control of his alcoholism and stabilizing his family life. As a Christian, I celebrate that. But the problem—and it is a serious problem—is that President Bush has attempted to nationalize his personal experience through the "faith-based initiative" program.

57. From the movie *Jerry McGuire*.

58. Ronald B. Flowers, "In Praise of the Separation of Church and State," *Lexington Theological Quarterly* 37 (Fall 2002): 161. I originally delivered a form of this article in a speech at Ministers Week, Texas Christian University, February 7, 2002.

59. This act never became law. It was referred to the House Committee on the Judiciary and then to the Subcommittee on the Constitution, where it died. However, when it was introduced, it made headlines and was indicative of considerable political grandstanding. Some members of Congress were even willing to trade on tragedy.

60. 351 F.3d 173 (2003).

61. 354 F.3d 438 (2003).

62. Richard E. Morgan calls Blaine "the prince of Republican opportunists" (*Supreme Court and Religion* [New York: Free Press, 1972], 51).

63. Anson Phelps Stokes, *Church and State in the United States* (New York: Harper & Bros., 1950), 2:722; Edward A. Crapol, *James G. Blaine: Architect of Empire* (Wilmington, DE: Scholarly Resources, 2000), 42.

64. The use of the word "accommodate" is interesting. The proper sense of the word is consistent with strict separation. Government should accommodate religion by getting out of its way and letting it flourish. That is what the First Amendment seems to demand. But "accommodationists" interpret the word to mean affirmative government aid or assistance to religion. I am using the word in their sense—in order to examine it critically and disagree with it.

65. 536 U.S. 639 at 645. Justice Breyer, in his dissent, at 724, makes the point succinctly: "Consider the voucher program here at issue. That program insists that the religious school accept students of all religions. Does that criterion treat fairly groups whose religion forbids them to do so?"

66. This is no longer as true under the charitable choice law. But it may be true in other forms of government aid, such as aid to parochial schools.

67. Russell H. Dilday Jr., "Jesus and Politics," *Church and State* 37 (October 1984): 20.

68. 426 U.S. 736 (1976).

69. 426 U.S. 736 at 744; see "Church Colleges: The Price of Tax Aid," *Church and State* 28 (June 1975): 10–12.

70. 426 U.S. 736 at 775.

71. Joseph L. Conn, "Breach of Faith? In Order to Keep State Funds Flowing,

Falwell and Company Drop Religion Requirements at Liberty University,"
Church and State 46 (July–August 1993): 12–13.

72. Defendant's trial brief, *McLean v. Arkansas Board of Education*, 14–15. The same concept is used in the latest permutation of creation science, "intelligent design."

73. Thomas Jefferson, "A Bill for Establishing Religious Freedom"; see appendix B.

74. In chapter 7 I pointed out that voluntary *individual,* nondisruptive prayer has never been forbidden by the Court.

75. Remember that RLUIPA is the final effort to soften the blow of *Smith* after Congress passed the Religious Freedom Restoration Act and the Court declared it unconstitutional as it applied to the states in *Boerne v. Archbishop Flores*, described in chapter 4. Also, the Court will decide in 2005 on the constitutionality of the institutionalized persons side of RLUIPA.

76. "A Memorial and Remonstrance against Religious Assessments," ¶ 6; see appendix A.

77. *Zorach v. Clauson* 343 U.S. 306 at 324–25.

78. 536 U.S. 639 at 686.

Epilogue

1. 370 U.S. 421 at 431–32. The phrase "unhallowed perversion" comes from Madison's "Memorial and Remonstrance," ¶ 5 (see appendix A).

Selected Bibliography

Boston, Robert. *Why the Religious Right Is Wrong about Separation of Church and State.* 2nd ed. Amherst, NY: Prometheus Books, 2003.

Carper, James C., and Thomas C. Hunt. *Religious Schooling in America.* Birmingham, AL: Religious Education Press, 1984.

Church, Forrest, ed. *The Separation of Church and State: Writings on a Fundamental Freedom by America's Founders.* Boston: Beacon Press, 2004.

Curry, Thomas J. *The First Freedoms: Church and State in America to the Passage of the First Amendment.* New York: Oxford University Press, 1986.

Davis, Derek. *Original Intent: Chief Justice Rehnquist and the Course of American Church/State Relations.* Buffalo, NY: Prometheus Books, 1991.

Davis, Derek, and Barry Hankins, eds. *New Religious Movements and Religious Liberty in America.* 2nd ed. Waco, TX: Baylor University Press, 2003.

Flowers, Ronald B. *To Defend the Constitution: Religion, Conscientious Objection, Naturalization, and the Supreme Court.* Lanham, MD: Scarecrow Press, 2003.

Gaustad, Edwin S. *Church and State in America.* New York: Oxford University Press, 1999.

———. *Neither King nor Prelate: Religion and the New Nation 1776–1826.* Grand Rapids: Wm. B. Eerdmans Publishing Co., 1993.

———. *Proclaim Liberty throughout All the Land: A History of Church and State in America.* New York: Oxford University Press, 2003.

Gilkey, Langdon. *Creationism on Trial: Evolution and God at Little Rock.* Minneapolis: Winston Press, 1983.

Hall, Kermit L., ed. *The Oxford Companion to the Supreme Court of the United States.* 2nd. ed. New York: Oxford University Press, 2005.

Hammond, Phillip E., David W. Machacek, and Eric Michael Mazur. *Religion on Trial: How Supreme Court Trends Threaten Freedom of Conscience in America.* Walnut Creek, CA: Altamira Press, 2004.

Ivers, Gregg. *Lowering the Wall: Religion and the Supreme Court in the 1980s.* New York: Anti-Defamation League, 1991.

Kramnick, Isaac, and R. Laurence Moore. *The Godless Constitution: The Case against Religious Correctness.* New York: W. W. Norton & Co., 1997.

Kraybill, Donald B., ed. *The Amish and the State.* 2nd ed. Baltimore: Johns Hopkins University Press, 2003.

Levy, Leonard W. *The Establishment Clause: Religion and the First Amendment.* New York: Macmillan Publishing Co., 1986.

McGraw, Barbara A. *Rediscovering America's Sacred Ground: Public Religion and Pursuit of the Good in a Pluralistic Society.* Albany: State University of New York Press, 2003.

Mead, Sidney E. *The Old Religion in the Brave New World: Reflections on the Relation between Christendom and the Republic.* Berkeley: University of California Press, 1977.

Michaelsen, Robert. *Piety in the Public School: Trends and Issues in the Relationship between Religion and the Public Schools in the United States.* New York: Macmillan Co., 1970.

Noll, Mark A., Nathan O. Hatch, and George M. Marsden. *The Search for Christian America.* Expanded ed. Colorado Springs, CO: Helmers & Howard, 1989.

O'Brien, David M. *Storm Center: The Supreme Court in American Politics.* 6th ed. New York: W. W. Norton & Co., 2003.

O'Connor, Sandra Day. *The Majesty of the Law: Reflections of a Supreme Court Justice.* New York: Random House, 2003.

Peters, Shawn Francis. *Judging Jehovah's Witnesses: Religious Persecution and the Dawn of the Rights Revolution.* Lawrence: University of Kansas Press, 2000.

Pfeffer, Leo. *God, Caesar, and the Constitution: The Court as Referee of Church-State Confrontation.* Boston: Beacon Press, 1975.

———. *Religion, State, and the Burger Court.* Buffalo, NY: Prometheus Books, 1984.

Rehnquist, William H. *The Supreme Court: How It Was, How It Is.* New York: William Morrow & Co., 1987.

Vecsey, Christopher, ed. *Handbook of American Indian Religious Freedom.* New York: Crossroad, 1991.

Wilson, John F., and Donald L. Drakeman, eds. *Church and State in American History.* 3rd ed. Boulder, CO: Westview Press, 2003.

Witte, John, Jr. *Religion and the American Constitutional Experiment: Essential Rights and Liberties.* Boulder, CO: Westview Press, 2000.

There are five regularly published periodicals completely devoted to church-state concerns:

Church and State, published every month except August by Americans United for Separation of Church and State, 518 C Street, N.E., Washington, DC 20002.

Journal of Church and State, published four times a year by the J. M. Dawson Institute of Church-State Studies, Baylor University, Box 97308, Waco, TX 76798-9989.

The Journal of Law and Religion, published twice a year at the Hamline University School of Law, 1536 Hewitt Avenue, St. Paul, MN 55104-1237.

Liberty: A Magazine of Religious Freedom, published bimonthly by the Review and Herald Publishing Association, 12501 Old Columbia Pike, Silver Spring, MD 20904-6600.

Report from the Capital, published ten times a year by the Baptist Joint Committee on Public Affairs, 200 Maryland Avenue, N.E., Washington, DC 20002-5797.

Index

223

Index